Breaking the Mold of Preservice and Inservice Teacher Education

Innovative and Successful Practices for the 21st Century

Edited by
Audrey Cohan
Andrea Honigsfeld

ROWMAN & LITTLEFIELD EDUCATION

A division of
ROWMAN & LITTLEFIELD PUBLISHERS, INC.
Lanham • New York • Toronto • Plymouth, UK

Published by Rowman & Littlefield Education
A division of Rowman & Littlefield Publishers, Inc.
A wholly owned subsidiary of
The Rowman & Littlefield Publishing Group, Inc.
4501 Forbes Boulevard, Suite 200, Lanham, Maryland 20706
http://www.rowmaneducation.com

Estover Road, Plymouth PL6 7PY, United Kingdom

British Library Cataloguing in Publication Information Available

Library of Congress Cataloging-in-Publication Data

Breaking the mold of preservice and inservice teacher education : innovative
    and successful practices for the 21st century / edited by Audrey Cohan
    Andrea Honigsfeld.
        p. cm.
    Includes bibliographical references.
    ISBN 978-1-60709-551-4 (cloth : alk. paper) -- ISBN 978-1-60709-552-1
(pbk. : alk. paper) — ISBN 978-1-60709-553-8 (ebook)
    1. Teachers—Training of—Cross-cultural studies. 2. Teachers—In-service
training—Cross-cultural studies. I. Cohan, Audrey. II. Honigsfeld, Andrea,
1965–
LB1707.B74 2011
370.071'1--dc22

                                                                        2010034853

∞™ The paper used in this publication meets the minimum requirements of
American National Standard for Information Sciences—Permanence of
Paper for Printed Library Materials, ANSI/NISO Z39.48-1992.

Printed in the United States of America

We dedicate this book to all teacher-educators and professional developers who prepare preservice and inservice teachers for the challenges of the twenty-first-century classroom.

We also dedicate this book to our respective families who are our daily inspirations: Barry, Jeffrey, Lauren, and Matthew; and Howie, Benjamin, Jake, and Noah.

Contents

Foreword

Thomas R. Guskey

Views on the preservice education of teachers vary widely. Some believe that we know exactly what needs to be done to prepare teachers to be knowledgeable, caring, well-skilled, culturally sensitive, technologically sophisticated, reflective, and highly effective practitioners. All we lack is the initiative and courage required to make the necessary changes in teacher preparation programs. Others contend that no matter what we do in the three or four years of preservice teacher education, it will never be sufficient to prepare new teachers for the challenging and exceedingly demanding situations they will face in modern classrooms.

The same is true regarding inservice education or professional development for teachers. Some see it as everything that a learning experience should *not* be. It is brief and rarely sustained, deficit oriented, radically underresourced, politically imposed rather than professionally owned, lacking in intellectual rigor or coherence, treated as an add-on rather than as part of a natural process, and trapped in the constraints of a bureaucratic system that poses barriers to even modest levels of success. In short, it is an ill-designed, pedagogically naïve, demeaning exercise that often leaves participants more cynical and no more knowledgeable, skilled, or committed than before.

Others, however, see inservice education and professional development for teachers very differently. Although they recognize that what passes for professional development in many contexts may be naïve and uninspiring, in other contexts it is an essential intellectual and emotional endeavor that rests at the heart of dedicated efforts to improve the quality of education. In these contexts, professional development for teachers uses our best knowledge about pedagogy, about professional renewal and growth, about individual commitment, and about organizational life and change. It enhances the preparation of new teachers, renews the professional skills and enthusiasm of classroom veterans (even those who may feel disenchanted or disenfranchised), and improves the professional expertise, self-confidence, and commitment of all. Amazingly, readers will find descriptions of preservice education and professional development similar to all of these perspectives included in this book.

As editors, Audrey Cohan and Andrea Honigsfeld have done a remarkable job of pulling together an outstanding collection of essays on preservice education and professional development that reflect this stunning diversity. They have done for readers what no one else has accomplished for some time: combine in a single volume a clear and concise description of preservice education and professional development's past, present, and projected future.

Readers are likely to have several reactions to these collected essays. Some, wanting one clear answer, might be discouraged by the many different views presented. Should preservice education be about nurturing inquiry, self-reflection, and individual professional identity, for example, or should it focus on an understanding of and conformity to specified reform agendas and improvement initiatives? Will improvements in professional development more likely arise from deepening teacher understanding of how children learn or from clarifying expectations, defining standards, and specifying practices shown to be effective? Should preservice education provide opportunities for individual, autonomous growth based on where individuals are in their personal and professional lives, or should it focus on collaborative work, shared responsibilities, and the development of cohesive learning communities? Can professional development of any form provide teachers with the time, skills, knowledge, commitment, and emotional energy needed to do the complex planning and implementation of the new practices required of them as agents of change?

Other readers will be concerned by the complicated nature of the issues involved and the wide variation in approaches to improvement recommended by the authors. All of the research described, for example, points to the complexity of teacher preparation and professional development, which mirrors the complexity of the purposes and practices of teaching. But the research different authors cite draws from different philosophical perspectives and different theoretical disciplines. As a result, it leads to different and sometimes competing understandings. Several authors argue that the purpose of preservice education and professional development is to deepen teachers' knowledge, strengthen individual practice, and build collective capacity for improvement of teaching and learning. Others suggest that both teacher preparation and professional development can be seen as political processes, used to achieve broader political agendas, particularly with regard to standards implementation and external accountability.

In the midst of this controversy and conflict, however, readers will be deeply impressed by the keen insights of the authors, the diversity of perspectives on improvement, and the creativity and breadth of the proposed solutions. They will see that preservice preparation and professional development for teachers are not about particular forms of activity but rather about a range of activities—formal and informal—that meet the thinking, feeling, acting, context, and change purposes of teachers over the span of their careers. They will recognize that teachers in different phases of their career and working in different contexts have learning needs that may be distinctly different from those of teachers in other phases, in different contexts, and at different times. They will see that to make significant progress, policy makers, strategists, researchers, professional associates, teachers, and parents all need to engage in an ongoing dialogue about what kinds of teachers are needed as we progress in the twenty-first century.

This is not a book that can be read lightly. The ideas and arguments set forth are too provocative and too complex to be skimmed. They require thoughtful analysis and careful probing. Readers should come to it prepared to argue with the authors, to contest their interpretations, and to suggest alternative perspectives. But they also must come with an open mind, ready to have their assumptions questioned, their ideas tested, and their understandings challenged.

Yet regardless of what they bring to the book, this book will affect readers in two important ways. First, they will see that there remains a considerable gap in our knowledge of the effects of both preservice preparation and professional development, in all their forms, on the thinking, planning, and practices of individual teachers, on schools as learning organizations, and on the learning outcomes of students. But second, the authors' commitment to informed and purposeful inquiry will undoubtedly renew efforts to improve. In today's world and in the foreseeable future, new teachers will need to be well prepared, and experienced teachers will need to engage in high-quality professional development if they are to keep pace with and respond to changes in society and, at the same time, retain their energy, enthusiasm, and commitment to high-quality teaching. Although the precise path we will take in this challenging endeavor remains uncertain, this book helps make our direction much clearer.

Preface

Audrey Cohan and Andrea Honigsfeld

What is the best way to prepare teachers for classrooms of ever increasing diversity, challenging curricula, and a growing number of standardized assessments? What are best practices to enhance and nurture practicing teachers' knowledge and skills necessary to stay up to date with the changing demands of instructional delivery? In a 2003 *Journal of Teacher Education* editorial, Cochran-Smith cautioned her readers regarding the unforgiving complexity of teaching and suggested avoiding simplistic solutions in the emerging age of accountability. In 2006, Darling-Hammond offered a comprehensive overview of changes she deemed necessary to overhaul teacher preparation practices and thus make the teachers more effective. She suggested that three critical components will overhaul traditional, outdated teacher education programs and help create highly effective teachers for the twenty-first century. The essential features of such a change include the following:

1. "tight coherence and integration among courses and between course work and clinical work in schools" (p. 306);
2. "extensive and intensely supervised clinical work—tightly integrated with course work—that allows candidates to learn from expert practice in schools" (p. 307); and
3. "closer, proactive relationships with schools that serve diverse learners effectively and develop and model good teaching" (p. 300).

Darling-Hammond, along with authors featured in this volume, readily acknowledges the underlying challenges of developing, implementing, and successfully maintaining such programs and concurs that innovative initiatives are needed to create teacher preparation and teacher development experiences that strengthen the profession and improve student learning outcomes.

There is much agreement among researchers and practitioners that making a commitment to deep-seated changes both in preservice and inservice teacher education is necessary. The specific approach to accomplish such reform efforts, however, varies greatly. Most recently, Caillier and Riordan (2009) have advocated for teacher training and ongoing teacher development to take place in carefully designed integration with K–12 school sites that serve a diverse student body and are also committed to continual renewal of practices. Lieberman and Pointer-Mace (2010) looked at best practices in the highest performing countries from around the world and suggested that teachers participate in networked learning opportunities through professional learning communities that are built around social networking sites and use new (Web 2.0) media tools. They maintained that "the teaching profession needs to open doors literally and metaphorically to share the wisdom of practice online" (p. 86).

At the same time, based on an extensive study of the types of highly specialized learning that improves teachers' practice and student learning in the United States and overseas, Darling-Hammond, Chung-Wei, Andree, Richardson, and Orphanos (2009) argued that teachers need to participate in (a) ongoing, sustained professional learning opportunities and (b) experiences that lead to transformations in their teaching practice that, in turn, will ultimately lead to improved student outcomes. Among several other practices they highlighted, Darling-Hammond et al. made a strong case for teachers:

> to participate in extended learning opportunities and productive collaborative communities in which [teachers] conduct research on education related topics; to work together on issues of instruction; to learn from one another through mentoring or peer coaching; and collectively to guide curriculum, assessment, and professional learning decisions. (p. 27)

OUR PURPOSE

As professors in a teacher education program, we recognize the important roles that effective and relevant teacher preparation and professional development can play in the lives of teachers and, ultimately, student learners. It is this shared passion for education, and the simultaneous goal of preparing successful, highly qualified teachers for the twenty-first century, that has motivated us to look for best practices and effective models in the preparation of preservice and the continued professional development of inservice teachers.

This book offers innovative ideas that have been documented as *breaking the mold* of traditional education ideas and practices. Similar to our first edited book also published by Rowman & Littlefield and entitled *Breaking the Mold of School Instruction and Organization: Innovative and Successful Practices for the Twenty-First Century* (Honigsfeld & Cohan, 2010), this volume chronicles reform-minded changes that have been successfully implemented in the context of teacher education. The contributing chapter authors may be well-established and well-published or first-time writers, all with diversified interests and research bases. Nonetheless they all share their authentic and compelling documentary accounts of initiatives and innovations.

In the first section of the book, preservice programs are highlighted and explored from the perspective of the future teacher, and in some narratives, from the perspective of the college or university faculty. In the next section, several chapters are dedicated to inservice teacher education or professional development that has an impact on the lives of teachers-in-practice. The themes include mentoring, the social and emotional competence of teachers, mindful teaching, technology, and teacher leadership. The showcased examples offer ways to make significant changes in the improvement of the profession.

In the third section, the collaborative elements of teaching and learning are examined with meaningful illustrations that affect students, teachers, and the communities in which they live. The community is brought into the school in many instances, and the concept of a seamless relationship is introduced, often bringing professionals and communities together in new ways.

To broaden the perspective of innovation, the final set of chapters includes educational practices with a global backdrop. The authors are from Canada, Scotland, China, and Malawi (in collaboration with their American colleagues). Although these initiatives span the world, they too improve children's lives one classroom, one idea, and one reform at a time.

As you visit the classrooms, districts, neighborhoods, faculty rooms, and college campuses featured in this volume, you will be introduced to successful and compelling experiences within teacher preparation and professional development. Take your time at each location; get to know the authors and their programs. Enjoy the journey!

REFERENCES

Caillier, S. L., & Riordan, R. C. (2009). Teacher education for the schools we need. *Journal of Teacher Education, 60,* 489–496.

Cochran-Smith, M. (2003). Editorial: The unforgiving complexity of teaching. *Journal of Teacher Education, 54,* 3–5.

Darling-Hammond, L. (2006). Constructing 21st-century teacher education. *Journal of Teacher Education, 57,* 300–314.

Darling-Hammond, L., Chung-Wei, R., Andree, A., Richardson, N., & Orphanos, S. (2009). *Professional learning in the learning profession: A status report on teacher development in the U.S. and abroad.* Retrieved July 1, 2010, from http://www.nsdc.org/news/NSDCstudy2009.pdf

Lieberman, A., & Pointer-Mace, D. (2010). Making practice public: Teacher learning in the 21st century. *Journal of Teacher Education, 61,* 77.

Acknowledgments

The editors would like to thank all contributing authors for sharing their innovative practices in teacher education and for inspiring our readers with their success stories.

We would like to personally recognize and extend a special note of appreciation to Dr. Drew Bogner, president, and Dr. Valerie Collins, vice president for academic affairs, of Molloy College, Rockville Centre, New York, who both encourage and value faculty scholarship. We offer a heartfelt thank you to the entire college leadership team, especially to Dr. Maureen Walsh, dean of the Division of Education, for recognizing the importance of innovative teacher education practices and faculty publications. We also wish to acknowledge individuals who have encouraged us to pursue this project, including Dr. Bernadette Donovan, O.P., Dr. Maria Dove, Dr. Charles Howlett, and Dr. Peter Lynch, as well as Kelley Cordeiro for her assistance with the manuscript preparation. We could not have completed this project without our colleagues and friends for supporting us on a daily basis—you know who you are!

Gratitude is extended to the staff at Rowman & Littlefield, who had the confidence in us to expand the first *Breaking the Mold* book into a four-volume series: Dr. Thomas Koerner, vice president and editorial director; Lindsey Schauer, assistant editor; and Maera Stratton, former assistant to Dr. Koerner.

1

PRESERVICE TEACHER EDUCATION

The expectations for teachers have risen dramatically over the last decade, in part prompted by legislation such as No Child Left Behind (NCLB) or accreditation requirements in schools of education urgently calling for highly qualified, certified teachers. This call for higher expectations and exemplary performance has simultaneously been undermined by the falling status of teachers. The criteria of what makes a professional and whether teachers' status is being reduced to that of a semiprofessional have been brought into question (Sadker & Zittleman, 2009). Teacher preparation has come under severe scrutiny as the profession is currently imposed by a strong accountability movement that is linking teacher performance with student academic achievement (Cochran-Smith, 2003). Furthermore, teachers are being encouraged to take ownership of their teaching and assume greater responsibility for student achievement (Hyslop-Margison & Sears, 2010).

Many professors and researchers have long been concerned with the preservice teacher programs that purport to *train* teachers at the undergraduate and graduate levels or through alternative preparation routes. These program leaders boldly claim that they adequately prepare future teachers, yet approximately half the teachers will leave the profession within the first five years of teaching (National Commission on Teaching and America's Future, 2007).

This section of the book examines varied preservice teacher education models and offers innovative accounts of democratization, collaboration, and implementation of effective practices designed to support the future teacher. Each of the ideas presented acknowledges that the teachers of tomorrow must master the knowledge, skills, and dispositions associated with professional teaching and learning.

First, Catherine McTamaney and Amy Palmeri discuss the development of their preservice teacher education program's conceptual framework, one in which they strengthen their own best practices to create a clearly defined teacher preparation program. Cultural and political vignettes are introduced by Jacqueline Darvin as a way for preservice teachers to apply culturally responsive practices when faced with the challenges of diverse classrooms. Through the community college lens, Laura R. Kates builds a bridge to four-year institutions as she addresses key ways to support future teachers in their understanding of professional literature. Next, Mark Warner, Cherry O. Steffen, Jim Cope, and Beth A. Peery offer a framework for enhancing preservice teachers' technological knowledge when coupled with problem-based learning pedagogy. Ken Zeichner and Morva McDonald describe how their teacher candidates benefit from the development of partnerships with community-based organizations.

In addition, Yi-Ping Huang details how teacher candidates can be immersed in a stimulating and supportive academic environment with high-impact experiences that bridge the contexts of residence, classroom, and the world beyond the campus. Peter Smagorinsky offers a programmatic innovation of service learning in alternative schools as a vehicle for future teachers to examine their own assumptions about the complexities of culture. Lastly, Sheryl L. McGlamery and Saundra L. Shillingstad offer a format for modeling best practices in assessment as they support their teacher candidates' assessment of literacy development.

REFERENCES

Cochran-Smith, M. (2003). Editorial: The unforgiving complexity of teaching. *Journal of Teacher Education, 54,* 3–5.

Hyslop-Margison, E. J., & Sears, A. M. (2010). Enhancing teacher performance: The role of professional autonomy. *Interchange, 41*(1), 1–15.

National Commission on Teaching and America's Future. (2007). *The high cost of teacher turnover* (Policy Brief). Retrieved July 2, 2010, from http://www .nctaf.org/resources/demonstration_projects/turnover/documents/CTTPolicy Brief6–19.pdf
Sadker, D. M., & Zittleman, K. R. (2009). *Teachers, schools, and society: A brief introduction to education* (2nd ed.). Boston: McGraw-Hill.

1

Mirrors, Maps, and Torchlights: Enacting a Conceptual Framework for Teacher Education

Catherine McTamaney and Amy Palmeri

Articulating a conceptual framework is nothing new for most teacher education programs. Indeed, for programs seeking national accreditation, such articulation is required (Dottin, 2001; NCATE, 2008). A sound framework can be a mirror of the beliefs currently held in the institution and a torchbearer for where the institution hopes to go. Like all tools, though, frameworks are limited by their users. Even the most profoundly articulated framework can go in one of two directions: toward relevance or toward obscurity. Who designs it, implements it, and assesses it will determine whether it becomes a powerful tool or an irrelevant paper trail.

Admittedly, our prior framework had fallen into obscurity and, candidly, few of us noticed. The articulation served policy requirements but offered little guidance beyond accreditation to those whose work it was designed to inform. Like many programs, our National Council for the Accreditation of Teacher Education (NCATE) accreditation cycle demanded we revisit our conceptual framework. Unlike some programs—and, indeed, in contrast to the precedent within our own program—this time, the leadership of practicing teacher educators, the support of our administration, and the availability of time and resources combined to elevate that process from a required component of accreditation to a trailblazing description of both where we were and where we hope to be. Ultimately, our framework emerged as a powerful, compelling vision that guides us to prepare candidates who understand research, implement

5

evidence-based practices, are reflective learners, and are educational leaders (Vanderbilt University, 2010).

WIPING THE MIRROR CLEAN

Our first task was to acknowledge that the existing framework was insufficient to inform or guide our current work. Designed by faculty who had since left the program, the framework described a process that, while appropriate, had no authentic link to the practices currently in place. Our dean appointed a task force of teacher educators, research faculty, and program directors, charging it with recommending ways to strengthen teacher preparation within our university.

The practical implication of reaccreditation helped structure our work in a serious manner and justified the allocation of resources, both in time and money, to the process. The task force convened a group of faculty to undertake the essential, if tedious, process of articulating a new framework. Faculty invited to participate had both deep knowledge of and the authority to make changes to our programs. Thus, we lost little time to establishing buy-in among the task force. Our intellectual effort quickly focused on clearing the path for innovations. The same individuals who designed the framework determined the ways it would be evident in our programs and, therefore, viewed aligning the framework and its implicit values with its explicit reflection in our practice as an opportunity not a burden. The process was organic, the impact immediate, and the outcome evident in stronger programs.

The new framework described both what we already did and what we sought to become. We took time, nearly eighteen months, to clarify, critique, and refine what we held as essential and what we would not sacrifice in the evolution of a process as dynamic as teacher education. That momentum inspired the designers of the framework to apply it as the central driving force in our work, allowing us to nudge program policies and refine our practices even while the framework emerged. Ultimately, the framework was sufficiently complex to reflect common beliefs across multiple programs, yet flexible enough to respond to and reflect the unique demands of individual programs (Ball, 2008; Feiman-Nemser, 2001; Grossman & McDonald, 2008).

The completed framework describes teacher preparation programs designed to prepare graduates who design, plan, enact, and refine instruction based on continuous investigation and analysis of student thinking and skill development. Our programs provide candidates opportunities to develop in four distinct but interrelated areas:

1. Subject Matter Knowledge for Teaching: Deep understanding of the content areas to be taught and how this content can be made accessible to students.
2. Understanding of Learners and Learning: Recognition of the ways in which learners' academic, behavioral, cultural, linguistic, and socioeconomic histories and repertoires inform learning and teaching.
3. Conceptions of the Practice and Profession of Teaching: How teachers construe their roles and relationships within their classrooms, schools, community, and the profession.
4. An Initial Repertoire in Curriculum, Instruction, Management, and Assessment: The understanding of and ability to use a well-chosen set of tools and techniques, as well as to transform materials to support student learning.

Following the formal adoption of the framework, we again faced two choices. We could view the framework as a means toward an end (merely completing documentation required for accreditation) or we could elevate it to strengthen the work we do and guide what we hope to do in the future. We chose the latter. Emphasizing practice, the framework articulated performance expectations, clarifying what successful graduates should know and be able to do by the end of their program. Because we described not only the theoretical underpinnings of our work but also the hallmarks we believed would be evident in a candidate who had been prepared through our program, the framework proved particularly useful as a tool guiding our daily work and shaping its path.

TAKING UP THE TORCH

Our department offers licensure in three undergraduate programs: Early Childhood, Elementary, and Secondary Education. Designing the framework highlighted common challenges across the multiple programs. In each, we faced a predictable obstacle of supporting our candidates as they navigate between their lives as undergraduates and their lives as potential teachers. Our programs exist within a unique setting as a private, elite Research I institution offering initial licensure to undergraduates. Our candidates transition between their on-campus lives of cocktail parties and the Greek row of sororities and fraternities and their off-campus professional lives as teaching candidates. Although we had believed we were already doing many of the things articulated in the framework, our surprise in realizing the common challenges our candidates experienced was profound.

By defining *conceptions of the practice and profession of teaching*, our understanding of our candidates' struggle grew. By articulating what we believed they would experience as they transitioned between their two lives, we were able to develop practices that responded more proactively to that transition. By applying the framework systematically to address this challenge, we were able to develop more effective ways of responding to candidates' internal discord.

THE BINARY LIVES OF CANDIDATES

We began with a presumption that familiarity with the language and emphases of the framework, as a reflection of the literature in the field and the values held at our institution, would strengthen candidates' ability to adopt coherent practices within our programs and beyond. We believed the challenges of their binary lives as college students and novice teachers were developmentally appropriate and that making such an understanding explicit would help them integrate those lives more effectively. To this end, the directors of our three programs created our *Teacher Candidate Policy and Performance Assessment Handbook* (Palmeri, Hardenbrook, & McTamaney, 2006).

Utilizing the metaphor of a journey to describe our expectations, we detailed candidates' likely experiences on the path: key features of the framework, the developmental trajectory we predicted for our candidates' performance, and the explicit means by which teacher candidates' knowledge, dispositions, and performance would be assessed. The handbook described explicitly the values reflected implicitly in our framework:

1. Teacher candidates and teacher educators undertake this journey together, with unique responsibilities for arriving at a predictable destination.
2. The journey is sensitive to and consistent with developmental principles.
3. Although the ultimate destination of our shared journey is known from the outset, we anticipate detours along the way; detours that provide opportunities to better understand our collective development as teachers.
4. Program policies should facilitate our response to these detours with sensitivity to the developmental needs of individuals without sacrificing alignment with the expectations of the programs.

Our desire to apply the new framework to our work of preparing teachers served to fuel the development of our handbook. The handbook provides a map for our candidates, field partners, and faculty, detailing the individual paths students may take through the program toward the horizon described by the conceptual framework. Taken together, we have a framework that defines programmatic values and a handbook that operationalizes these values in a developmental context.

The final innovation securing the influence of our intellectual work on the practices in our program lay in how well we articulated to our candidates the expectations for performance described in our handbook. We wanted candidates to internalize the values of the framework. To do so, we believed candidates needed repeated exposure to the framework and that such exposure was needed to mirror the same teaching practices it emphasized. Thus, we planned for regular and scaffolded opportunities to educate our candidates.

Each year, we introduce them to the framework and performance handbook during an orientation held in the freshman year, include a summary of the framework in all course syllabi for licensure courses, and implement the performance expectations in all field experiences. Finally, our explicit goal of seamlessly integrating the scholarly work of the framework's development with its practical implementation led us to develop new tools to bring coherence to our programs and inform ongoing program development.

LIGHTING OUR PATH AND
ILLUMINATING OUR PRACTICE

We developed a framework that was reflective of our programs and articulated the specific performances we believed would demonstrate candidates' internalization of the values it embraced. Knowing that we wanted our framework to be both a mirror of and a torchlight for our program, we recognized that we needed ways to measure its impact in practice. Toward that end, we developed critical assessment documents consistent with and reflective of the language and concepts within our framework.

New assessment tools included checklist-based assessments used in early field experiences, dispositional assessments used in licensure courses, open-ended observation tools guiding the mentoring of teacher candidates, and extended narrative assessments used in student teaching. Focused on assessing the internal coherence of our framework, we were careful to design assessments that could be used in a variety of courses and by multiple professors. These assessment tools move the framework from ideals on paper to the measures by which we hold our candidates and ourselves accountable to those ideals.

In developing assessments, we incorporated language directly from the framework and organized the tools to describe performance in each strand. Because our framework emphasizes knowledge in practice, we linked the theoretical language of the framework to its potential demonstration in candidates' practice (Cohen, 2005; Schön, 1987). We designed assessments bridging the static theoretical foundation of the framework and its enactment in dynamic performance.

Consistent with theoretical foundation of the framework and the application of developmental principles in our programs, all of our performance assessments, regardless of when in the program they are utilized, are measured against end-of-program expectations, allowing us to describe candidates' knowledge in practice along a continuum of development. Candidates, therefore, have a clear sense of where they are going and a constant reference point providing insight into their individual progress. Carrying this particular torch required us to define the levels of performance we expected at benchmark points within our programs.

COMPASS ROSES: DESIGNING TOOLS FOR MEASURING CANDIDATE DEVELOPMENT

In each assessment tool, we describe the spectrum of performance within each strand of our framework, measured as *not yet evident, emergent, proficient,* or *accomplished.* We include criteria for knowledge and skill evident *in planning* and knowledge and skill evident *in practice.* This differentiation reflects our awareness that practice does not always mirror intention. From a developmental perspective, we expect candidates to have knowledge they do not yet know how to put into practice. At the same time, they are expected to enact practices and yet often lack the ability to justify them theoretically.

Developing assessment tools that are explicitly aligned with our framework allows feedback of our candidates' performance to be both formative to their development and informative to our understanding of how the framework is evidenced in our programs. In the same way that we hope our candidates will view their own teaching, we frame knowledge and performance in terms of candidates' strengths while pointing to areas for continued growth. Because the assessment framework is consistent among multiple programs, faculty and candidates can objectively discuss candidates' knowledge and practice with a common language, identifying where each candidate lies at any particular moment and the candidate's trajectory toward our shared goals.

Our framework emphasizes candidates' ability to diagnose student thinking as it influences instructional choices and assessments in a highly collaborative, evidence-based practice. Likewise, strong alignment of teacher education course work and fieldwork, frequent conversations among program faculty focused on candidates' thinking and learning, and systematic mentoring documenting candidates' performance over time contribute to the scaffolding of candidates' opportunities to discuss, examine, and critique their own knowledge and practice. Once engaged in an analysis of one's practice, it is easier to refine and extend that practice.

The repeated use of the same assessment tools tracks our candidates' developing knowledge and skill, illuminating the trajectory articulated in our handbook as it is reflected in candidates' performance. Our explicit focus on modeling effective practice and our candidates' involvement in the assessment process enable teacher education faculty to support candidates moving toward the independent, self-sustaining habits of self-assessment we intend them to maintain after they graduate.

WHAT WE HAVE LEARNED: AN IMAGE REFLECTED

What began as a decision to articulate a framework that was more than just words on a page had a profound impact on how our faculty thinks about and implements our work as teacher-educators. Because assessments of our candidates' performance are measured against the specific strands of our framework and at predictable benchmarks throughout the programs, we have found the collective performance of our candidates to be its own measure of our programs' internal coherence. Aligning our theoretical base with a measurable accountability to candidates' learning protects the integrity of our programs and enables us to learn more about our work as teacher educators and to better understand beginning teacher development.

By insisting on programmatic assessments that explicitly reflected the strands of our conceptual framework, we were able to easily identify times when our program did not align with the intent of the framework. Our first application of the performance assessment tools, for example, suggested that the sequence through which candidates completed required course work influenced the proficiency with which they were able to demonstrate more nuanced qualities of their practice. Thus, we adopted a prescribed sequence we believed supported the most effective construction of candidate knowledge. Our assessments helped us defend a policy change that more accurately reflected our understanding of how candidates learn. In doing so, we modeled at a programmatic level the same closed loop of inquiry, intervention, and assessment that we encourage candidates to adopt in their teaching.

Additionally we designed an assessment to measure candidates' pedagogical content knowledge (Ball, Thames, & Phelps, 2008; Phelps & Schilling, 2004; Shulman, 1986). We sought the expertise of content professors in literacy, social studies, science, and math education to develop scenarios that could elicit candidates' general pedagogical knowledge, specific content knowledge, and pedagogical content knowledge, then situated this assessment between completion of candidates' required course work and the beginning of student teaching. Consistent with the framework, this assessment again models our belief that pedagogical content knowledge should persist beyond the completion of each class and measures our proficiency in eliciting it in candidates.

The framework became powerful, not only because it helped us understand candidates' development but also because we have used it to illuminate a path toward increasingly coherent programs. Our engagement in the refinement of our practice is a powerful model for our candidates and answers a common challenge in aligning the methods of teacher education with the methods candidates adopt themselves. We *mirror* in our practice as teacher educators as complex and nuanced an image of teaching and learning, complete with its compelling and intellectually engaging challenges, as we hope our candidates will demonstrate when they leave.

REFERENCES

Ball, D. (2008). *The work of teaching and the challenge for teacher education.* Hunt Lecture presentation to the annual meeting of the American Association of Colleges of Teacher Education, New Orleans, LA.

Ball, D. L., Thames, M. H., & Phelps, G. (2008). Content knowledge for teaching: What makes it special? *Journal of Teacher Education, 59,* 389–407.

Cohen, D. (2005). Professions of human improvement: Predicaments of teaching. In M. Nisan & O. Schremer (Eds.), *Educational deliberations* (pp. 278–294). Jerusalem, Israel: Keter.

Dottin, E. S. (2001). *The development of a conceptual framework.* Lanham, MD: University Press of America.

Feiman-Nemser, S. (2001). From preparation to practice: Designing a continuum to strengthen and sustain teaching. *Teachers College Record, 103,* 1013–1055.

Grossman, P., & McDonald, M. (2008). Back to the future: Directions for research in teaching and teacher education. *American Educational Research Journal, 45,* 184–205

National Council for Accreditation of Teacher Education. (2008), *Professional standards for the accreditation of teacher preparation institutions.* Retrieved March 29, 2010, from www.ncate.org/documents/standards/

Palmeri, A., Hardenbrook, M., & McTamaney, C. (2006). *Teacher candidate policy and performance assessment handbook: Your guide to practica and student teaching*. Nashville, TN: Vanderbilt University.

Phelps, G., & Schilling, S. (2004). Developing measures of content knowledge for teaching reading. *Elementary School Journal, 105*(1), 31–48.

Schön, D. (1987). *Educating the reflective practitioner*. San Francisco: Jossey-Bass.

Shulman, L. S. (1986). Those who understand: Knowledge growth in teaching. *Educational Researcher, 15*(2), 4–14.

Vanderbilt University. (2010). *Peabody College of Vanderbilt University: Conceptual framework*. Retrieved May 20, 2010, from http://peabody.vanderbilt.edu/ Documents/NCATE/Conceptual%20Framework%20Exhibits/Conceptual Framework.pdf

2

"I Would Rather Feel Uncomfortable in an Education Class Than at the School Where I Teach": Cultural and Political Vignettes as a Pedagogical Approach in Teacher Education

Jacqueline Darvin

Some of my students have started drawing themselves with blonde hair. I try to emphasize that they're beautiful the way they are, but it's interesting to take notice of how they emulate my looks and aspects of my culture because I'm their teacher. All my kids are darker because they are Asian, Hispanic, Indian. . . . They all have darker hair and eyes. So for me to walk in there with blonde hair and blue eyes, I'm different to them. They see me as their teacher, so I'm pretty—no matter what. . . . It's funny how now I'm so much more in tune to things like this. I would have never noticed or questioned it before working with CPVs.

The preceding excerpt was taken from an exit interview with a second-year elementary school teacher who had just completed a graduate course at Queens College of the City University of New York, in which cultural and political vignettes (CPVs) were employed and researched as an innovative teacher education practice. CPVs are cultural and political scenarios that are presented to teachers, first in a written format and later enacted as situated performances. They are designed to ask teachers to reflect on the cultural and political factors that influence their own decision making and that of others in the school community, including students, parents, administrators, and colleagues.

CPVs ask respondents to work out possible solutions to conflicts that are complex, open ended, and closely mirror the kinds of difficult situations that teachers of today often face but are seldom addressed or even acknowledged in teacher preparation programs (Sleeter, 2001). Examples of several of the vignettes that were performed and discussed at length by teachers in the CPV study at Queens College included the following:

- It is parent–teacher conference night and the parents of a student in your class come to see you. Their son is doing poorly in your class and they blame you and the school for their son's problems in your class. What are some of the things you can say and do to try and improve this situation? What pitfalls should you avoid?
- You are a new teacher in a culturally diverse high school. One day, you are in the faculty room eating lunch and three other teachers from your department are present. You overhear one of the teachers using racial slurs when referring to a student and his parents. What, if anything, can you do and why?
- There are several foreign-born students in your fourth-period class. As English language learners, you know that it is important for them to be given many opportunities to speak English, but when they try and participate in discussions, the native speakers of English make fun of their accents and tease them. How would you deal with this issue?
- As a novice teacher (the year before you come up for tenure), your principal tells you to write your own annual performance evaluation and she will sign it. She says she's very busy, she knows you are doing a fine job, and no one will ever know. What would you say and do?

It is important to note that thought-provoking CPVs compel the responding teachers to consider problems through several cultural and political lenses and encourage them to contemplate aspects of culture or politics with which they may not be entirely familiar or comfortable. CPVs allow teachers to share and dialogue about experiences that they have had as both students and teachers and to make decisions collectively as they unpack the various aspects of the situations and discuss possible approaches and repercussions to their decisions.

CHALLENGES IN TEACHER EDUCATION

Although many leading teacher educators have written about the need for teachers to be given opportunities to challenge assumptions, broaden belief systems, and develop more complex understandings of teaching and learning in culturally, linguistically, and politically diverse settings (Cochran-Smith, 2005; Hoffman & Pearson, 2000; Ladson-Billings, 1995), very few advocate *actual pedagogical practices* designed to meet these intricate goals (Sleeter, 2001). Absent from their analyses and recommendations are suggestions of how teacher educators can actually help students to become more culturally and politically aware through targeted course work and class activities.

Teachers who participated in two recent studies of the impact of CPVs on their graduate course work at Queens College acknowledged in a survey that ways for teachers to approach culturally and politically sensitive issues were topics rarely, if ever, addressed in their undergraduate teacher education programs. Instead, they indicated that the emphasis in their prior teacher preparation was placed much more heavily on training teachers in the more mechanical aspects of teaching, such as creating assessments and lesson plans. The mismatch between teacher education course work and the real challenges teachers face in diverse classrooms can create tremendous problems for novice teachers as they increasingly encounter culturally and politically sensitive issues in their classrooms.

The National Commission on Teaching and America's Future (2008) reported that every school day, nearly a thousand teachers in the United States leave the field of teaching and another thousand change schools. This incredibly high rate of attrition does not exist solely because new teachers cannot write effective lesson plans. It exists, in part, because teacher education programs need to do a better job of preparing teachers for the realities of teaching, including the myriad of culturally and politically sensitive issues and problems that occur.

It is interesting to note that the National Council for Accreditation of Teacher Education (NCATE) appears to be moving in a similar direction in their recent call for an enhanced clinical preparation of teachers. In January 2010, they announced the formation of an expert panel called the NCATE Blue Ribbon Panel on Clinical Preparation, Partnerships, and

Improved Student Learning. According to NCATE (2010), "Significantly enhanced clinical preparation may mean, for example, more extensive use of simulations, case studies, analyses of teaching and other approximations of teaching, as well as sustained, intense, mentored school-embedded experiences" (p. 1). It is for the aforementioned reasons that cultural and political vignettes (CPVs), particularly in the form of situated performances, have the potential to help break the mold in teacher education.

THEORETICAL FRAMEWORK

In the two studies of CPVs conducted at Queens College, participants indicated that the most powerful aspect of the CPVs came to light during the situated performances and the class discussions that followed those performances. As a practice or methodology, situated performance finds its roots in situated cognition research and is also connected to research on dramatic role-play, simulation, and other experiential forms of learning (Finders & Rose, 1999). However, situated performance differs from these other forms of learning in several important ways. According to Finders and Rose,

> Situated performances are role-taking activities with the following characteristics: 1) learners actively participate by assuming specific subject positions (as opposed to merely observing others' actions or imagining their own actions); 2) the social, cultural, institutional and interpersonal contexts for the actions and situational constraints are fore-grounded; and 3) the performed actions, motives, and circumstances are subjected to critical reflection and revision. (p. 208)

Critical reflection and revision of the performed actions and dialogue are integral parts of situated performances and the ensuing dialogue. Situated performances differ from other role-plays in the sense that participants are asked to reflect on their actions, comments, gestures, and other aspects of both verbal and nonverbal communication in a more in-depth way. Additionally, participants are asked to articulate the cultural, political, institutional, and interpersonal contexts of their actions and those of the others in the performance in ways that they would not in a typical role-play.

The essence of the theory behind how and why CPVs can be effective in teacher preparation is that when teachers have opportunities to engage in situated performances as part of their teacher education course work, they have virtual or simulated cases stored in their memories to compare and contrast with the new, real situations they encounter. This allows them to use their past experiences to help determine appropriate responses. The self-reflective and self-analytical components of situated performances lend themselves perfectly to a teacher education context because these are aspects of good teaching that are touted as being important but are not usually taught explicitly in education classes.

DATA COLLECTION

Data collection included written reflections from students throughout the semester and videotapes of the CPV situated performances and the class discussions that followed. Ethnographic observations were made in the form of detailed observational notes by the primary investigator, and exit interviews of all participants were conducted. All videotaped and audio-taped data were transcribed, coded, and analyzed for recurrent themes.

HOW CAN CPVS HELP BREAK THE MOLD
IN TEACHER EDUCATION?

The analyses of the situated performances of CPVs by the participants themselves is the hallmark of what makes it more powerful than some of the traditional case-study approaches that are employed regularly in teacher education contexts to help students come to understand issues of culture, power, and politics. An example of this was illustrated in a class discussion that followed a CPV situated performance. In the performances, participants were asked to conduct mock parent–teacher conferences with angry parents who were making false accusations toward the teachers and blaming them for their children's failures in school. At the conclusion of the performances, the teachers analyzed their own comments and body language during the situated performance. They believed that the teachers (actors) in the vignette had made degrading comments about the children and the way their parents were raising them.

The teachers engaged in a lot of finger-pointing and tended to blame the parents for their children's academic difficulties. They failed to say anything positive to the parents about their children and made no offers to partner with the parents or provide any additional assistance to the children. In analyzing their body language, the teachers noticed that the teachers in the situated performances did not even stand up when the mock parents entered the room, indicating that the teachers did not welcome them or make them feel important.

This self-reflective, constructive dialogue emerged as a valuable tool because it asked the teachers to evaluate *their own* verbal and nonverbal communication in ways that would be difficult in their real classrooms. The CPV situated performances provided them with opportunities to evaluate the positions of both the parents and teachers in the situation and to unpack not only aspects of the performance that could be clearly seen by the audience members but also other highly influential ones that often cannot be visually interpreted.

The conversation continued to center on other issues that could not be observed directly during the situated performances but may have affected the parents' and teachers' actions. For example, the teachers discussed parents who may be English language learners and nervous because of their limited English proficiency. They discussed political factors that may influence people's views of the institution of school and how even the concept of parent–teacher night is an American construct with which foreign-born parents might not be familiar or comfortable. Finally, the discussion concluded with ways that teachers can facilitate the process of making parents feel comfortable and open lines of communication within and beyond the classroom walls.

One of the exceptional aspects of using situated performances of CPVs as a pedagogical tool in teacher education is that they enable the teachers who are engaged in these performances to see themselves and others in new ways. They aid in the discussion of not only the things that were said in the situated performances, but *how* they were said, *why* they may have been said in particular ways, and *what* implications these nuances of communication have for teachers in a variety of situations involving students, parents, colleagues, and administrators. During and after the situated performances, participants can actually pinpoint and discuss these fine distinctions and learn to hone their communication skills accordingly. The ability to do this is greatly enhanced when the situated performances are videotaped and repeatedly reviewed by the class.

EVIDENCE OF SUCCESS

One major theme to clearly emerge from the data in the CPV studies was labeled Teachers' Increased Awareness. This theme was seen across all of the participants' interview responses. The first subtheme about which teachers reported increasing their awareness concerned the ways in which student behavior, academic achievement, class participation, motivation, engagement, and even attendance are actually affected by culturally and politically sensitive issues in the classroom.

Another subtheme was related to teachers increasing their knowledge about the complex relationships between culture and identity and how their own cultures come into play in the classroom, including stereotypes that others may have about them. Most of the participants expressed an increased awareness of the need for teachers to think more carefully before reacting to culturally and politically sensitive situations in their classrooms and school communities. Many of the class discussions also centered on the complexity of culturally and politically sensitive situations and the need for teachers to consider and approach them from multiple perspectives.

In addition, there were findings that were specific to the situated performances themselves, when analyzing both the verbal and nonverbal communication of the students. One of the things revealed in the analysis of the situated performances was that the teachers were not aware of many of the things that they communicated nonverbally. They even expressed things physically about which they were completely unaware. These included (a) not standing up when an actor who was portraying a *parent* role entered the classroom, (b) not greeting actors that were portraying *students* at the classroom door or acknowledging their entrance into the room with smiles or nods, and (c) acting in a subservient manner with actors portraying *administrators*, such as stooping their shoulders, speaking in quiet, inaudible tones, and stuttering. Other teachers interrupted one another or spoke loudly when acting as *colleagues* in a situated performance, said words "like" or "um" repeatedly when they were nervous, and did not allow actors portraying *students* any wait time after asking questions, just to name a few examples.

Another phenomenon that was revealed in and through the situated performances was that, more often than not, the teachers' first responses to the CPVs were not what they later determined to be the best ones. They often believed that they reacted too quickly or emotionally and then after considering the situation more carefully, revised their actions and comments in the situated performance. This led to many discussions that centered on taking more time to listen to others before reacting. The participants unanimously agreed after reviewing the situated performances that their listening skills needed to be strengthened, particularly in dealing with sensitive issues in their classrooms and school communities.

CONCLUSIONS

In their exit interviews, 80 percent of the participants in the CPV studies were able to provide concrete, specific examples of how working with the CPVs influenced their decision-making processes and subsequent actions in their classrooms and school communities. The remaining 20 percent indicated that they believed the CPVs were helpful in influencing their thinking and subsequent actions but were unable to provide definitive examples in which they may have acted differently in particular situations as a direct result of working with the CPVs.

In her exit interview, one participant referred to an interaction that she had with a Mexican student and how the CPV work influenced her thinking regarding the culturally sensitive issue of the kinds of foods that people from various cultures eat that may be different from American foods:

> A little girl was sharing that in Mexico they eat crickets. And so I said, "Oh, that's wonderful, that's so great. Why don't you bring some? I would like to see what they look like." So the other day, she came to school, took her little hand out of her pocket and had a handful of fried crickets. The other Mexican students were very happy and wanted to share her fried crickets. And then some of the children were saying, "Ugh, that's disgusting, that's disgusting; I can't believe you're doing that; that's disgusting, that's disgusting." I

scolded them, and I told them that's part of her culture; that's part of what they do and who they are. That's not very nice of you. Then she offered me a fried cricket, and said to me, "So why don't you try one?" I said, "Okay," and I did. I didn't really want to, but I felt it was more important to model for the children and to be culturally responsive in this situation.

This example illustrates one of many self-reported ways in which CPV activities positively influenced the teachers' thinking and decision-making processes in their classrooms and school communities. Although examples such as this one can be viewed as small in the overall context of decisions that teachers face, they do indicate that this pedagogical approach made some difference for the majority of participants in the study.

CPVs have the potential to help break the mold in teacher education because rather than simply discussing the challenge of making educators more culturally and politically savvy, which already has been done at length, they are practices that can actually be used to assist in accomplishing these worthy goals.

REFERENCES

Cochran-Smith, M. (2005). The new teacher education: For better or for worse? *Educational Researcher, 34,* 3–17.

Finders, M., & Rose, S. (1999). "If I were the teacher": Situated performances as pedagogical tools for teacher preparation. *English Education, 31,* 205–222.

Hoffman, J., & Pearson, P. (2000). Reading teacher education in the next millennium: What your grandmother's teacher didn't know that your granddaughter's teacher should. *Reading Research Quarterly, 35*(1), 28–44.

Ladson-Billings, G. (1995). Toward a theory of culturally relevant pedagogy. *American Education Research Journal, 32,* 465–491.

National Commission on Teaching and America's Future (NCTAF). (2008). *No dream denied: A pledge to America's children.* Washington, DC: Author.

National Council for Accreditation of Teacher Education (NCATE). (2010). *NCATE news: NCATE blue ribbon panel initiates a mainstream move to more clinically based preparation of teachers.* Retrieved January 23, 2010, from http://www.ncate.org/public/010410_BRP.asp

Sleeter, C. (2001). Preparing teachers for culturally diverse schools: Research and the overwhelming presence of whiteness. *Journal of Teacher Education, 52,* 94–106.

3

Building a Bridge from the Experiential to the Textual: Preparing Critical Readers for a Complex Teaching Terrain

Laura R. Kates

COMMUNITY COLLEGE TEACHER EDUCATION STUDENTS' TRANSFER EXPERIENCES

Community colleges are currently viewed as an essential resource for diversifying the teaching force, bringing needed new teachers into the workforce, and improving teacher retention (Center for Community College Policy, 2006; Townsend, 2007). Ayers (2010) noted that close to half of all undergraduates in the United Sates attend a community college, most of whom are from lower socioeconomic backgrounds. In addition, many are the first in their families to ever go to college.

Although data on enrollment, alignment, credentialing, and retention abound (Center for Community College Policy, 2006; Ignash & Slotnick, 2007; Townsend, 2007), community college education students' own accounts of their professional preparation are rarely found in the literature. In an effort to examine students' own perceptions, a study was conducted that endeavored to fill this gap in the knowledge base. The project began by interviewing a cohort of graduates of a community college's early childhood education program. Students' experiences at the two-year college and at the nearby four-year college they had transferred to under an articulation agreement between the two campuses, which are both part of a large public urban university system, were explored (Kates, 2010).

Although the interviewees were quite diverse in terms of age, ethnicity, and level of academic achievement, their perceptions of the successes and challenges encountered at each institution were remarkably similar. Most strikingly, community college students experienced difficulties in making the transition from the *experiential* emphasis of the two-year college to the *textual* emphasis of the four-year institution. Students enjoyed and found much value in the two-year college's early childhood focus—especially the actual enactment of such activities as baking, painting, block building, and reading aloud—but they struggled with the four-year college's expectation of constructing interpretations of and personally responding to assigned readings. In addition to learning about early childhood curricula in their education classes, now they experienced a major shift and also had to integrate references to peer-reviewed research into their writing. Most community college students tend to be unfamiliar with such tasks and unclear about how to approach them. Many are unable to do so successfully, frequently failing required classes or finding themselves barred from matriculating in their majors because of low GPAs (Shkodriani, 2004).

An innovative solution to these challenges has led to the development of new approaches that can sustain the social, interactive, practice-oriented approach the students are drawn to and with which they have become so successful. This initiative also offers the much-needed opportunity for them to become more accustomed to textual engagement and analysis as an integral part of their classroom and professional life. This chapter describes such innovative practices and the students' responses to them.

PREPARING CRITICAL READERS FOR
A COMPLEX TEACHING TERRAIN

In thinking about how to bolster the textual dimension of course work at the community college, there needs to be an emphasis not just on surface comprehension of text but also on such critical reading skills as questioning, analyzing, synthesizing, and identifying assumptions and intentions (Richardson, Okun, & Fisk, 1983). Such skills are crucial for success at the four-year college. Additionally, they are essential if teacher candidates are to become informed, aware early childhood and elementary education professionals, particularly given the current complex terrain of mandated assessments, as well as local, state, and national standards, prescribed curricula, and forms for accountability and reporting that are now so predominant in the workplace. Without the ability to read critically, graduates of two-year college teacher education programs will be unable to thoughtfully analyze the substance, source, and purpose of the many mandates they are sure to encounter.

In aiming to develop pedagogical strategies that bolster such critical reading skills, this innovation has been influenced by the literature, often authored by practitioners of undergraduate education, on methods that allow students to thoughtfully engage with texts through processes that are lively, active, and collaborative (Barkley, Cross, & Major, 2005; Nilson, 2003). Most influential has been the work on seminaring, developed by faculty collaborating with the Washington Center for Improving the Quality of Undergraduate Education. In the context of undergraduate education, the term *seminaring* means a "focused, collaborative group discussion of a text" (Washington Center for Improving the Quality of Undergraduate Education, n.d., p. 1). Students prepare for the seminar by reading the text and writing beforehand about the author's essential points and purposes as well as about the questions and personal responses the text generates for them (Hamish, 1995). As students become more familiar and comfortable with the seminaring process, discussions are increasingly student led rather than teacher directed (Hamish, 1995).

In addition to the literature on seminaring, these innovative practices were informed by Barkley et al.'s (2005) work on collaborative learning techniques and Nilson's (2003) thinking on process-oriented writing-to-learn activities. In combination, these resources provided a framework for designing assignments that allow students to become more familiar and comfortable with text-based course work while engaging in manageable, interesting, and educative learning experiences.

BUILDING A BRIDGE FROM
THE EXPERIENTIAL TO THE TEXTUAL

At the urban community college in which this innovation takes place, a simplified version of the seminar is being implemented in the introductory *Foundations of Education* course. All students who indicate an interest in the early childhood or childhood education major at the college must first take this course and pass it with a grade of C or better in order to matriculate in either major. Many students come to the class straight from high school and have not been assigned readings before other than those found in a textbook. Rarely have they been asked to or taught how to actively synthesize and interpret what they have read. It is critical to work with the incoming freshmen so that, from the outset, they can deepen their meaning-making strategies. Future teachers must acquire the awareness that attention to text and the practice of critical reading are essential for success in college and professional life.

As with any effective learning experience, it is crucial to tailor teaching to the needs of the learners. In this Foundations course, there are many English language learners (ELLs), as well as both native and nonnative speakers of English enrolled in developmental English courses. The reading material must, therefore, be selected so that it is both accessible to and stimulating for students with highly varied abilities, experiences, and prior knowledge.

Although much of what is written about seminaring focuses upon discussion and analysis of full-length books, the seminars described here focus upon short articles from professional journals and periodicals. This is done because shorter readings are more manageable for many of the students, allowing them to get a feel for the range of topics and issues educators are currently addressing in their writing. In addition, students can gain an overview of the variety of publications and formats in which education professionals both read and write.

Articles are chosen that include discussion of theory and research but also offer strong links to classroom practice and real-world schooling. This is done so that students can engage with the practice-oriented content they tend to be most curious about while also gaining an understanding of the ways in which sound approaches to practice are, by necessity, rooted in rigorous theory and scholarship. Topics of the assigned articles include (a) the usefulness of reading multicultural children's books aloud, (b) the implementation of an inquiry-based approach to elementary science education, (c) the enormous academic pressures currently being placed on kindergartners, and (d) the approach being taken by some different preschools to closing the achievement gap.

Guided note-taking is assigned instead of the traditional seminar paper. The focus is to be on reading the articles as deeply and reflectively as possible rather than on the preparation of a formal written assignment. To scaffold this assignment, note-taking sheets are attached to the front of the articles. Open-ended questions are asked on these sheets so that students can both deepen their understanding of the assigned reading specifically and become more aware of the elements of text to which critical readers generally attend. These questions include what the author's most important points are, what the author's intents and purposes are, how this reading compares to others on similar topics, what questions are raised for the reader, what prior knowledge may be helpful to access, and what personal responses and opinions are evoked.

In addition to the cover sheets, students are encouraged to highlight, underline, and make notes in the margins as they read. How to do this is demonstrated early on in the semester, and successful examples from the class are shared on an ongoing basis.

Seminars are conducted in class approximately every other week. The following procedure is followed:

- Students are given a few minutes to read over their marked-up articles and filled-in note-taking sheets and to discuss them with a partner.
- Discussion begins with an exchange of perspectives about what the most important points are for each section of the article. Students are encouraged to attend to section headings and to substantiate their assertions by citing specific passages from the text.
- After reaching some consensus about the most important points, perceptions of the author's purposes are discussed, taking into account the type of publication in which the article has appeared and any biographical information offered. For this segment of the discussion, referring back to the text as evidence to support one's argument is, once again, highly encouraged.
- Students share personal responses to and opinions about the content of the article. This is, invariably, the liveliest segment of the seminar.

Many of the students in this introductory course arrive at the college having only had the experience of being asked to speak in class for the purpose of providing a brief, factual answer to a closed question posed by a teacher. Participating regularly in the open-ended exchanges of ideas that the seminar fosters makes for a comfortable, supportive context in which to articulate analysis of written texts. Further, by hearing consistently from others, students become aware of the multiple interpretations that can be made of a single reading and the ways in which prior knowledge and personal experience may shape those interpretations.

With their note-taking sheets as guides, students do a closer, more critical reading ahead of time, both because they know the sheets will be collected and because they know they will be expected to air their views in class. By providing a predictable structure while also embracing divergent opinions and ideas, the seminar is at once a rigorous and welcoming forum for teacher education students to collectively, critically consider the meaning of texts pertinent to their future practice and professional preparation.

LOOKING DEEPER WITHIN A TEXT

At the end of each semester, the students describe the learning opportunities the seminar offers in a survey about their experiences. This survey first asks, "Do you approach reading differently now than you did at the beginning of the semester?" Invariably, a majority of students answer affirmatively. When asked to describe just what has changed, most describe an enhanced ability to make meaning of text. Student comments have included:

- "This class really taught me to look deeper within a text and 'read between the lines.'"
- "These readings made me think deeper about the message of the author and read more carefully to understand the main idea."

Many students point to the need to take notes and to mark up the text as instrumental in their improved understanding:

- "I learned that for me to really understand and be engaged in reading, I have to highlight and sometimes annotate or else I get lost or lose interest."

- "I've become a more careful reader. I really try to zone in now and take notes on what the author is trying to say."

The most widely cited reason for improved comprehension is the social opportunity that has been provided to co-construct the meaning of text. As students have described it:

- "Most helpful was discussing what I read with classmates so I can hear another person's point of view and possibly change the way I think based on evidence and people's opinions."
- "Discussing it was the best part because getting to hear how others view things is really insightful and helpful."

Many share that they read much more carefully on their own when they know they are preparing to participate in a discussion.

Informal observations mesh with the students' evaluation of their learning process. As the semester progresses, more and more students come to class with passages carefully highlighted and notes made in the margins. More frequently, students turn to their notes before speaking in order to substantiate what they are going to say. A wider range of students, including more ELLs, participate readily in discussions. The seminar provides a framework that allows students to enjoy reading more, engage more deeply with what is read, and more confidently and competently voice interpretations and impressions.

CONCLUSION

The author's earlier research revealed that text-based assignments are often de-emphasized in community college teacher education programs because of a concern that students might struggle with such assignments or find them uninteresting (Kates, 2010). The experiences with seminaring indicate that this does not have to be the case if students are supplied with needed supportive scaffolds. In this instance, the note-taking sheets and class discussions, in particular, functioned as such scaffolds. The note-taking sheets provide accountability for doing the reading because they are collected after each seminar. Further, they spur students to read more thoughtfully because information about the authors' ideas and intents have to be categorized, recorded, and articulated to others.

The discussions provide a meaningful context in which to share and further analyze what has been recorded and an opportunity to learn through the spirited social modalities most teacher educations students prefer (Korthagen, Loughran, & Russell, 2006; Proefriedt, 1994). Although further study with more students in varied settings is clearly needed, these findings indicate that—if supportive conditions are created—two-year college teacher education students can and will read critically as well as enthusiastically.

REFERENCES

Ayers, D. F. (2010). Putting the community back into the college. *Academe, 96*(3), 9–11.

Barkley, E., Cross, P., & Major, C. (2005). *Collaborative learning techniques.* San Francisco: Jossey-Bass.

Center for Community College Policy. (2006). *Teacher preparation policy toolkit.* Retrieved July, 20, 2008, from http://www.communitycollegepolicy.org/html/toolkit/default.asp

Hamish, J. (1995). *What is in a seminar?* Retrieved March 15, 2009, from http://www.cfkeep.org/uploads/seminar_materials_copy2.pdf

Ignash, J. M., & Slotnick, R. C. (2007). The specialized associate's degree in teacher education: Effective pathway or degree proliferation? *Community College Review, 35*(1), 47–65.

Kates, L. R. (2010). Student perspectives on transfer and articulation: Implications for teacher education pedagogy and practice. *The New Educator, 6,* 30–55. Retrieved June 2, 2010, from http://www1.ccny.cuny.edu/prospective/education/theneweducator/upload/2nd-article-4.pdf

Korthagen, F., Loughran, J., & Russell, T. (2006). Developing fundamental principles for teacher education programs and practices. *Teaching and Teacher Education, 22,* 1020–1041.

Nilson, B. L. (2003). *Teaching at its best: A research-based resource for college instructors.* San Francisco: Anker.

Proefriedt, W. A. (1994). How teachers learn: Towards a more liberal education. New York: Teachers College Press.

Richardson, R. C., Jr., Okun, M. A., & Fisk, E. C. (1983). Literacy in the open-access college. San Francisco: Jossey-Bass.

Shkodriani, G. (2004). *Seamless pipeline from two-year to four-year institutions for teacher training.* Retrieved June 27, 2010, from http://www.ecs.org/clearing house/49/57/4957.pdf

Townsend, B. K. (2007). Pre-service teacher education in the community college. *Community College Review, 35*(1), 4–9.

Washington Center for Improving the Quality of Undergraduate Education. (n.d.). *Seminars: A collection of materials on seminar approaches and evaluation strategies.* Retrieved June 27, 2009, from http://www.evergreen.edu/ washcenter/natlc/pdf/seminars.pdf

4

Raising the Bar for Twenty-First-Century Teacher Preparation

Mark Warner, Cherry O. Steffen,
James Cope, and Beth A. Peery

BACKGROUND

Since students entering schools today differ from those of the past in terms of their technological literacy and educational experiences, educators must discover relevant curriculum (Martin, Warner, Brown, & Coffey, 2006) that enables constructivist pedagogy and *real-world* technology-rich, authentic assessment that address national content standards to have an impact on the learning of all students. Additionally, school systems that marshal the strengths of technology tools and implement their correlation to curriculum reform will stimulate students to cultivate critical thinking skills and increase the likelihood of students' successful performance in the world beyond the classroom (Means, 1997). Consequently, preservice teachers' acquisition of the knowledge, skills, and dispositions that attend to Technological Pedagogical Content Knowledge (TPACK) is essential to address the diverse learning challenges indigenous to twenty-first-century learners (Koehler & Mishra, 2008).

THEORETICAL FRAMEWORK AND FOCUS

The TPACK framework (Koehler & Mishra, 2008) connects technology to curriculum course content and specific pedagogical approaches (Shulman,

1987) and describes how teachers' understanding of technology, pedagogy, and content can interact with one another to produce effective content-based teaching with educational technologies. As we address the significance of TPACK's power to integrate elementary school curriculum and its ability to increase students' depth of understanding, we also underscore problem-based learning (Torpe & Sage, 2002; Warner & Leonard, 2004). Problem-based learning is a vigorously relevant pedagogy that incorporates a quality standards-based curriculum, instruction, and assessment for learners whose individual differences are influenced by such demographics as socioeco-nomic status, home language, and culture. Thus, the confluence of TPACK and problem-based-learning pedagogy results in an effective model that improves the development of teacher candidates' skills to meet the learn-ing challenges presented by students who are more diverse, technologically savvy, and more media molded than yesterday's learners.

MEETING THE CHALLENGE

This chapter not only demonstrates how TPACK and problem-based learning differentiate instruction for students who bring individual differ-ences to the classroom, it also evidences a successful teacher preparation course designed to engage preservice teachers in a semester-long whole-class collaboration to resolve *real-world* problems. As a final project, the student cohort in our integrative math, language arts, science, and social studies pedagogy courses are required to work together in three-person teams to produce an integrative unit of the highest quality that includes the following:

1. An authentic problem situation;
2. External links to student-made research-based graphic presentations providing social science-, language arts-, math-, and science-related information for children to assist with completing the tasks embed-ded in their problem situation;
3. An external link to a movie made by the various cohort groups us-ing Windows Movie Maker to provide more relevant information to introduce the essential questions concerning the problem presented;

4. An external link to a united streaming Discovery Channel video that also addresses and provides instructional insights into the problem situation; and

5. An interactive bulletin board (glog) using the free educational web software provided at www.Glogster/Education.com.

INTEGRATING THE CONTENT AREAS

A culminating project, entitled the *turboquest*, was designed to subsume all of the various formative assessments assigned in each of the following four content areas: social studies, language arts, science, and math. The turboquest simulation is an adaption of the webquest (Dodge, 1997) and so named for its insistence on the inclusion of specific student-generated, technology-enhanced learning products. This project provides the organizing element for all of the activities explored in the content pedagogy courses and also offers a twenty-first-century context for the learning that eventuates as a result of the project.

In addition to identifying the project as the organizing element, we used the National Council for Social Studies (NCSS) standards (1994) since they provide excellent themes from which to draw content-specific problem issues. The preservice teachers who register for this cohort are assigned to all the same methods course sections, and each preservice teacher is also assigned a specific K–5 field placement with a collaborating teacher.

Preservice teachers are divided into grade-alike teams and instructed in their first class session to have a conversation with their respective collaborating teacher concerning the content they are expected to teach during the field placement occurring at the end of the course. After the preservice teachers return the following week, the teams meet to discuss the most suitable grade-level social studies theme that provides the engine for developing one turboquest that each preservice teacher could use to teach the required integrated unit in his or her respective field placement. Once the developmentally appropriate thematic problem issues are identified by each team in their social studies methods course, the students were then responsible to negotiate how they were going to integrate the requirements

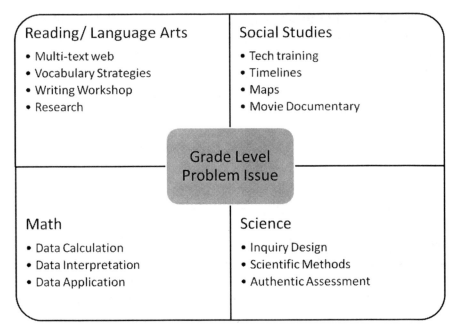

Figure 4.1.   Integrated Unit Turboquest Planning Guide

of their other methods courses to fit seamlessly into their final project. Figure 4.1 illustrates the planning guide for the kinds of content-specific applied learning that is included in the turboquest integrated unit.

UNPACKING TPACK

Making Social Studies Social

Since the final turboquest project is developed using various technology tools, the students acquire the necessary technology skills to complete their project in a technology lab in the context of a three-hour block devoted each week to the social studies methods course. Time is carved into the social studies methods course to allow the teams of students to work collaboratively on their group projects. For the first four social studies class blocks, students are given advanced instruction in presentation software for developing the turboquest slideshow, spreadsheets for generating charts and graphs to display data, desktop publishing for creating an announcement or invitation, and Windows Movie Maker for producing a documentary movie.

Presentation software enables a slide show that allows children to navigate through the different phases of the turboquest format, including the title, introduction, task, process, evaluation, and conclusion slides. Each slide type is designed for a specific purpose and guides the children to complete the formative and summative assessments embedded in the turboquest. In addition to the advanced instruction given in the software applications, students receive instruction in browsing for and saving content-specific graphics that are inserted as engaging visuals throughout the turboquest and used to produce an appealing documentary movie.

For example, the turboquest entitled "Dinner with Famous Americans" invites children to travel back in time to explore the lives of famous Americans who left behind legacies of leadership, activism, and caring. This turboquest simulation is inspired by the social studies standard stating that students will (a) discuss the lives of Americans who expanded people's rights and freedoms in a democracy, (b) be able to explain social barriers, restrictions, and obstacles that these historical figures had to overcome, and (c) describe how they overcame them (NCSS, 1994).

The Role of the Student Learners

Children placed in groups of four are given the task to research the lives of Frederick Douglass, Susan B. Anthony, Eleanor Roosevelt, and Thurgood Marshall. Since access to the Internet is often blocked in schools, the children conduct their research by viewing the individual presentation created by the preservice teachers concerning information associated with each famous American. These individual presentations contain required tables, graphs, charts, graphics, textual information, and links to Discovery Channel documentaries about these famous Americans and the times in which they lived.

Children are prompted to interpret this information to resolve problems associated with completing their final project. As a final project in this turboquest, the children must plan a dinner party that includes invitations and relevant discussion topics that pertain to their assigned American. Students then take on the role of their influential person by performing a short dinner-party skit for the class.

During the process of planning the dinner party, students make decisions about menu items, appropriate background music, proper period attire, and relevant dinner discussion topics. Members of the group assume the identity of their chosen American and role-play that individual for the duration of the dinner party. The classroom teacher participates as a guest at each dinner party to sustain conversation flow if necessary. Students are evaluated on the basis of individual participation in the conversation, relevance of the conversation, and appropriate menu, props, and entertainment.

The Role of the Professor

As we review the role of the professor in the social studies methods course, it is clear that the turboquest activity provides a meaningful environment for learning and interacting with relevant twenty-first-century instructional strategies and designing curriculum that promotes authentic assessment in a performance context. In this methods course, the professor is constantly moving from group to group asking probing questions and challenging students in order to generate opportunities for children to engage critical thinking skills. More important, the professor fosters a situation in which preservice teachers must take responsibility for their own acquisition of technological pedagogical content knowledge.

Integrating Reading/Language Arts

In the reading/language arts class, students focus on instruction for teaching K–5 students reading strategies that are easily integrated into all content areas. Course assignments require preservice teachers to collect and implement a variety of best practices—including vocabulary strategies—that assist their students in achieving state performance standards (Snyder, 2004). The turboquest provides the context for preservice teachers to implement these strategies through their group projects.

Another technology-enhanced assignment that is required to be embedded in the turboquest is the twenty-first-century interactive bulletin board. This project leverages the traditional concept of an interactive bulletin board and enables preservice teachers to use the free educational web software provided at Glogster/Education.com to create electronic interactive bulletin boards. Each group's *glogs* are used by students on classroom computers but are most effective when used on interactive white boards. Each glog must include original artwork or photographs that are attractive and appealing to students at the designated grade level. The glogs integrate reading and language arts with content that is developmentally appropriate. More specifically, each glog consists of the following:

- Clearly defined procedures that are represented as text and audio
- One or more links to an online lesson for the student to complete
- Provisions for student self-checking, if appropriate
- Examples of ideas or resources for open-ended projects
- Ideas based on a constructivist perspective

In addition to the reading/language arts activities in the glogs, the preservice teachers are required to include science and math activities to fulfill assignments in those courses. The final glogs are then integrated into each group's turboquest. This one activity used cutting-edge, user-friendly, free educational software to integrate the four content areas into a single interactive activity that would engage student learning.

Contextualizing Science

The design of this program has also proven to be an effective format for developing strategies for using science as an alternative foundation for teaching math, reading, and social studies. In many cases the central theme for the turboquest is a science topic. For example, one group titled their turboquest "Going Green." The problem that is presented is one in which pollution has devastated the Earth in the future. Students are charged with the task of developing a plan for today that prevents this from becoming a future reality.

As with each of the turboquests, all four subject areas are incorporated as the students develop a solution to the problem. As students complete the activities, they have the opportunity to learn about animal habitats, branches of government, data analysis, and persuasive letter writing. Teacher candidates develop a standards-based curriculum map as a means of crafting the technology project. In addition, class participants prepare backward design plans for the individual presentation section of the turboquest.

Once topics for turboquests and associated standards are determined, teacher candidates are asked to research the topics and produce an appropriate graphic organizer showing their findings. Graphic organizers must include at least twenty concepts (ten from science and ten from various other disciplines) and show the connections between the concepts. Subsequent to the general curriculum and development, all other assignments in the science methods class are designed to reinforce the advancement of the turboquest while supporting the students in learning to design science curriculum in the elementary school.

Making Mathematics Relevant

The turboquest offers a more meaningful, real-world connection of math to the content areas of social studies, language arts, and science. At the inception of the math methods course, the first assignment involves technology, math manipulatives, and literature. Prior to the assignment, the professor models literature connections to mathematics. Then, the preservice teachers are instructed to select their thematic topic and choose a children's literature book (fiction or nonfiction) appropriate for their small group's grade level. In large grade-level groups, they then discuss and list ideas of how math can be integrated with the literature using the state standards. The literature is then used with, or scanned into, the turboquest.

Each preservice teacher creates at least one math word problem presentation related to the theme and the literature. As the problems are posed, the children use math journals to show their work by incorporating manipulatives, pictorial representations, and finally an algorithm. Subsequent slides provide *hints* for solving the problem. Links to math websites of step-by-step skill demonstrations support children in the learning process. The final slide provides possible solution approaches. This allows for immediate feedback whereby the teacher may remediate misconceptions in small-group, guided math lessons.

During the creation of this learning experience, preservice teachers are able to grasp firsthand how technology-, math-, and social studies–related problems work as a team to reinforce teaching for understanding (Perkins, 1993). Technology engages children in math situations that connect to the real world. The turboquest's social studies portion requires tables, graphs, and charts. During math class, the preservice teachers study the K–5 standards for graphing. They work in groups to present similar data for each grade level on chart papers. This demonstrates the need to build upon previous years' standards, since the children do not use all possible data collection methods at every grade level. The small groups then create appropriate graphs in the turboquest to support the unit theme as a whole or within individual content areas.

The final math methods assignment connected to technology is the Twenty-First-Century Interactive Bulletin Board (glog). During math class, discussions of math connections for integrative grade standards allow preservice teachers to generate effective activities that are posted to the glog and eventually to the turboquest. This further demonstrates an interactive, interdisciplinary model of instruction.

A FINAL WORD

Final turboquest projects implemented in the subsequent five-week field experience immediately following the integrative content courses proved to be successful and rewarding for the preservice teachers and the students in their respective classrooms. Preservice teachers' formal final presentations indicate that the turboquests enable the learning process to become more relevant and meaningful by contextualizing integrated content for children. Turboquests also involve dynamic group learning and opportunities for independent investigations.

Preservice teachers achieve their learning goals and develop their knowledge and social skills in the process of meeting the problem situation in the turboquest, solving the problem using creative and critical thought-provoking venues, and sharing their authentic products as a culmination of their learning. Reflections by preservice teachers following their field experience indicate an increase in self-efficacy concerning their preparation for the classroom.

Preservice teachers also indicate that their respective collaborating teachers are impressed with their technological pedagogical content knowledge preparation and view them as potential teacher-leaders. For example, one preservice teacher stated, "Prior to this class, technology was intimidating to me. We learned many valuable and practical skills for successfully integrating technology for all subjects in our future classrooms." Another preservice teacher reported, "Collaborating with my peers on this project forced me to realize the weight of responsibility that falls on my shoulders as a team member." Finally, another preservice teacher captured one of our primary learning outcomes for developing this program as she reflected, "This project also helped me to realize that I can use technology to design curriculum that is not easy to teach to today's children when children no longer respond to the same methods used when I was in school."

REFERENCES

Dodge, B. (1997). *Some thoughts about webquests.* Retrieved December 14, 2009, from http://webquest.sdsu.edu/about_webquests.html

Koehler, M., & Mishra, P. (2008). *Handbook of technological pedagogical content knowledge (TPCK) for educators.* New York: Routledge.

Martin, D., Warner, M., Brown, T., & Coffey, D. (2006). Technology in education. In T. Deering (Ed.), *Perspectives in American education* (pp. 87–110). Dubuque, IA: Kendall Hunt.

Means, B. (1997). *Critical issue: Using technology to enhance engaged learning for at-risk students.* Retrieved February 7, 2009, from http://www.ncrel.org/sdrs/areas/issues/students/atrisk/at400.htm

National Council for Social Studies. (1994). *Expectations of excellence: Curriculum standards for social studies.* Washington, DC: Author.

Perkins, D. (1993, Fall). Teaching for understanding. *American Educator, 17*(3), 8, 28–35.

Shulman, L. (1987). Knowledge and teaching: Foundations of the new reform. *Harvard Educational Review, 57*(1), 1–22.

Snyder, A. (2004). *Vocabulary strategies.* Unpublished document.

Torpe, L., & Sage, S. (2002). *Problems as possibilities: Problem-based learning for K–16* (2nd ed.). Alexandria, VA: Association for Supervision and Curriculum Development.

Warner, M., & Leonard, J. (2004). An emergent problem based course for prospective middle grades teachers. *Middle School Journal, 35*(4), 33–41.

Practice-Based Teaching and Community Field Experiences for Prospective Teachers

Ken Zeichner and Morva McDonald

Traditionally, college- and university-based preservice teacher education programs have been based on an *application of theory* model where prospective teachers are supposed to learn theories at the university and to practice or apply what they learned in schools (Tom, 1997). Although most college- and university-based programs have incorporated school-based experiences paired with college course work, this increase in the amount of time that preservice teacher candidates spend in schools during their preparation programs has not altered the application of theory model.

TRADITIONAL TEACHER EDUCATION PROGRAMS

Teacher candidates are still placed in schools where they do not always have opportunities to observe, practice, and receive feedback on the particular teaching practices that the teacher education program wants them to acquire. In fact, it is still very common for cooperating teachers in whose classrooms teacher candidates are placed *not* to be knowledgeable about the specific content of the university courses, and similarly course instructors are unfamiliar with the classrooms in which candidates are placed (Zeichner, 2010). One consequence of this disconnect is that teacher candidates often do not learn how to enact the teaching practices that they are being taught (Clift & Brady, 2005; Valencia, Martin, Place,

& Grossman, 2009). This problem has been referred to as the *Achilles' heel* of teacher education and as the *two-worlds pitfall* (Feiman-Nemser & Buchman, 1985; Darling-Hammond, 2009).

College-Recommending Programs

One response to the lack of planned connections between school-based and campus-based experiences in *college-recommending* preservice teacher education—where most of the preparation is completed prior to candidates becoming teachers of record—is the attempt to develop school–university partnerships. In such cases, where clinical placements for teacher candidates take place in professional development or partner schools, there is an effort of universities and schools to collaborate across different stages of teachers' careers to support teacher learning. There is substantial evidence, however, that this partnership movement has not adequately addressed the problem of fragmentation. Additionally, the lack of coherence between the campus and field has not provided teacher candidates with opportunities to observe, practice, and receive high-quality feedback on their enactment of teaching practices emphasized in course work (Bullough et al., 1999; Zeichner, 2007).

Early Entry Programs

Alternatively, in many of the *early entry* models of teacher education— where candidates assume full responsibility for a classroom with very little preservice preparation—it is often assumed that most of what novice teachers need to learn about teaching can be learned in the midst of teaching practice and that the role of academic knowledge about teaching can be minimized without serious loss (Grossman & Loeb, 2008). Although the research on entering teaching through an early entry or college-recommending program is somewhat mixed, there is some evidence that teachers who become teachers of record without having completed carefully structured and supervised clinical experiences are less effective in promoting student learning in their first few years of teaching than teachers who completed carefully supervised clinical experiences (Boyd et al., 2008; Zeichner & Conklin, 2005).

Neither early entry nor college-recommending programs pay much attention to providing community-based field experiences for teacher candidates. There is substantial empirical evidence that carefully mediated experiences for teacher candidates in the communities served by their placement schools help develop important personal qualities and teaching skills that enhance their ability to educate all students (Boyle-Baise & McIntyre, 2008). In the rest of this chapter, we briefly discuss work under way in teacher education programs at the University of Washington, Seattle, to address both the *two-worlds pitfall* and the lack of community-based field experiences that undermine the quality of teacher learning for prospective teachers.

PRACTICE-BASED TEACHING AND MEDIATED FIELD EXPERIENCES

In both the elementary and secondary programs at University of Washington (UW), Seattle, faculty have moved a portion or most of content-area methods courses into urban partner schools, strategically aiming to give teacher candidates innovative opportunities to observe, practice, and receive feedback on the kinds of *high-leverage practices* (Windschitl, Thompson, & Braaten, in press) that university courses emphasize. Motivated by their own research that showed that their students were not taking up the ideas and practices that were advocated in their campus courses, the elementary and secondary teacher education faculty who teach methods courses committed to mediate the gaps between their campus courses and candidates' school experiences. In and of itself, however, moving methods courses to elementary and secondary schools does not mean that the course will be any different in terms of its impact on teacher learning than when it was taught on campus.

Our approach to on-site practice-based teaching provides prospective teachers with guided assistance in enacting teaching practices in real time with real children—rather than leaving prospective teachers to negotiate the uneven terrain between university course work and K–12 schools in isolation. Our approach potentially creates a new space for teacher learning to occur where both academic and practitioner knowledge are carefully coordinated to support the learning of new teachers, and challenges the application of theory model of teacher education.

Faculty enact a variety of pedagogical approaches in these field-based courses, including (a) candidates observing and debriefing with K–12 teachers, (b) university faculty modeling lessons or working with students using specific teaching practices, (c) candidates rehearsing alone or in small groups some of these same practices, and (d) debriefing the teaching and sometimes reteaching. Methods courses, taught at the school in the different content areas, vary in terms of how many sessions per quarter are held in schools, ranging from nine in secondary mathematics to two or three in secondary social studies.

We have been collecting data seeking to document the complexities and tensions associated with this work and its impact on the ways in which the courses are taught, what candidates learn from the courses, and what they are able to enact in urban classrooms. Initial analysis suggests that the practice-based teaching has helped candidates learn how to more successfully enact teaching practices emphasized in the methods courses. For example, Campbell (2008) reported that where interns participated in mediated instruction in secondary mathematics methods, they developed a deeper understanding of the promoted best teaching practices and were more successful in enacting these practices in diverse urban secondary schools.

COMMUNITY-BASED LEARNING FOR ELEMENTARY TEACHER CANDIDATES

"Your teachers don't know our kids," a sentiment reportedly expressed by community members, resonated with the faculty of the elementary teacher education program. This statement captured in a concise, compelling way a problem faculty to some extent already recognized—that we had not yet figured out how best to prepare teachers to learn about students from diverse backgrounds and their communities. To improve the preparation of our candidates, particularly to prepare them to teach in high-needs schools with students who have been traditionally disadvantaged by the educational system, faculty initiated a number of structural and curricular revisions to the elementary teacher education program.

First, along with staff, K–12 teachers, principals, and other stakeholders, they decided to commit to placing our candidates in high-needs schools for their school-based, yearlong practicum. This represented a shift from placing candidates in a range of schools with loose connections to the university. The elementary program currently works closely with eleven partner schools and clusters candidates in groups of three to seven in these schools. The intent of this practice is to (a) place candidates in cohorts so that they can support each other during their practicum, and (b) concentrate our candidates in the hopes that by doing so we will make a more significant contribution to the schools and to students' opportunities to learn.

Second, faculty committed to offering a strand focused on differentiated instruction, which includes foundational and pedagogical information regarding the teaching of English language learners and students identified with special needs. This course cuts across all four quarters of the program and supports candidates' learning in content methods and foundational courses.

Third, recognizing the tension between integrating and isolating the content of the multicultural education course, the faculty decided to retain a separate course focused on multicultural education while attempting to include related content in other courses and experiences.

Finally, faculty agreed to develop partnerships with community-based organizations (CBOs) and require every candidate in the first quarter of the program to intern in a CBO. This effort stemmed from faculty awareness that K–12 students' opportunities to learn are improved when teachers bridge school knowledge with students' informal knowledge (Moll, Vélez-Ibañez, & Greenberg, 1990).

Community-Based Organizations as a Learning and Cultural Bridge

A number of goals undergird the placement of the elementary candidates in the community-based organizations, including supporting candidates to:

1. Deepen preservice teachers' understanding of the lives and knowledge of children by expanding opportunities for *seeing* children (Ayers, 2001);
2. Broaden their familiarity with prospective networks, beyond schools, that support children's growth and development;

3. Build connections between preservice teachers, community organizations, and local schools;
4. Acknowledge education and learning as a process that occurs in multiple contexts; and
5. Develop a view of teaching in which students, families, neighborhoods, and communities are central to teaching and learning.

Structural Aspects of the Innovation

For the past two years, we have partnered with eleven community-based organizations to support the preparation of our candidates. We use the following criteria to select the community organizations:

- Willingness of the director to work with the university to prepare teachers;
- Proximity of the CBO to one of our school partners;
- Capacity to support placements of at least three candidates;
- Broad range of activities that support elementary-aged children's learning opportunities (for example, we wanted candidates to see and participate in more than homework help or tutoring after school); and
- Strong reputation within the community of after-school providers.

We often selected organizations that fit many but not all of these guidelines. The CBO partners range from locally based community centers, to national affiliates like Boys and Girls Clubs and YMCAs, to culturally oriented programs that address the needs of particular groups of children. After two years of implementation, we have begun to identify more specific features of organizations that seem to matter for candidates' learning. These include organizations in which the directors have long-term ties to and relationships with the particular neighborhood or community that the organization serves.

We often partner with organizations that primarily support the needs of a particular group of children and youth—such as Asian students, Latino students, or African American students. For example, we have placed candidates in the Chinese Information Service Center, which helps Chinese and other Asian immigrants achieve success by providing information, referral services, and programs, including an after-school program that supports children and youth to develop their academics, bilingual and bicultural identities, and leadership skills to name a few. Similarly, we have placed candidates at El Centro de La Raza, whose mission is to "build unity across all racial and economic sectors, to organize, empower, and defend our most vulnerable and marginalize populations and to bring justice, dignity, equality, and freedom to all the peoples of the world" (http://www.elcentrodelaraza.com/AboutUs/mvo.htm).

Through their participation in these organizations, our candidates have had opportunities to learn not only about individual children's experiences after school but also learn about the range of ways in which children, often identified under one socially constructed category such as Latino or African American, enact their cultural identities and knowledge. In addition, these placements offer candidates opportunities to see in action how community organizations play an integral part in the lives of children, youth, and families, as well as support children's capacity to learn during the school hours. For a number of our candidates, these placements, at the very minimum, meant exposure to resources outside of school that they could garner to support their work as teachers with individual children in school.

During the first two years of implementation, each candidate spent six hours per week for ten weeks as an intern in the community-based organization. Candidates were assigned organizations that would support and challenge their perspectives on children, youth, and families and, ultimately, inform their conception of what it means to be a teacher—specifically, one who does not simply drive in and out of communities but rather learns about specific communities to enhance his or her teaching. While interning in the CBOs, candidates also took five university courses: multicultural teaching, literacy methods, differentiated instruction, social studies methods, and a community-based organization seminar.

As we know from research, a persistent challenge in teacher education is structural and conceptual fragmentation among the various program components (Feiman-Nemser, 2001). We also know from research and scholarship that preservice teachers' appropriation of principles and practices for teaching improves when programs better connect teachers' opportunities to learn across courses and field experiences and among courses (Darling-Hammond, 2006). In addition, research on multicultural education and the placement of preservice teachers in schools serving a diverse population of students suggests that unless those experiences are facilitated they run the risk of supporting preservice teachers' negative stereotypes and perspectives on children from diverse backgrounds, their families, and their communities (Boyle-Baise, 1998; Sleeter, 2008; Zeichner & Melnick, 1996). With this research in mind, an essential element of the implementation of the CBO partnership and placements was the integration of this experience, at the very least, into the first-quarter courses.

Four of five of the courses mentioned above intentionally designed assignments to facilitate candidates' experiences in their placements and to capitalize on their learning in the field to support course concepts. Course assignments, such as a portrait of one child in the CBO as well as a project for the CBO developed in consultation with the children and staff, were designed to facilitate a candidate's development of learning about an individual child, as well as how to *give back* to the community in which he or she was learning. One assignment in the social studies class required the candidates to map the community surrounding the CBO and to consider how these organizations facilitated civic engagement. The differentiated instruction course required students to conduct an in-depth case study of one child—an assignment they continued into the school year and that dovetailed with the CBO seminar assignment.

Professors of each of these courses had to reconsider and modify the assignments of previous years in order to help the candidates to value their community experiences as part of their learning to teach. The literacy course, for example, had to be redesigned so some of its assignments could help candidates' understand the opportunities for literacy in nonschool environments. As one would predict from relevant research in teacher education, evidence from a longitudinal study of the implementation of this project suggests that the integration across courses and between courses as well as the CBO experience enhanced our candidates' experiences and opportunities to learn in those settings significantly (McDonald et al., in press).

CONCLUSION

In the elementary and secondary teacher education programs at the University of Washington, Seattle, we have moved content-area methods courses into the field in order to strategically bring academic and practitioner expertise together, and thus better support teacher candidates' learning to enact specific teaching practices. We have also provided field experiences for candidates in our elementary program in community-based organizations and have sought to draw on the expertise in these organizations to improve the preparation of teachers who are able to work in culturally responsive ways. Underlying both of these efforts is a commitment to bring academic, practitioner, and community-based knowledge together in new ways to support the development of successful urban teachers (Zeichner, 2010).

REFERENCES

Ayers, W. C. (2001). *To teach.* New York: Teachers College Press.

Boyd, D., Grossman, P., Hammerness, K., Lankford, R. H., Loeb, S., McDonald, M., et al. (2008). Surveying the landscape of teacher education in New York City: Constrained variation and the challenge of innovation. *Education Evaluation and Policy Analysis, 30,* 319–343.

Boyle-Baise, M. (1998). Community service learning for multicultural education: An exploratory study with preservice teachers. *Equity and Excellence in Education, 31*(2), 52–60.

Boyle-Baise, M., & McIntyre, D. J. (2008). What kind of experience? Preparing teachers in PDS or community settings. In M. Cochran-Smith, S. Feiman-Nemser, & D. J. McIntyre (Eds.), *Handbook of research on teacher education* (3rd ed., pp. 307–330). New York: Routledge.

Bullough, R., Burrell, J., Young, J., Clark, D., Erickson, L., & Earle, R. (1999). Paradise unrealized: Teacher education and the costs and benefits of school-university partnerships. *Journal of Teacher Education, 50,* 381–390.

Campbell, S. S. (2008, March). *Mediated field experiences in learning progressive teaching: A design experiment in teacher education.* Paper presented at the annual meeting of the American Educational Research Association, New York City.

Clift, R., & Brady, P. (2005). Research on methods courses and field experiences. In M. Cochran-Smith & K. Zeichner (Eds.), *Studying teacher education: The report of the American Educational Research Association panel on research on research on teacher education* (pp. 309–424). New York: Routledge.

Darling-Hammond, L. (2006). *Powerful teacher education.* San Francisco: Jossey-Bass.

Darling-Hammond, L. (2009, February). *Teacher education and the American future*. Charles W. Hunt Lecture. Presented at the annual meeting of the American Association of Colleges for Teacher Education, Chicago.

Feiman-Nemser, S. (2001). From preparation to practice: Designing a continuum to strengthen and sustain teaching. *Teachers College Record, 103*, 1013–1055.

Feiman-Nemser, S., & Buchman, M. (1985). Pitfalls of experience in teacher education. *Teachers College Record, 87*, 49–65.

Grossman, P., & Loeb, S. (Eds.). (2008). *Taking stock: An examination of alternative certification*. Cambridge, MA: Harvard Education Press.

McDonald, M., Tyson, K., Brayko, K., Bowman, M., Delport, J., & Shimomura, F. (Forthcoming, 2010). Innovation and impact in teacher education: Community based organizations as field placements for preservice teachers. *Teachers College Record*.

Moll, L. C., Vélez-Ibañez, C. G., & Greenberg, J. (1990). *Community knowledge and classroom practice: Combining resources for literacy instruction. A handbook for teachers and planners*. Washington, DC: U.S. Dept. of Education, Office of Educational Research and Improvement, Educational Resources Information Center.

Sleeter, C. (2008). Preparing white teachers for diverse students. In M. Cochran-Smith, S. Feiman-Nemser, & D. J. McIntyre (Eds.), *Handbook of research on teacher education* (3rd ed., pp. 559–582). New York: Routledge.

Tom, A. (1997). *Redesigning teacher education*. Albany, NY: SUNY Press.

Valencia, S., Martin, S., Place, N., & Grossman, P. (2009). Complex interactions in student teaching: Lost opportunities for learning. *Journal of Teacher Education, 60*, 304–322.

Windschitl, M., Thompson, J., & Braaten, M. (in press). Fostering ambitious pedagogy in novice teachers: The new role of tool-supported analyses of student work. *Teachers College Record*.

Zeichner, K. (2007). Professional development schools in a culture of evidence and accountability. *School-University Partnerships, 1*(1), 9–17.

Zeichner, K. (2010). Rethinking the connections between campus courses and field experiences in college and university-based teacher education. *Journal of Teacher Education, 89*(11), 89–99.

Zeichner, K., & Conklin, H. (2005). Teacher education programs. In M. Cochran-Smith & K. Zeichner (Eds.), *AERA panel on research in teacher education* (pp. 645–736). Washington, DC: American Educational Research Association.

Zeichner, K., & Melnick, S. (1996). The role of community field experiences in preparing teachers for cultural diversity. In K. Zeichner, S. Melnick, & M. L. Gomez (Eds.). *Currents of reform in preservice teacher education* (pp. 176–196). New York: Teachers College Press.

6

High-Impact Practices and the Preparation of Educators in the New Era

Yi-Ping Huang

TEACHER EDUCATION IN TIMES OF ACCELERATED TRANSITION

With the urge for "revolutionary change—not revolutionary tinkering" from the Obama administration, transformation of teacher education is at a critical juncture. Education leaders have been engaged in change initiatives ranging from conceptual re-envisioning to strategic modifications in practice, with an overarching mission of developing a national teaching force capable of helping P–12 students succeed and thrive in the new era.

To better support teaching professionals, better position the teaching profession, and better address urgent P–12 needs, Darling-Hammond (2006) cited three critical components in constructing twenty-first-century teacher education:

1. Tight coherence and integration among courses and between course work and clinical work;
2. Extensive and intensive clinical work linking theory and practice; and
3. New school–university relationships leading to changes in the content of schooling as well as teacher training.

The initiative described is one example that strives to better prepare and support teaching professionals in the new era. Drawing upon the experience of implementing a living learning community (LLC) for aspiring teachers, this model highlights a vision for embracing a liberal arts tradition within a progressive-oriented teacher preparation program; it shares the processes of co-constructing teacher education through both intentional adoption of high-impact practices and purposeful alignment of higher education learning outcomes and P–12 priorities; and it explores the potentials of transforming teaching professionals, teacher educators, and teacher education programs through collective investment in mutual accountability and reciprocal transformation.

LIBERAL EDUCATION IN THE NEW GLOBAL CENTURY

Aspirations for producing informed and fully engaged citizens in the new global century have led to initiatives across levels of schooling in the United States. In the realm of higher education, the Association of American Colleges and Universities (AAC&U, 2007) has been serving as a primary vehicle for advancing and communicating a framework for educational excellence, demonstrated through four Essential Learning Outcomes (ELOs) that are critical to success in work, life, and citizenship. Deeply grounded in the liberal arts tradition, the ELOs are:

1. Knowledge of human cultures and the physical and natural world;
2. Intellectual and practical skills;
3. Personal and social responsibility; and
4. Integrative and applied learning.

To help address challenges and achieve outcomes, a collection of innovative, high-impact teaching and learning practices were identified (AAC&U, 2007). These include (a) first-year seminars and experiences, (b) common intellectual experiences, (c) learning communities; (d) writing-intensive courses, (e) collaborative assignments and projects, (f) undergraduate research, (g) diversity/global learning, (h) service learning and community-based learning, (i) internships, and (j) capstone courses and projects.

In the discussions on effectiveness of the high-impact practices, Kuh (2008) asserted that these activities help promote engagement in *deep learning*, and as a result, help elevate levels of learning and development outcomes. Though varying in characteristics and effects, high-impact practices tend to create contexts and conditions that foster greater personal investment and self-directedness; demand authentic interactions with content, peers and mentors; and require integration, synthesis, and application of knowledge, often through project-oriented and performance-based activities that connect classroom learning to the real world.

A LIVING LEARNING COMMUNITY
FOR ASPIRING TEACHERS

The University of Maryland, Baltimore County (UMBC), is recognized as a national leader in providing outstanding opportunities for undergraduate research and creative projects, "combining the traditions of the liberal arts academy, the creative intensity of the research university and the social responsibility of the public university" (*UMBC Vision*, n.d., para. 1), UMBC actively creates contexts and conditions for high-impact practices aiming to engage and enhance student success. Among the many endeavors are first-year seminars and experiences, learning communities, writing-intensive courses, undergraduate research, service learning, community-based learning, internships, and capstone courses and projects.

Committed to preparing educators for the new era, a living learning community entitled Aspiring Teachers at UMBC (AT@UMBC) was created in fall 2008 for undergraduates interested in pursuing teaching as a profession. The initiative is jointly supported by the Office of Undergraduate Studies, the Office of Residential Life, and the Department of Education at UMBC. Two faculty members and one professional staff member serve as mentors of the LLC. Combining high-impact practices in addressing the four ELOs and twenty-first-century skills, program activities are created as *purposeful pathways* that integrate knowledge construction with practical application, and connect academic preparation with real-world experience. These activities are summarized below.

Creating a Living Learning Community (LLC)

Grounded in the learning community vision of integration, involvement, and engagement, LLCs are learning communities with a residential component. Varying in frameworks and modalities, LLCs are increasingly being adopted by institutions to enhance retention, persistence, and performance. Common characteristics of LLCs include:

1. Living in a specially themed and intentionally clustered portion of the residence hall;
2. Participating in common academic and intellectual experiences through curricular activities;
3. Engaging in cocurricular and social activities that facilitate growth and development in and out of the classroom; and
4. Accessing resources and activities that are unique to the participants (Inkelas, Johnson, Lee, & Alvarez, 2005; Kuh, 2008).

AT@UMBC participants are immersed in a stimulating and supportive environment with high-impact experiences that bridge the contexts of residence, classroom, and the real world beyond campus. Participants are engaged in activities such as field-based experiential learning, community-based service learning, peer and faculty mentoring, course work on issues in education, workshops on twenty-first-century skills, enrichment activities in the arts and sciences, and an e-Portfolio capstone project, as well as social gatherings.

A resource and supply center for arts and crafts was established to encourage creativity and integration of arts in teaching and learning. A multimedia lab was established on the AT@UMBC resident floor to help advance skills such as technology and information literacy, as well as learning and innovation skills. A high-tech lounge was also designed on the floor to further engage and integrate learning and social networking in both traditional and new media environments. Social activities such as field trips, movie nights, and picnics were held to facilitate transitions to higher education and connections to peers and the university.

Common Intellectual Experiences

Evolving from the concept of core curriculum, colleges and universities offer a variety of formats ranging from general education programs to required common courses. Combining broad themes with curricular and cocurricular options, these programs often emphasize the development of *intellectual and practical competencies* (ELO 1) within the broad context of *human cultures and the physical and natural world* (ELO 2). These intellectual and practical skills include inquiry and analysis, critical and creative thinking, written and oral communication, quantitative literacy, information literacy, teamwork, and problem solving.

The teacher preparation program at UMBC requires the completion of both an academic major as well as the teacher certification program. This combination is designed to ensure that teacher candidates know and are able to demonstrate their content expertise through discipline-specific experiences, and their professional knowledge, skills, and dispositions through professional preparation experiences. With participants having majors and minors in over twenty fields of study and working collaboratively toward their teacher certification, the AT@UMBC initiative helps establish connections between general and specialized studies. It also facilitates interactions that build candidates' capacities as teaching professionals and creates linkages to the teaching profession.

AT@UMBC participants are required to complete an additional one-credit course each academic year. Topics of the course range from media representation of teachers and the teaching profession to contemporary issues and viewpoints about teaching. Participants actively engage in and serve as lead facilitators in both face-to-face and online learning environments. Weekly journals documenting experiences are signature activities intended to cultivate reflective practitioners.

Participatory workshops addressing twenty-first-century skills and themes such as diversity and conflict resolution, as well as media and technology literacy, are delivered to help teacher candidates understand the changing expectations of modern education. As an extension of the course on media representation of teachers, participants initiated Friday night movie screenings at the AT@UMBC's residential lounge. Participants noted that the movie experience provides opportunities to learn and share differing viewpoints, as well as strengthen friendships, collegiality, and the sense of community.

Service Learning

Field-based experiential learning with community partners engages participants in an iterative process of knowledge construction and understanding building. Common characteristics among the various experiential learning models include:

1. An exploratory process engaging learners with a "concrete experience" (Kolb, 1984) in real-world settings;
2. A reflective process engaging learners in building capacities for "reflection-on-action" and "reflection-in-action" (Schön, 1987); and
3. A "conceptualization" process engaging learners in deepening of understanding through applications (Kolb, 1984).

With the learning activity embedded in schools and communities, service learning fosters the development of *personal and social responsibilities* (ELO 3).

In collaboration with various campus units, local P–12 schools, and community centers, participants are required to conduct fifteen hours of service learning per semester. Each service-learning project is collaboratively designed by the participant and the faculty advisor to meet individual goals and needs. These experiences include tutoring in local schools, conducting activities in senior centers, assisting in campus learning resource centers, and planning and hosting UMBC campus tours for P–12 students, especially from high-need schools.

The service-learning activities have initially focused on deepening and broadening the understanding of self and the teaching profession. As time progresses, more attention has focused on connecting pedagogical and leadership development with real-world capabilities. Individual and collective reflections are conducted through classroom discussions, online postings, and journal entries, as well as frequent interactions with faculty mentors and peers.

Capstone Project

Capstone projects are cumulative experiences that require learners to demonstrate competencies, through integration and application, of knowledge, skills, and capabilities. Projects may be in forms such as research papers, exhibits, performances, or portfolios. Increasingly capstone courses and projects have been adopted for *integrative and applied learning* (ELO 4) that facilitate the advancement and accomplishment across general and specialized studies.

The UMBC Teacher Education Program has institutionalized a *ProcessFolio* consisting of course-embedded key assignments, field-based performance assessments, and a cumulative final capstone (*Teaching-Folio*) that highlights competencies and achievements during clinical practice. Though limited in scope and scaled for developmental appropriateness, participants are supported to explore process, content, standards, technology, and assessment associated with the creation of an electronic portfolio.

At the individual level, participants are immersed in deeply personalized learning and empowered to become both adaptive experts and knowledge creators. At the collective level, participants are involved in establishing a *community of creators*, extending interactions beyond classrooms to a *community of practice*, and expanding teacher development beyond core subjects to include twenty-first-century themes and skills (Huang, 2006).

CO-CONSTRUCTING TWENTY-FIRST-CENTURY TEACHER EDUCATION

As a new initiative, the AT@UMBC advisors and participants have been engaged in a dynamic process of co-constructing the agenda for *reciprocal transformation*. This incorporates the transformation of new and veteran teachers to be able to help P–12 students succeed and thrive, and the transformation of teacher education programs and teacher educators to be able to help teachers succeed and thrive in the new global environment.

To establish mutual accountability and to better understand elements that affect the participants, a series of formative and summative assessments, as well as focus groups and a survey, were conducted. Though limited in scope, ongoing and informal assessment results have also helped shaped the program design, implementation, assessment, and resource management.

Assessing Progress

The first two cohorts of participants have excelled in their program's required courses. Embedded in the courses were direct and indirect assessments on personal, academic, and civic developments. In addition, a recent study was conducted on *overall experience* and *participant outcomes*. The instrument mirrors the National Study of Living Learning Programs (NSLLP) (http://www.livelearnstudy.net) with additional items that are specific to the AT@UMBC initiative. The overall experience focused on satisfaction with the LLC, university experience, learning experiences, peer mentoring, faculty mentoring, and the reasons for joining the LLC. The participant outcomes focused on ten categories: oral communication, written communication, critical thinking, technological competency, information literacy, teamwork, leadership, time management, career, and self-understanding.

The findings reflected rather vividly the need to better integrate the liberal-education-based ELOs, twenty-first-century skills, and P–12 priorities in the preparation of new teachers as public intellectuals. The results also indicated the need to enhance the curriculum and instruction within the entire teacher preparation program, as well as to provide professional development for teacher educators.

Addressing the Challenge

With the commitment to transforming teaching professionals, teacher educators, and teacher education programs, the AT@UMBC is striving to integrate new understandings, promising practices, and contemporary priorities in the preparation of highly effective teachers. Lessons learned from participant outcomes, feedback, and survey results are guiding strategic changes. These include

- Restructuring both academic and social activities with explicit alignment of living learning experiences with higher education outcomes and P–12 priorities;
- Incorporating experiences designed to address specific ELOs and twenty-first-century skills; and
- Inclusion of additional faculty mentors with expertise in these areas.

Professional capacity is being further developed through faculty research and through networking with an emerging Community of Practice established by the Office of Residential Life, the Office of the Undergraduate Study, and faculty and staff advisors of the nine LLCs across disciplines on campus.

A CALL FOR INVESTING IN MUTUAL ACCOUNTABILITY AND RECIPROCAL TRANSFORMATION

Accompanying the accelerated transitions in the economy, culture, and politics of the twenty-first century are increased demands for global competitiveness and increased urgency to re-envision our notions of educational excellence. With the call of policy makers, accreditation agencies, and the general public demanding revolutionary change, the potentials of transforming P–12 education can only be fully realized with equal commitments to transforming teaching professionals, teacher educators, and teacher education programs. The promise of developing highly effective teachers capable of helping all students succeed and thrive in the new era may only be actualized through collective investment, such as through high-impact practices that foster mutual accountability and reciprocal transformation.

REFERENCES

Association of American Colleges and Universities (AAC&U). (2007). *College learning for the new global century: A report from the national leadership council for liberal education & America's promise.* Washington, DC: Author. Retrieved April 16, 2010, from http://www.aacu.org/leap/documents/Global Century_final.pdf

Darling-Hammond, L. (2006). Constructing 21st-century teacher education. *Journal of Teacher Education, 57,* 300–314.

Huang, Y. (2006). Sustaining ePortfolios: Progress, challenges, and changing dynamics in teacher education. In A. Jafari & C. Kaufman (Eds.), *Handbook of research on ePortfolios* (pp. 503–519). Hershey, PA: IGI Global.

Inkelas, K. K., Johnson, D., Lee, Z., & Alvarez, P. (2005, November). *Facilitating the early success of women in STEM majors through living-learning programs.* Paper presented at the annual meeting of the Association for the Study of Higher Education, Philadelphia, PA.

Kolb, D. A. (1984). *Experiential learning: Experience as the source of learning and development*. Englewood Cliffs, NJ: Prentice Hall.

Kuh, G. (2008). *High-impact educational practices: What they are, who has access to them, and why they matter*. Washington, DC: AAC&U.

Schön, D. (1987). *Educating the reflective practitioner: Toward a new design for teaching and learning in the professions*. San Francisco: Jossey-Bass.

UMBC Vision. (n.d.). Retrieved April 16, 2010, from http://www.umbc.edu/aboutumbc/mission.php#vision

7

Service Learning as a Vehicle for Examining Assumptions about Culture and Education

Peter Smagorinsky

SERVICE LEARNING IN ENGLISH EDUCATION

Christopher's parents force him to go to school because it is the law but they pay no attention to his success or failure once he is outside their house, outside their sphere of control. In a way, Christopher Taylor [a pseudonym] is a product of his surroundings. His parents do not care whether or not he succeeds, so neither does he. People look at him and all they see is a black nineteen-year-old male with dreadlocks and a big nose heading nowhere fast, so he too sees himself in that light.

Tatum (2003) writes in her book, *Why Are All the Black Kids Sitting Together in the Cafeteria? and Other Conversations about Race: A Psychologist Explains the Development of Racial Identity*, that "our self-perceptions are shaped by the messages that we receive from those around us" (p. 53). For example, if a ten-year-old girl is constantly told that she is tall for her age then she will eventually see her above-average height as a part of her identity. Similarly if Chris is continually told, verbally or otherwise, that he will only ever be a nobody in life, then he has no incentive to better himself through education. If he is ceaselessly bombarded with the prototypical image of the young black man as a criminal with no education, then eventually he will see himself as such.

So often one forms one's identity based on a compilation of ideas and images of oneself as seen by other people. Unfortunately these images frequently originate from stereotypes and prejudices. Therefore, Christopher's lack of motivation might have developed as a result of his self image of worthlessness and a man with an unpromising future as planted in his mind by a prejudiced society.

This observation and insight has come from a teacher candidate enrolled in a service-learning course at the University of Georgia (UGA). The teacher candidate, like most students at her state's namesake institution, has been a highly successful student throughout her education. The state's lottery proceeds provide free college education to students who maintain a B average or better, a move that has helped keep the top students in state universities. As a result, the typical student admitted tends to come from a relatively privileged background and has moved through school in an elite curriculum: honors and Advanced Placement courses, gifted and talented programs, International Baccalaureate curriculum, and other enriched programs. Once on campus, they are again subjected to an admission process in order to enter the teacher education program, which in a typical year can only accept 60–65 percent of its applicants.

UGA thus draws a student population from a fairly exclusive group; the teacher candidates tend to be white, relatively affluent, suburban, female, high achieving, and with an academic bent given their aspiration to teach. Throughout their education, and no doubt throughout their lives, they have had little contact with poor, minority, immigrant, disaffected, or otherwise marginalized students. When they initially consider the prospect of teaching, they tend to envision themselves in a professorial role, discussing the fine points of Shakespeare and Milton with the sorts of students with whom they have shared classrooms over the years.

Yet when UGA graduates begin their teaching careers, they are often assigned classrooms filled with students who are decidedly different from themselves in terms of their orientation to school, given that early career teachers are often assigned to lower-track classes (Kelly, 2009). The course described here was designed to disrupt their exclusive experiences through their work in an alternative school, their reading of books that attend to cultural differences, and their discussion of those books in book club settings. The excerpt from a course final paper that opens this chapter reveals the sorts of new understandings that become available through this cultural exchange.

MUTUAL EDUCATIONAL EXPERIENCES

The syllabus for the course is available at http://www.coe.uga.edu/~smago/ SL/SLSyllabus.htm. The course meets on campus each week for up to three hours and requires an additional hour each week of tutoring and mentoring a student in one of Athens's two alternative schools. The students in this alternative school typically come from a radically different cultural environment from that experienced by our teacher candidates in terms of race, ethnicity, social class, educational aspiration, family situation, and other factors.

The course is designed to develop mutually educational experiences for the teacher candidates and the young people they tutor. The teacher candidates provide service to the community by helping struggling students with their schoolwork as they progress toward graduation and to enter a mentoring relationship that goes beyond academics and into other life issues; and the students being tutored educate the teacher candidates about their perspective on school, the subject of English (the discipline in which the service-learning course is grounded), the value of an education, their short- and long-term goals with their lives, and whatever else emerges from their extended conversations.

The students in the alternative school meet the profile of the students envisioned in the course design. The alternative school is designated a Performance Learning Center (PLC) and serves students who have had difficulty fitting in with conventional schooling. They represent a range of races but tend to come from lower socioeconomic classes; a number bring their own young children to school with them to take advantage of the school's nursery; some hold hands with same-sex partners, a behavior unlikely in the mainstream schools; and for the most part, they hate school and are forthcoming in their reasons for their antipathy. Thus, they provide the sort of interaction that helps the university students learn about how school may be viewed by students whose life experiences and perspective on education are considerably different from their own.

SUSTAINED MENTORING: WHAT REALLY WORKS

For their course project, each teacher candidate may choose from among three topics (see http://www.coe.uga.edu/~smago/SL/SLCourseProjects

.htm). If it is possible to develop a stable and sustained tutoring and mentoring relationship with a single student at the alternative school, the course paper could be a case study of the student. Many teacher candidates, however, have difficulty establishing such continuity with an alternative school student. The environment is, to say the least, often in flux. Some teacher candidates tutor students who drop out or are dismissed from the school because of excessive absences or violations of rules.

Some of the students from the Performance Learning Center are undependable so that when the teacher candidates make the trip to the campus—something around which they plan their day—their mentee never shows up. On such occasions, they meet with another available student or otherwise try to help with what needs to be done at the school. Because several teacher candidates have such capricious experiences, alternative assignments have been developed so that those who make good-faith efforts to meet the course requirements can also write a course paper outlining what they have learned, even if they need to weave together their experiences with a variety of students with whom they do not have the opportunity to develop a sustained relationship.

An online library of course projects written by university students who provide permission to have their work posted has been assembled at the syllabus website so that future teacher candidates may get some sense of how others have undertaken this task (see http://www.coe.uga .edu/~smago/SL/SLCourseProjects.htm). It also allows anyone interested in the reflections of the teacher candidates to consult this library to see what they have produced, and to see what they have learned through their service to the community.

BOOK CLUBS

Class sessions on campus focus on three areas. Early on, teacher candidates learn how to conduct a tutoring session and are given class time to ask questions about how to develop their course projects. The majority of the class sessions, however, are devoted to book club meetings. Book clubs have become established as a legitimate pedagogy in English education (Daniels, 1994; Faust, Cockrill, Hancock, & Isserstadt, 2005; McMahon, Raphael, Goatley, & Pardo, 1997; O'Donnell-Allen, 2006; Raphael, Pardo, Highfield, & McMahon, 1997). The menu of readings represents a range of issues that might arise in teacher candidates' engagement with high school students of various cultural backgrounds and include attention to socioeconomic class, race, culture, youth culture, urban education, immigration, bilingualism, gender, and related issues (see http://www.coe.uga.edu/~smago/SL/SLBookClubs.htm).

The class is structured so that each book club group of three to five teacher candidates discusses three books during the course of the semester. During the first session, they discuss the book however they wish; during the second session, they continue this discussion while also planning for what they will do during the third session. During the third session, they present their book to the class through whatever means they think will be most interesting, informative, and compelling for their classmates. The idea behind this approach is to put both the selection of topics (within the boundaries of the course's goals) and the means of discussion in the hands of the participants. The pedagogy is thus designed to help them see that there are alternatives to the lecture-and-discussion approach to teaching that they have experienced throughout much of their school lives.

This approach also allows the teacher candidates to discuss issues that they might resist exploring without the faculty member's initiating and directing their inquiries. In the Deep South, most students come with conservative political values and often reject professorial attempts to reroute their values to more progressive beliefs. The course is not designed to reeducate them so that they adopt progressive views wholesale, something that research on teacher development suggests will not happen regardless of what professors hope (Smagorinsky, Cook, & Johnson, 2003). Rather, given the value systems and experiences with which they enter the course, they choose books and undertake discussions during which they raise the questions most relevant to their growth as educators.

HOW BOOK CLUBS FOSTER CRITICAL THINKING

The problem is a delicate one for any progressive educator working with students from conservative political backgrounds: how to invite a consideration of issues without trampling on students' prior beliefs. The book club format enables the candidates to express their beliefs honestly and forthrightly in the company of their classmates without concern for how their professor might interpret them as people in light of what they say.

The intersection of teacher candidates' prior beliefs, their tutoring and mentoring experiences at the alternative school, their engagement with books from the book club menu, and their discussions and class presentations often produce a perplexing dissonance. One group, for instance, selected Kozol's (1992) *Savage Inequalities: Children in America's Schools*, which contrasts the resources available in one wealthy suburban high school outside Chicago and one deeply impoverished urban school in East St. Louis.

The teacher candidates became deeply vexed over how to resolve their prior beliefs about social problems with the portraits presented by Kozol (1992) of the dramatic differences between the conditions of schooling in the two districts and the potentials afforded students through the resource differential of the two communities. This is the type of comment students frequently made:

> Now, I don't buy Obama's socialism, but this situation is unfair. One school has computers in every classroom and in the other, ceiling tiles are falling on kids while they're trying to learn. I don't think we should raise taxes or redistribute wealth, but the kids in the poor school need a better learning environment.

The candidates' raised awareness of this dilemma was the sort of jarring recognition that the course professor hoped to achieve in designing the course. Had he stood before them as a (perceived) Northern liberal (even though having lived most of his life in the South) and explained to them these inequalities and the solution of redistributing wealth to promote equal learning opportunities, they could have more easily rejected his position as an outsider, a liberal, a university pinhead, and other means of dismissal.

Because the book club format required that candidates wrestle with such issues on their own terms, they had greater ownership over their conclusions and thus a greater stake in considering the problem and how to resolve it. Indeed, the student who most frequently invoked "Obama's socialism" as an unacceptable solution was easily the most passionate proselytizer of Kozol's (1992) book, saying that she was making everyone in her family and wider friendship circles read it to raise their awareness of educational inequities.

WHY SERVICE LEARNING CAN BE INNOVATIVE AND A VEHICLE FOR EXAMINING ASSUMPTIONS

This course is heading toward institutionalization in candidates' preservice teaching experiences. The critical reflection available through the book club discussion is a key component of the teacher candidates' engagement with students in the alternative schools. Students' educational experiences, including teacher education, serve largely to perpetuate schooling as historically conducted: Students spend twelve or more years in apprenticeships of observation in authoritarian school systems, take general education courses in large lecture halls, engage with their content area in courses typically dominated by professors' soliloquies, and are steeped in school-based field experiences that replicate top-down educational processes. In addition, teacher candidates often take one semester of courses in education that might critique these practices but that the National Council for Accreditation of Teacher Education (NCATE) is attempting to eliminate in place of yet more field experiences in authoritarian school settings, and then take jobs in which their teaching is evaluated according to its proximity to the status quo (Smagorinsky, 2010).

This service-learning course provides one means of interrupting this extensive socialization to traditional school norms. The teacher candidates engage with high school students who hate school and refuse to play by its authoritarian rules; the book club setting and accompanying readings provide both an alternative pedagogy in which the university students control the content and process of their discussions, and a set of challenges to their assumptions about culture and education. Because a multicultural perspective is engaged with on their own terms, whatever concept change they experience (see Smagorinsky et al., 2003) is one over which they have complete ownership, and thus presumably is one that will be more durable than any changes in perspective that would follow from hortatory efforts for them to teach more inclusively.

CONCLUSION

The course thus helps to challenge norms of schooling and white-collar assumptions about families from outside the circles of privilege in which most of students at this university have lived their lives. The following conclusion to one teacher candidate's course paper perhaps captures the sorts of insights produced through the interrelated experiences provided through the class:

> Throughout the Book Club readings this semester, every group has recognized the multitude of issues among conventional schools as well as those that resemble the PLC, but the books have left the solutions open-ended. In *Jocks and Burnouts*, Eckert [1989] primarily focuses on the differences that exist among students and how they view high school through different lenses. For the jocks, or students who value education, a desire to contribute to the school resonates, and so they actively participate in academics and extracurricular activities. The burnouts, on the other hand, tend to slack off, frequently miss school, as well as carry themselves with a defiant attitude. Students are very easily categorized as a burnout, because so few students correlate perfectly with the ideal student model that is set by schools. In reality, high school solely opens up opportunities for college bound students. But most burnouts do not see themselves as college material, and they will more than likely partake in a blue collar vocational job—so high school loses practicality for many students. It is very unlikely for burnouts and students like John to better fit the conventional model of school, so schools should consider better adapting to these students who need a push.
>
> All of our book clubs and class discussions have raised compelling arguments and problems with conventional schools. Some students believe that schools like the Performance Learning Center are a successful answer to our problems, and others see it as a way out for kids who refuse to cooperate with conventional schools. I believe the PLC is a magnificent thing and I am absolutely blown away by this transformation. Students are given a chance to prove themselves and are treated with respect, as their slates are wiped clean when they enroll at the school. John is a PLC success story and with his pending high school diploma, he is ready to continue his success in college. I believe the one key to inspiring the unmotivated student lies in respect. If a teacher is flexible, encouraging, and respectful—he or she is bound for success in the classroom. I hate that the burnout students have

such a stigma placed with them and that the bad reputation follows them throughout high school. With each passing year, semester, or even within the separate classes—each child should be given the opportunity to succeed, a fair chance for a clean slate. I could almost guarantee a student is more likely to fulfill a teacher's expectations if they are given the chance. I am positive that there are more students like John than there are like me in public schools, and sometimes a second, third, or even a fourth chance is all that those kids need to regain the self-confidence that is required to succeed.

As this candidate's reflection shows, the course allowed the participating preservice teachers considerable latitude in how they made sense of their school experiences, their readings, and their book club discussions. By selecting books that were relevant to the sorts of students they were meeting, they were able to customize their reading to their teaching and mentoring. Their leading of a class discussion then enabled each group to share insights with their classmates, expanding the range of issues explored through the course to the experiences of each class member at the PLC in conjunction with the different texts discussed by each book group. The following remarks on an end-of-course evaluation are representative of how many students responded to the class:

I believe this class has helped me more for my career as an educator than any other education class I've taken at the University. Most of the classes have a service component, but it's not very long nor gets much attention in the classroom. Since the service portion is the largest part of the class and dominates the classroom discussion of how to operate a classroom, what to expect from students, as well as how to motivate a student—I was encouraged and learned more about my future classroom than any other class.

Candidate satisfaction tended to follow from the control that they were given over the success of the class. The innovative component of this project was a direct result of the cultural exchange and the opportunities for the teacher candidates to take control over their own learning. The course gave future teachers opportunities to take charge of their own learning by providing services to students who greatly appreciated them, as well as through reading and discussing books that raised issues that provoked them to new levels of understanding.

REFERENCES

Daniels, H. (1994). *Literature circles: Voice and choice in the student-centered classroom.* York, ME: Stenhouse.

Eckert, P. (1989). *Jocks and burnouts: Social categories and identity in the high school.* New York: Teacher College Press.

Faust, M., Cockrill, J., Hancock, C., & Isserstadt, H. (2005). *Student book clubs: Improving literature instruction in middle and secondary schools.* Norwood, MA: Christopher Gordon.

Kelly, S. (2009). Tracking teachers. In L. J. Saha & A. G. Dworkin (Eds.), *International handbook of research on teachers and teaching* (pp. 451–461). New York: Springer.

Kozol, J. (1992). *Savage inequalities: Children in America's schools.* New York: Harper Perennial.

McMahon, S. I., Raphael, T. E., Goatley, V. J., & Pardo, L. S. (1997). *The book club connection: Literacy learning and classroom talk.* New York: Teachers College Press.

O'Donnell-Allen, C. (2006). *The book club companion: Fostering strategic readers in the secondary classroom.* Portsmouth, NH: Heinemann.

Raphael, T., Pardo, L., Highfield, K., & McMahon, S. (1997). *Book club: A literature-based curriculum.* Littleton, MA: Small Planet Communications.

Smagorinsky, P. (2010). The culture of learning to teach: The self-perpetuating cycle of conservative schooling. *Teacher Education Quarterly, 37*(2), 19–32.

Smagorinsky, P., Cook, L. S., & Johnson, T. S. (2003). The twisting path of concept development in learning to teach. *Teachers College Record, 105,* 1399–1436.

Tatum, B. (2003). *Why are all the black kids sitting together in the cafeteria? And other conversations about race: A psychologist explains the development of racial identity* (5th ed.). New York: Basic Books.

8

Modeling Assessment and the Impact on K–16 Student Learning

Sheryl L. McGlamery and Saundra L. Shillingstad

Schools of education across the nation send teacher candidates into class-rooms for field experiences to enrich their knowledge, skills, and dispositions in the process of learning to teach. Field experiences are designed and implemented to provide the opportunity for candidates to observe and interact with teachers, students, and other support personnel in diverse school settings.

WHAT DOES RESEARCH SAY?

The need for an extensive field experience is well documented in the literature on learning to teach (Kagan, 1992; Tang, 2004). Field experience combined with methods classes is essential to the professional development of beginning teachers. Among the many goals of field-based methods courses is helping beginning teachers to do the following:

1. Make connections between theory and practice,
2. Construct curriculum that is meaningful and developmentally appropriate,
3. Model best practices, and
4. Assess student learning in effective ways (Darling-Hammond et al., 2005).

While observing in the field, preservice teachers have the opportunity to observe best practices being modeled, including best practices about assessment. This is good experience, yet it does not always mean the teacher candidate understands when and why the assessment is given, or how the assessment relates to future teaching objectives.

Research in the area of assessment indicates that most beginning teachers need much more assistance to develop a good understanding of assessment in general (McTighe & O'Connor, 2005; Wiggins & McTighe, 2008). More specifically, candidates need to know how to use assessment to further student learning (Stiggins, 2009).

The field or clinical experience—in conjunction with the methods courses—is one additional place where preservice teachers may be introduced to concepts such as formative and summative assessment. These assessment concepts are powerful when applied appropriately in classroom settings (Stiggins & Chappuis, 2008), and it is critical that preservice teachers have experience with assessment application and are schooled in formative and summative assessment strategies and techniques (Stiggins, 2007).

A COLLABORATIVE INQUIRY

Following extensive discourse and observation (2001–2009) of preservice teacher candidates' engagement in an academic service-learning field experiences in math, science, and social studies methods courses, we noted that many of the candidates struggled in the area of making connections between theory and practice and applying the principles of assessing student learning in their field experiences. Our collaboration documents the impact that modeling and demonstration of formative and summative assessment measures had on candidates' understanding of assessing student learning. Additionally, candidates gained a greater awareness of the integration of authentic formative assessment measures into lessons they planned to teach in elementary, middle, and secondary classrooms.

A predominant focus of our innovative work is on how the integration of authentic assessment practices that were first modeled in the higher education classroom were then transferred to K–12 classrooms. Both of us, as professors, strive to provide a field experience built upon differentiated instruction and assessment practices. Over the past eight years, we have strongly integrated and collected data on candidates' abilities to access K–12 student learning through formative and summative assessment measures reported in candidates' reflective journals following their teaching in K–12 field experience placements.

ARRIVAL IN METHODS
(MATH, SCIENCE, AND SOCIAL STUDIES)

To draw upon prior learning experiences in the field and in the university classroom, candidates were asked at the start of the semester to reflect on what they knew about assessment of student learning. Responses included:

- "I know that assessment is very important to determine if your students understand a lesson or unit."
- "Assessment is often done after the lesson and it is used to track student learning and progress."
- "Assessment is a way to measure student learning at the end of a lesson."

As we reflected on candidates' responses, it was not surprising that candidates' knowledge of assessment focused predominately on *when* assessment took place (summatively). Candidates shared that the majority of lessons they had observed in the field were lessons that teachers assessed student learning at the culmination of the lesson.

A concern was that if our candidates identified assessment as a summative process, much work would be needed to prepare them for future field-teaching placements. Having identified an area that candidates needed improvement resulted in our rethinking how assessment literacy was delivered in our university classrooms.

RETHINKING ASSESSMENT

We determined that changes in instructional delivery and methodology in the university classroom was a place to start. We also recognized that explicit instruction, demonstration, and guided discussions were needed to assist candidates in identifying why teachers assess, when assessment can take place, and how to identify or recognize if student learning has occurred. Six guiding questions were written as prompts to assist us in rethinking how we were presenting assessment literacy to our teacher candidates.

- Question 1: How are we defining assessment?
- Question 2: Could the lesson-plan template be used as a tool to assist candidates in developing lessons that included both formative and summative assessment measures?
- Question 3: Could candidates make a greater connection with assessment if they recognized that lessons could include differentiated assessment measures?
- Question 4: Could teacher candidates' understanding of formative and summative assessment strategies improve if higher education faculty provided models and demonstrated the assessment strategies in the higher education classroom?
- Question 5: Could the integration of formative and summative assessment measures as part of the performance objectives heighten candidates' ability to assess in multiple parts of a lesson?
- Question 6: Could the integration of formative and summative assessment measures into science, math, and social studies lesson plans improve the candidates' ability to recognize and document student learning?

Question 1: Defining Assessment

We began by strongly reinforcing to candidates that assessment of student learning in K–12 classrooms was more than a summative event. We emphasized that assessment was part of the process of teaching and learning and needed to be built into the planning of teaching.

McTighe and O'Connor (2005) noted that assessment falls into three categories: (a) summative assessments (summarize learning at the conclusion of the instructional segment), (b) diagnostic assessments (precede instruction), and (c) formative assessment (occur concurrently with instruction).

Assessment is a fundamental educational tool for teachers. To move candidates along the continuum of understanding, we needed to reiterate that linking assessment and instruction is critical to effect learning for the candidates and for their future K–12 students.

Question 2: Lesson Template

We began with a review of a lesson-plan template that guided the development of lessons taught in math, science, and social studies field placements. It was determined that candidates needed to see, hear, and witness how our twelve-step lesson plan could assist them in integrating assessments before, during, or following instruction.

Candidates were required to revisit the template, which guided the development of their lessons. The goal was for candidates to understand that all parts of the lesson-plan template were interconnected. An effort was made to move candidates' understanding of assessment as one of the steps in the lesson plan to the notion that all of the steps on the lesson plan are interconnected and assist teachers in monitoring student progress and learning.

- Steps 1–4: Includes lessons' content and materials needed;
- Step 5: Outlines how the lesson is to be differentiated by content, process, and product;
- Step 6: Identifies the content standard(s);
- Step 7: States the rationale for teaching the lesson;
- Step 8: Notes the performance objectives that guide assessment throughout the lesson;
- Step 9: Sets the stage for learning;
- Step 10: Guides instruction and integration of formative and summative assessment;
- Step 11: Provides opportunity to assess summatively; and
- Step 12: Provides content closure of the lesson objectives (see figure 8.1).

Question 3: Differentiation

Entering our methods courses, candidates know that differentiation is comprised of three areas: content, process, and product (Tomlinson, 2000).

---

1. Content/Grade Level:

2. Lesson #:

3. Lesson Title:

4. Materials:

5. Differentiation of Instruction:
   - Content (materials utilized)
   - Process (instructional strategies implemented throughout the lesson)
   - Product (formative and summative assessment measures to assess student learning)

6. Standard(s):

7. Rationale:

8. Performance Objectives:

   Pre-Instruction: Formative assessment implemented prior to lesson or during anticipatory set
   During Instruction: Formative assessment implemented in the middle of the lesson
   Post-Instruction: Summative assessment at lesson's end

9. Anticipatory Set:

10. Instructional Input/Procedure:

11. Assessment:

12. Closure:

Figure 8.1.   Lesson Plan Template (used in all field experiences and in curriculum unit planning)

Across the math, science, and social studies methods courses, candidates are moved from general awareness of differentiation to applying differentiated ideas and strategies in the lessons they planned for the field experience.

Content

Candidates have a firm understanding that the curriculum in K–12 schools is typically aligned with local and state standards. Therefore, an emphasis was directed to *how* teachers could teach *differently* via differentiated teaching strategies. It was noted that although content may remain static, the opportunity to differentiate outside of the textbook can come in many forms, to include:

- Primary resources: curriculum guides and supplementary materials.
- Secondary resources: newspapers, periodicals, novels, fiction and non-fiction works, electronic resources, movies, songs, poems, or plays.

Process

Students learn in various ways; therefore, it was essential for candidates to understand and have the ability to apply a range of instructional strategies during instruction in the field. Candidates were reintroduced to direct (presentations, demonstrations, questions, recitations, practice and drills, reviews, guided practice, and homework) and indirect (inductive, independent, and social approaches) instructional strategies in an effort to help them do the following:

- Differentiate between direct and indirect instructional strategies; and
- Determine which instructional strategies would work best with their content.

Product

Assessment is a complex process. The goal was for candidates to understand that there are numerous ways to integrate formative and summative assessments into the objectives written for the lessons taught in the field placement. Candidates were asked to assimilate the content, process, and product into a performance objective.

Question 4: Formative and Summative Assessment Strategies

Throughout the semester, we made an effort to continually assess what our candidates knew about the learning-to-teach process. We asked ourselves over and over the following questions: Could they construct curriculum that is meaningful and developmentally appropriate to meet the needs of the K–12 students? Could they model best practices through differentiated instruction? Could they assess student learning in effective ways?

In teaching assessment literacy to candidates, we noted that the terms *formative* and *summative* were at times challenging for the candidates to understand. We reinforced the concept that in a balanced assessment system, both formative and summative assessments are an integral part of information gathering.

The goal was for candidates to understand that there are numerous ways to check and assess student learning via formative and summative assessment. We reinforced that formative assessment can be integrated throughout the lesson—beginning, middle, or end. Through integration of formative assessment strategies, candidates could begin to identify the following:

- Students' prior knowledge
- Students' strengths and weaknesses
- Students' learning and progress
- Teacher effectiveness

We modeled the following formative assessment strategies in our higher education classrooms throughout the teaching of the lesson-planning process. We demonstrated how formative assessment strategies could assist in informing the teacher if students were learning the goals and objectives of the lessons they were teaching.

Formative Assessment Strategies

- T-charts
- Venn-diagrams
- Concept or word webs
- Three-way Venn diagrams
- KWL charts
- Compare/contrast charts
- Five Ws chart
- Time-order charts
- Timelines
- Cause and effect
- Flow charts

- Step-by-step charts
- Oral questioning
- *I Learned* statements
- Learning illustrated
- Key identification
- Displays
- Self-reporting
- Circle meetings
- Feedback forms
- Sequence charts
- Cluster/word webs

Summative Assessment Strategies

In building up candidates' assessment literacy, we modeled and demonstrated throughout our instruction that summative assessments included more than standardized tests and state assessments. Summative assessments provide for teachers at the district or classroom level an accountability measure that is generally used as part of the grading process.

• Chapter tests	• Final copies
• Unit tests	• District benchmarks
• Final exams	• Statewide tests
• Projects	• National tests
• Performances	• Entrance exams

Question 5: Writing Performance Objectives

Teaching candidates to write performance objectives required explicit modeling. Candidates at this point in their course work have spent a great deal of time becoming familiar with Bloom's (1984) levels of learning. Following a review of Bloom's classification chart, we modeled how to write three-part performance objectives.

Candidates were asked to check out a curriculum guide from the education curriculum lab and we modeled and demonstrated the following to the candidates:

- We discussed how to *read* a curriculum guide and demonstrated how the guide was broken into units, chapters, lessons, activities, and assessments.
- Candidates chose a unit, focused on one chapter, and the accompanying lessons.
- Candidates located individual lesson objectives.
- Candidates recorded objectives from the curriculum guide.
- Finally, we then modeled and demonstrated how to turn the objectives from the curriculum guide into observable, measureable teaching objectives.

We revisited Step 8 of the lesson-plan template. Candidates were reminded that performance objectives include: (a) an action statement, (b) a condition statement, and (c) a criterion statement. The lesson template includes three objectives that include the integration of two formative and one summative assessment measures:

- Pre-Instruction: Formative assessment implemented prior to lesson or during anticipatory set;
- During Instruction: Formative assessment implemented in the middle of the lesson; and
- Post-Instruction: Summative assessment at lesson's end.

We explicitly modeled and demonstrated how the curriculum guide objectives can be rewritten as performance objectives to include an action statement, a condition statement, and a criterion measure. Example objectives are:

- Formative: Before the lesson, the students will brainstorm with a partner and record four to six ideas on a concept web regarding what they know about the term *geography*.
- Formative: During the lesson, the students will develop a t-chart and stop and record four or five tools and one or two ways geographers use those tools to study the world of geography.
- Summative: Following the lesson, the students will complete the ten items on workbook page 41 with 80 percent accuracy.

Why three objectives? The goal was to move candidates away from assessing only at the end of the lesson. Requiring them to write two formative objectives and one summative objective enhanced their understanding that assessment was not a single event in the teaching process.

Question 6: Student Learning:
The Field Experience and Lesson Plan Connection

Once the candidates planned and wrote the lessons, they were ready to teach their lessons in the field context. While the lesson-plan template helped candidates to construct a notion of assessment, actually teaching the lesson led to the construction of understanding about assessment. In order to capture the learning and understanding developed by the candidates, they were asked to write about their experiences in a field journal.

Candidates were asked to reflect on the learning-to-teach experience. Following their teaching in the K–12 settings, they were asked to analyze the lessons they taught. Some of the prompts we offered below guided their reflections:

- Describe the classroom environment.
- What instructional materials and strategies were used?
- What were the objectives of the lesson?
- Did the instructional strategies assist in meeting the objectives?
- How were the students grouped for instruction?
- Did you have to modify the lesson from the original plan?
- How did you assess the lesson?
- Did the assessment measures assist in meeting the objectives?
- What did you learn as a result of this learning-to-teach experience?

The use of the lesson-plan template and field experience led to the construction of the cycle shown here:

LEARNING TO ASSESS: STEPS CANDIDATES PROCEED THROUGH DURING THE FIELD AND METHODS COURSES

Step 1: Plan lessons (university classroom).
Step 2: Teach lessons in the field (diverse field placement).
Step 3: Reflect on the lessons and assessment outcomes of student learning.
Step 4: Debrief with colleagues (university classroom).
Step 5: Repeat Steps 1 through 4.

A moment of reflection-on-practice and reflection-in-action brought one beginning teacher to the Aha! moment, when the purpose and meaning of assessment were understood. The moments of reflection after teaching brought opportunity to the candidates to make sense of the learning process. Reflection on-action helped the candidates to: (a) learn and organize content, (b) follow student learning, (c) document student learning through formative and summative assessment, and (d) plan for new teaching based on data (from assessments) about student learning.

DISCUSSION AND IMPLICATION OF OUTCOMES

Following eight years of observations in the field with our candidates, we have noted that the best place to assess student learning is in the field placement. Candidates need to be provided with opportunities to transfer learning from the higher education classroom to the K–12 setting to develop a strong understanding of assessment.

Through our observations—in and outside of the university classroom—we have noted that modeling and demonstration of assessment in the higher education classroom is critical to the transfer into K–12 classrooms. At the end of a recent semester, an elementary social studies candidate noted:

> Looking back, prior to this semester I knew somewhat little regarding the assessment of student learning. I was aware of the terms *formative* and *summative* assessment and knew that it was important to include these forms of assessment into the curriculum in order to reach every student. However, I did not know enough about either assessment form that would allow me to confidently implement them into lessons. I also knew that standardized tests and traditional forms of assessment are not always the most effective tools to assess students' learning as they do not give a well-rounded example of the student's knowledge of the material. I am now more confident in my ability to include various assessment methods into my lessons in order to gain a stronger understanding of my students' knowledge.

REFERENCES

Bloom, B. S. (Ed.). (1984). *Taxonomy of educational objectives. Handbook 1: Cognitive domain*. New York: Longman.

Darling-Hammond, L., Banks, J., Zumwalt, K., Gomez, L., Sherin, M. G., Greisdorn, J., & Finn, L. (2005). Educational goals and purposes: Developing a curricular vision for teaching. In L. Darling-Hammond & J. D. Bransford (Eds.),

Preparing teachers for a changing world: What teachers should learn and be able to do (pp. 169–200). San Francisco: John Wiley and Sons.

Kagan, D. M. (1992). Professional growth among pre-service and beginning teachers. *Review of Educational Research, 62,* 129–169.

McTighe, J., & O'Connor, K. (2005). Seven practices for effective learning. *Educational Leadership, 63*(3), 10–17.

Millard Public Schools. (2009). *Elementary schools.* Retrieved March 11, 2009, from http://www.mpsomaha.org/mps/index.cfm?action=202&bt=16,53&bt1 =64&id=345

Omaha Public Schools. (2009). *Schools.* Retrieved March 11, 2009, from http://www.ops.org/district/SCHOOLS/SchoolInformationPages/Elementary Schools/tabid/95/Default.aspx

Stiggins, R. (2007). Five assessment myths and their consequences. *Education Week, 28*(8), 28–29.

Stiggins, R. (2009). Assessment for learning in upper elementary grades. *Phi Delta Kappan, 90,* 419–421.

Stiggins, R., & Chappuis, J. (2008). Enhancing student learning. *District Administration, 44*(1), 42–44.

Tang, S. Y. F. (2004). The dynamics of school-based learning in initial teacher education. *Research Papers in Education, 19,* 185–204.

Tomlinson, C. (2000). Reconcilable differences? Standards-based teaching and differentiation. *Educational Leadership, 58*(1), 6–11.

Wiggins, G., & McTighe, J. (2008). Put understanding first. *Educational Leadership, 65*(8), 36–41.

II

INSERVICE TEACHER EDUCATION

There is much written about effective inservice teacher development, but there is little agreement as to what comprises a quality program. In the 2001 *Standards for Staff Development*, the National Staff Development Council (NSDC) targeted three areas to consider—context, process, and content of programs—that improve the learning of all students.

The chapters selected for this section share these three key elements and offer documentary accounts of innovations as evidence of successful professional development initiatives. Each of these programs describes the setting or context in which the innovative change takes place and pays careful attention to the roles of teachers and students. Similarly in terms of process, enhanced instructional strategies that lead to improved student performance are detailed. In addition, the contents of the programs are highlighted so that they can be used as models in other teaching and learning environments.

Joseph Corriero and Lynn Romeo introduce a multiyear induction program, and they document how novice teachers become engaged in practices that support teaching in reform-minded ways. The Schools of Promise in New York state are showcased by George Theoharis and Julie Causton-Theoharis through a whole-school reform project that embedded professional development initiatives within the goals of inclusion. Diane Lapp, Thomas DeVere Wolsey, Douglas Fisher, and Sharon Walpole collaborate to describe ways in which technology can enhance teacher knowledge through blended instruction and increased opportunities for web-based interactions designed for literacy coaches. Challenged by the demand for science, technology, engineering, and mathematics (STEM) education, Susan K. Parry, Valerie B. Brown-Schild, Lisa B. Hibler, Charles R. Coble, and Ruben G. Carbonell present how the Kenan Fellowship program successfully cultivates teacher leadership through a comprehensive model for professional advancement. Finding a path to promote teachers' social and emotional competencies—as a support for teacher efficacy and commitment to the profession—is the goal of Patricia A. Jennings's work. Nita A. Paris, Harriet J. Bessette, Traci Redish, and Dawn Latta Kirby describe an innovative, practice-oriented educational doctorate as a teacher leadership model.

REFERENCE

National Staff Development Council (NSDC). (2001). *NSDC's standards for staff development.* Retrieved July 2, 2010, from http://www.nsdc.org/standards/index.cfm

9

When Mentoring Is Not Enough: A Multiyear Induction Program

Joseph Corriero and Lynn Romeo

NOVICE TEACHER INDUCTION

Teaching is difficult, challenging work, and learning to teach is often a daunting process in which teachers find themselves on their own with little support or encouragement. This is most evident in the initial years of teaching, as novice teachers struggle to fulfill their two major responsibilities—teaching and learning to teach (Lampert, 2010).

Given the complexities of being a teacher, it is not surprising that many novice teachers decide to leave teaching during this turbulent time. Some reports indicate that as many as 50 percent of new teachers leave the profession within five years, and three out of ten move to a different school or stop teaching altogether after their first year (Ingersoll & Smith, 2004). Many states and school districts have attempted to resolve the problem of novice teacher attrition by creating, and in some cases mandating, mentoring programs.

What the Research Tells Us

Traditionally, the goal of mentoring has been to provide new teachers with a smooth transition into the existing school culture and to forge mentoring relationships focused on helping beginning teachers retain their jobs and adapt to their environments (Wang, Odell, & Schwille, 2008). A review of the professional literature provided insight into practices that have proven to be effective in attaining these goals. Ingersoll and Smith (2004) reported that *packages* of formal induction that include a mentor from the same subject area, a common planning time with other teachers who teach a similar subject, regularly scheduled collaboration, and being part of an external network of teachers are associated with reduced levels of teacher turnover.

A study of the effects of mentoring and induction on beginning teachers' practices in an early childhood setting (K–3) revealed that a comprehensive induction program can foster teaching expertise (Davis & Higdon, 2008). In their extensive review of the literature, Wang et al. (2008) cited the following as qualities of effective induction programs:

1. Comprehensive and continuing throughout the initial teaching experience;
2. Built into the context of the teacher's work environment;
3. Based on a vision of effective teaching and learning that is linked to student achievement;
4. Part of a cohesive professional growth plan that is focused on how and what teachers need to learn to become effective practitioners; and
5. Grounded in continuous reflective practice.

The problem is not a scarcity of professional resources involving mentoring and induction, but a lack of clarity regarding the desired outcomes.

The Challenge

There is evidence that beginning teachers view mentoring as effective in supporting classroom management, curriculum resources, and their relationship with students (Wang et al., 2008). Although the research supports the effectiveness of mentoring for enhancing the comfort level and job satisfaction of novices, there is less evidence that mentoring affects the quality of their teaching and learning practices (Wang et al., 2008; Ingersoll & Smith, 2004).

A recent study sponsored by the U.S. Department of Education indicated that the intensive teacher induction programs they examined had no impact upon changing teachers' instructional practices, improving student achievement, or retaining teachers (Isenberg et al., 2009). This is sobering news for those who advocate mentoring as a means to ease the transition into teaching. Some researchers found that mentoring reinforces traditional norms, thereby promoting the status quo and hindering change efforts (Puk & Haines, 1999). These limitations raise a number of issues, such as (a) the nature of mentoring relationships, (b) the quality of induction practices, and (c) the question of whether traditional mentoring is appropriate to prepare teachers who can not only survive but also thrive in complex educational environments.

MENTORING AND REFORM-MINDED TEACHING

The popular perception of mentoring as providing new teachers with emotional and psychological support may not be consistent with reform-minded teaching practices that are characterized by instruction that relies on curriculum and teaching standards developed by professional organizations. Wang and Odell (2002) noted that "this kind of teaching includes more student-centered instruction and features a progressivist perspective on education and constructivist ideas of knowledge and learning" (p. 484). Supporting novices to become reflective problem solvers who teach in this manner requires a different set of skills and dispositions than those found in traditional mentoring relationships where *surviving* and *adapting* are the priorities.

Retaining new teachers in the profession is a concern, but the more important issue is keeping quality teachers who are going to have a positive impact on student achievement. The challenge in our work with a partnership district, Hazlet Township, located in New Jersey, was to create a research-based induction program that not only retained teachers but also assisted them to become reflective, highly competent, reform-minded professionals who promote student achievement.

THE SAVE MODEL

Collaborating as university faculty with school district partners, we always begin our work by acknowledging that the first few years of teaching are difficult, complex, challenging, and critical to a teacher's career. Consequently, to meet the needs of novice teachers during this important time, we promote a three-year induction program aligned with school district goals and consistent with research-based *best practices.* We begin our collaborative dialogue by discussing the major goals of our induction program with local school faculty and administrators:

1. *Survival:* Initially, the focus is on survival skills, such as classroom management and developing relationships with students. The emphasis is on technical assistance, which is usually provided by an assigned mentor who functions as a supportive colleague.
2. *Adaptation:* The major focus of this goal is on socialization and emotional support for novice teachers. One-on-one mentoring is the principle delivery form, and the major role of the mentor is to acculturate the new teacher to the norms of the school and district.
3. *Vision-building:* The third goal assists novices in developing a personal style and professional persona through lifelong practices of self-assessment, reflection, and the continuous examination of their core values and beliefs.
4. *Effective reform-based teaching:* The final goal focuses on assisting novice teachers in designing responsive curriculum and instruction that is consistent with reform-minded practices and national and state standards, and promotes student achievement.

OUR MULTIYEAR INDUCTION PROGRAM

Year One

In year one of our program with the Hazlet Township Public Schools, teachers were paired with supportive mentors who had a similar teaching responsibility. Professional development sessions were provided for both the novice and the mentor by district and university faculty in the summer before the initial teaching year and during the first school year. Although the mentoring relationship was primarily related to *survival* and *adaptation* goals, the process was infused with opportunities for novice teachers to develop the dispositions, knowledge, and skills necessary for reform-minded teaching.

We were hopeful that the novice teachers would begin to acquire a repertoire of reform-minded teaching strategies based on essential teaching behaviors collaboratively constructed by the school district and university. We identified what reform-minded teaching looks like in practice and set expectations for the novice teachers. Mentors and novice teachers were given some common planning time to design lessons collaboratively, and observe, reflect, and provide feedback regarding the essential teaching behaviors and the effect on student learning. The novice teachers were encouraged to use discussion and journaling to reflect on their lessons and to set goals for improving their teaching.

What is the role of reflection? From the initial introductory meeting, novices were engaged in reflective practices. During their orientation meeting, novices participated in a vision-building exercise to reflect upon their core values and beliefs regarding teaching. They were encouraged to keep this vision as their central focus as professional identities evolved and took shape. We emphasized reflection as a means to foster the new teachers' abilities to self-assess and *learn how to learn*.

Realizing that the term *reflection* is overused and is open to different interpretations, we intentionally taught, modeled, and provided practice in reflective experiences using Valli's (1997) classification as a guide: technical reflection, reflection in- and on-action, deliberative reflection, personalistic reflection, and critical reflection. Novices were exposed to the different types of reflection, and attempts were made to match the reflective practices with the intended outcomes of our induction activities.

Technical reflection is limited to the comparison of the effectiveness of one's teaching to prespecified teaching strategies. It can be used to support the survival goal. Reflection-on-action represents the retrospective thinking teachers do after a lesson has been taught. Reflection-in-action refers to the spontaneous, intuitive decisions made during the act of teaching that support the adaptation goal.

Deliberative reflection emphasizes decision making based on multiple perspectives and a variety of sources: research, experience, advice of colleagues, personal beliefs, and values. Personalistic reflection gives meaning and purpose to one's work; it is within our vision that we derive our passion, motivation, and commitment. Critical reflection focuses on the consequences of actions, taking into account the broader social, political, and cultural issues (Valli, 1997).

Year Two

In year two, the novice teacher was not assigned a specific mentor. The emphasis was on exposing the second-year teacher to reflective practices related to reform-minded teaching. Guided and supported by district and university faculty, the novices engaged in the development of a *reflective portfolio*. The components of the portfolio included the following:

- A personal vision statement;
- A case study involving a contextualized problematic situation with a student;
- A unit plan using the district-developed backward design template;
- A self-critique of a lesson taught by the novice, focusing on one of the components of the district-created essential teaching behaviors;
- *Wondering:* Novice teachers considered their classroom and teaching practices as potential research studies as they contemplated "what if . . ." or "I wonder . . ." scenarios; and
- A teacher-directed professional growth plan.

Year Three

During the third year, teachers were engaged in an action research project that generally evolved from their questions or "wonderings" developed in their second year. The third-year teachers were introduced to action research by university faculty as practical, user-friendly, systematic inquiry aimed at improving teaching and learning (Ross-Fisher, 2008). They were guided through the process of identifying a problematic area and transforming it into a question that was investigated by reviewing the related literature, followed by the collection and analysis of data.

In response to the initial question, a plan of action was developed that provided the teacher with a methodical way to improve practice. The teachers were supported in their research by district and university faculty. At this stage, the focus was on refining reflective practices and taking responsibility for one's professional growth. In both years two and three, the experience culminated in a professional sharing in which the novice teachers were provided a public forum to share their work with colleagues and the community.

OUTCOMES AND EVIDENCE OF SUCCESS

Novice Teacher Perspectives

The novice teachers were interviewed and also completed surveys regarding their mentoring experiences. Content analysis was used to analyze the data. Most participants had positive experiences; for example, one mentee indicated, "Having a mentor was definitely a benefit. She always provided support and encouragement." However, they indicated some challenges as well.

It appears that, in most cases, mentoring accomplished the traditional goal of transitioning the novice teachers into the routines, procedures, and culture of their schools while sustaining practices needed to become reflective practitioners. The reflective portfolio produced during the second year was seen as helpful in supporting this process. One novice pointed out that the case study enhanced her sense of efficacy by demonstrating that she "can make a difference." Another teacher indicated that the most valuable component of the second year was the articulation of her vision of teaching as part of the portfolio process: "I found it meaningful to examine my core beliefs and values and realize that everything you do in your practice stems from that. It's really important to step back and look at yourself as an individual and see what you believe in."

Although most of the teachers had not previously been exposed to action research, the year-three teachers reported that this turned into a very rich experience. A teacher of basic skills pointed out that she focused her action research question on the district's targeted reading program and used this experience to support the work she was already involved in with her colleagues, thereby integrating her research into everyday practice.

In general, the novice teachers believed they had become more reflective. However, it appears that most of their reflection involved technical reflection and reflection-in-action regarding what went well during teaching and what was problematic. They indicated that their research encouraged them to become more collaborative. Further, they also began to make connections between their own teaching practices and student learning.

Challenges Identified by Novices

The novice teachers were asked about the challenges they encountered in the induction activities; several themes emerged from the data:

1. The need for more time to meet with mentors, to observe other teachers, to network with other novice teachers, and to work with district and university faculty to refine their portfolios and action research projects.
2. The need for additional resources that novice teachers can use as models. They requested exemplars of the components of reflective portfolios (vision statements, case studies, unit plans, lesson critiques, personal growth plans) and previously completed action research projects.
3. The request for novices to have contact with teachers who have gone through the induction process.

Feedback from the Superintendent

Interviews were also conducted with administrators in the school district where the program was initiated. They were asked about their appraisal of the program's impact upon their novice teachers. The superintendent indicated the induction program individualized the learning for the novice teachers, allowing them to improve upon all aspects of their professional responsibilities, setting them on the road to becoming highly effective teachers. The involvement with the university allowed the district to prioritize their goals for novice teachers and provided specific, best-practice teaching models for them.

IMPLICATIONS AND CONCLUSIONS

Based on the sustained, three-year induction program, novice teachers moved beyond the limited goals of traditional mentoring and became engaged in practices that supported the developing skills and dispositions needed to teach in reform-minded ways (Wang & Odell, 2002). It is important to remember that induction is not an isolated activity but is a part of a coherent, sustained, professional growth plan linked to student achievement (Darling-Hammond, Wei, Andree, Richardson, & Orphanos, 2009).

In this context, our future work must include enriching and extending the reflective activities beyond technical reflection and the consideration of *what went right and what went wrong.* Engaging novices in critical reflection that challenges them to question existing assumptions, address issues regarding social justice and democratic values, and consider how to infuse this into a culturally responsive instructional design would be a significant step forward in the development of reform-minded teachers (Wang & Odell, 2007).

We also need to provide sustained professional development for mentors with the expectation that they will assume a more active role in promoting novices' effective teaching practices. We must ensure that mentors are committed to assumptions underlying reform-minded teaching and are capable of teaching in this manner. The expectations of mentors must be raised beyond promoting novices' transition into the existing culture and norms of teaching. Ideally, mentors will assume roles as *agents of change* who are able to enhance the novices' abilities to engage in reflective practices and develop the dispositions to support reform-based teaching (Wang & Odell, 2002).

Finally, we must more fully extend and enrich the partnership between the university and school district faculty as we collaboratively investigate the issues surrounding learning, both for students and adults.

REFERENCES

Darling-Hammond, L., Wei, R., Andree, A., Richardson, N., & Orphanos, S. (2009). *Professional learning in the learning profession: A status report on teacher development in the United States and abroad.* Oxford, OH: National Staff Development Council.

Davis, B., & Higdon, K. (2008). The effects of mentoring/induction support on beginning teachers' practices in early elementary classrooms (K-3). *Journal of Research in Childhood Education, 22*, 261–274.

Ingersoll, R. M., & Smith, T. M. (2004). What are the effects of induction and mentoring on beginning teacher turnover? *American Educational Research Journal, 41*, 681–714.

Isenberg, E., Glazerman, S., Bleeker, M., Johnson, A., Lugo-Gil, J, Grider, M., Dolfin, S., Britton, E., & Ali, M. (2009). *Impacts of comprehensive teacher induction: Results from the second year of a randomized controlled study* (NCEE 2009–4073). Washington, DC: U.S. Department of Education, Institute of Education Sciences, National Center for Educational Evaluation and Regional Assistance.

Lampert, M. (2010). Learning teaching in, from, and for practice: What do we mean? *Journal of Teacher Education, 61*(1–2), 21–34.

Puk, T. G., & Haines, J. M. (1999). Are schools prepared to allow beginning teachers to re-conceptualize instruction? *Teaching and Teacher Education, 15*, 541–553.

Ross-Fisher, R. (2008). Action research to improve teaching and learning. *Kappa Delta Pi Record, 44*(4), 160–165.

Valli, L. (1997). Listening to other voices: A description of teacher reflection in the United States. *Peabody Journal of Education, 72*(1), 67–88.

Wang, J., & Odell, S. J. (2002). Mentored learning to teach according to standards-based reform: A critical review. *Review of Educational Research, 72*, 481–546.

Wang, J., & Odell, S. J. (2007). An alternative conception of mentor-novice relationships: Learning to teach in reform-minded ways as a context. *Teaching and Teacher Education, 23*, 473–489.

Wang, J., Odell, S. J., & Schwille, S. (2008). Effects of teacher induction on beginning teachers' teaching: A critical review of the literature. *Journal of Teacher Education, 59*, 132–152.

10

When All Really Means All: Schools of Promise, School Reform, and Innovative Professional Development

George Theoharis and Julie Causton-Theoharis

Imagine schools in which all self-contained settings, resource rooms, pullout programs, and overloaded or cluster classrooms for students with disabilities are eliminated. Each classroom now has a balance of student needs and *all* teachers are responsible for teaching *all* students. In addition to students having increased access to peers and the general education curriculum, these schools have experienced promising achievement gains.

SCHOOLS OF PROMISE

This chapter focuses on an inclusive whole-school reform project titled Schools of Promise (SOP). The SOP approach is designed to harness the integration of school resources (Frattura & Capper, 2007), the power of inclusive practices (Peterson & Hittie, 2003) with aspects of effective whole-school reform (Edmonds, 1979; Fashola & Slavin, 1998), and a school district–university partnership (Darling-Hammond, 1994; Holmes Group, 1990; Teitel, 2004).

SOP is a partnership between Syracuse University School of Education and local school districts that provides an innovative example of teacher inservice. This partnership aims to improve elementary schools for all students, particularly those students who have traditionally not been successful in schools: students with disabilities, English language learners, students of color, and students from low-income families. SOP is essentially about inclusive school reform. At its core, SOP centers on issues of belonging and creating school structures, staffing plans, schedules, class placements, teaching teams, and daily instruction that are designed to include *all* students in the general education setting.

SCHOOLS OF PROMISE BACKGROUND

Consider the history of segregation in public schools and the history of separation in special education as a backdrop to this chapter. Pair that with the current pressures to target instruction and to remediate students when schools are faced with diverse learning needs in order to raise achievement on state tests (Huefner, 2000; Reese, 2005). In light of these educational realities, researchers argue that success for all students requires a proactive, whole-school approach (Frattura & Capper, 2007; McLeskey & Waldron, 2006; Theoharis, 2009).

This means recognizing that there are and will be a range of learners and learning challenges or strengths within any school. A proactive, whole-school approach implies using existing resources and staff to meet those needs by building collaborative support in general education that improves the educational experience for all students. This is a direct contrast to the approach used to address students who struggle in many schools. Often this involves waiting for students to fail and using resources reactively and in a targeted manner to remediate for some, removing them from their peers and general education classrooms, while other students receive no additional support.

SOP began with a planning process that was facilitated by the university faculty that involved teachers and administrators reconfiguring the use of staff to create teams of specialists and general education teachers to collaboratively plan and deliver instruction to heterogeneous student groups. This resulted in all students (including students with significant disabilities, students with mild disabilities, students with emotional disabilities, students with autism . . . *all* students) being placed into inclusive classrooms with their supports and services delivered to them seamlessly in the context of general education. Through this partnership, the entire school team received professional development and support for three years (Causton-Theoharis, Theoharis, Bull, Cosier, & Dempf-Aldrich, 2010).

INNOVATIVE PROFESSIONAL DEVELOPMENT

The SOP partnership involved examining and redeploying school resources, which necessitated multiple levels of ongoing professional development for teachers and administrators. It was important to see that this school reform was not only about students with disabilities; this was about *all* students through a focus on creating systems and learning to raise achievement and create a sense of belonging.

Innovative professional development through the SOP partnership involved:

1. Gaining an authentic understanding of the system and use of resources, and creating plans to use human resources to match the goals of inclusion and belonging for all;
2. Offering university graduate courses on site for graduate students and practicing teachers;
3. Embedding professional development initiatives within goals of inclusion and belonging (science lesson study, writing projects);
4. Developing authentic collaborative instructional teams;
5. Problem solving and mentoring with administrators and instructional teams; and
6. Leading conversations with the entire faculty.

Understanding the System and Creating Plans to Use Human Resources Differently

For each SOP, the first step was that the university faculty facilitated the school staff in the development of goals relating to belonging, inclusion, and access. Examples of these brainstormed goal statements include:

- Students in balanced classrooms with positive role models.
- Students do not leave to learn.

- Purposefully built classroom and school climates that are warm and welcoming for children and staff and fosters active/engaging learning.
- Child-centered, differentiated, research-based instruction that challenges children of all abilities, supported by targeted staff development.

After the goals were decided, the next step in the SOP partnership was to complete a visual map of how the school was using resources. This involved creating visuals of how teachers and assistance were arranged and deployed, and where students with disabilities were served and by whom. For an example of this, see figure 10.1.

Many school staff had never considered the macro view of their school. Given the daily pressing realities of teaching, they did not have the opportunity to understand the ways in which the school operated as a system. Thus, this process offered a practical, hands-on way for teachers and staff to gain new understanding of the school. For example, in the school depicted in figure 10.1, the teachers involved in the process commented, "I had no idea we had 10.5 special education teachers" and "this map [of

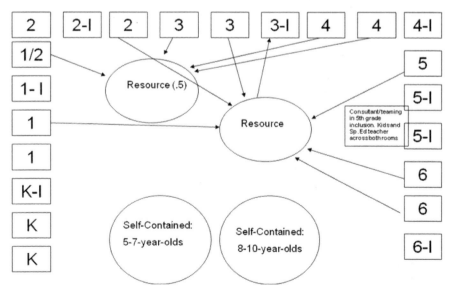

Figure 10.1. Visual Representation of Summer Heights K–6 School: Service Delivery/ Use of Human Resources for Students with Disabilities

the services] gives me a picture of why I feel overwhelmed by the needs in my class."

Following the creation of a visual map of how services were offered, the staff created plans for redeploying resources to better meet the SOP developed goals. This engaged school staff members in learning about the school as a system and in turn they recognized that a focused alignment of resources was needed to meet the goals of the school. The faculty at the school depicted in figure 10.1 chose to redeploy their resources as depicted in figure 10.2.

This restructuring used the 10.5 special education teachers in new ways. All students were placed and became members of the general education classrooms, keeping in mind the idea of creating balanced classrooms without an overload of students with disabilities. This eliminated pullout services and self-contained programs and allowed for the teachers previously assigned to work in those programs to collaborate and co-teach. All teachers—general education and special education—currently collaborate, co-teach, and plan together about how to meet the range of needs in their classroom.

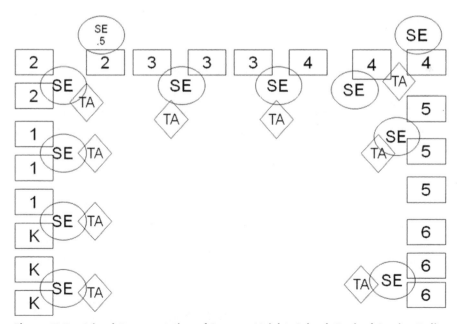

Figure 10.2. Visual Representation of Summer Heights School: Revised Service Delivery and Redeployment of Human Resources

This process of creating new service delivery and redeploying human resources gave the school staff insight about how to align resources with priorities. Every spring this process is now part of the yearly planning for the upcoming school year—how to allocate staff to meet the needs of students through the lens of their inclusive vision.

Offering Innovative University Graduate Courses On-Site

During the first year of implementation of the restructured services, the university offered an on-site graduate course titled Collaboration for Inclusive Schooling at the SOP. Before SOP, this course was only offered at the university and only for graduate students. For the SOP partnership, the location of the course moved to the SOP schools and opened to inservice teachers as well as graduate students. The population of the class consisted of thirty graduate students in the school of education taking the course for university credit and thirty inservice teachers from the SOP schools receiving professional development credit and not paying university tuition.

The purpose of the course was to explore a variety of strategies for professionals to collaborate in order to promote the learning of all elementary students. The course participants examined how general and special education teachers plan and teach collaboratively and focused on best practices for differentiation of curriculum. They explored different ways to collaborate with other professionals, young people, and families, and identified benefits and complexities of collaboration. Additionally, they reconsidered traditional adult roles in inclusive school settings. Further, they practiced strategies in the area of communication, running effective team meetings, creative problem solving, and conflict resolution.

The format of offering the class at one of the SOP sites and combining university graduate students with SOP teachers who took the class for school district professional development hours enabled the practicing teachers to work with university faculty to learn how to collaborate effectively. The course professors worked to create a classroom community where both groups of participants (SOP teachers and university graduate students) worked together on group assignments. Additionally, it allowed the university students to learn alongside teachers in the field who were challenged by the daily issues of teaching. The learning by both groups was greatly enhanced by the presence of the other.

Developing Collaborative Instructional Teams

Another important feature of the SOP partnership was that the university faculty sat with the school teams to provide support as they placed students in classrooms for the upcoming school year. During this student placement process, the schools' inclusive goals were displayed visually, so that the decisions were made with respect to those goals. Next, the group determined the collaborative instructional teams. For example, two general education teachers, one special education teacher, and one paraprofessional might be responsible for teaching two classrooms of students. These teams ultimately learned to co-plan and co-teach together.

One of the benefits of the formation of these teams was that not only did they receive professional development instruction about how to work together as a team, but they also shared their expertise with each other. For example, general educators learned about modifying and adapting, and special educators became familiar with the fourth-grade content, as they were responsible for co-teaching and co-modifying the curriculum. This partnership developed an increased capacity in the teachers to work with all students.

Embedding Other Professional Development Initiatives within Goals of Inclusion and Belonging

The SOP partnership created a focus at the participating schools on issues of belonging and inclusion. This focus was kept central as each school engaged in other professional development initiatives. For example, two years into the SOP partnership, many of the staff at one school began to participate in a professional development initiative on elementary science. This involved rethinking how they taught science and the ways they engaged students in science.

The university faculty leading the elementary science professional development worked with the school staff to incorporate the new learning as an extension of the SOP partnership. As they rethought the ways they brought science into their classrooms, this meant they engaged in planning to differentiate and meet the range of learners' needs inclusively. There was no distinction between the SOP inclusive reform and the science learning; they worked together to enhance teaching and learning for all students in heterogeneous classrooms.

Another school focused on improving their teaching and learning of writing. Again, this became a complement of SOP and not something that was happening separately from newly created heterogeneous classrooms. A member of the SOP team met with the grade-level teams weekly as they were learning and working on writing instruction in order to help maintain the focus on serving all students inclusively.

By the end of the first year of this writing focus, the teachers were amazed at the gains in writing for students they initially were hesitant about including. For example, a boy who according to the teachers was "unable to express his thoughts, he has no ideas" and was "way too low academically to engage in 5th grade writing" was included in the heterogeneous project. For the final project, he wrote a book about the careers he is interested in pursuing. One of the teachers reflected, "I would never in a million years have thought he could have even participated in this writing, and his writing has developed so much."

These two examples demonstrated the power of harnessing other professional development initiatives through the goals of the SOP partnership. While specific learning took part to enhance the collaborative skills and abilities to differentiate, in part SOP was seen and was described as "not one more thing on the plate, but *the* plate." Infusing other professional development activities into the SOP goals was one way inclusion and belonging became *the plate* and not an add-on or an extra program, but rather a driving force for the school and all the learning that happened there.

Problem Solving with Administrators and Instructional Teams

A key aspect of the SOP partnership was how the university team responded to the needs of teaching and administrative teams as issues arose. This took diverse forms; some examples included the following:

- University faculty observed students with challenging behaviors and held problem-solving sessions;
- University faculty met with administrative teams to problem solve about scheduling and the participation of paraprofessionals;
- University graduate students worked weekly with instructional teams to integrate diverse co-teaching models into the weekly plan; and
- University graduate students provided short-term assistance in classrooms so staff could learn new assistive technologies.

This aspect of the partnership was certainly not scripted but evolved out of the fluid needs of the school professionals. One staff member commented that "the support we needed our first year we no longer need because we now have the skills to make decisions and adjustments with the [university SOP team] support."

Holding Whole-Staff Conversations and Learning Experiences

One of the continual aspects of the SOP partnership was that the university faculty led whole-staff conversations and learning experiences that were tailored to the needs of the school. In one school, they engaged in the topics of differentiation, modifications, and racial diversity. In another school, the conversations focused on supporting students with challenging behaviors and the involvement of paraprofessionals. Some of the discussions involved having the school staff read a book or an article prior to the discussion.

Other conversations included video examples of co-teaching or assuming competence about students with disabilities along with discussion questions. These professional exchanges served to help address upcoming concerns and also to keep all staff focused on the more noteworthy goals of the school reform effort.

CONCLUSION: RESULTS OF SCHOOLS OF PROMISE

SOP takes significant time, energy, and persistence from the university team and the participating school professionals. As with all school reform, not everybody involved agrees with or supports this partnership, but in these schools, over 85 percent of staff and 100 percent of administrators report being *supportive of this effort* at this point in time. Many students who previously received their education in separate or self-contained settings, or who were removed from the general education setting to receive services, are now being educated with their peers by teams of professionals.

At one school, previously 42 percent of third graders were reading at grade level and now 68 percent are. Where 50 percent of fourth graders were reading at grade level two years ago, 71 percent of these same students are reading at grade level now. One school went from no students with disabilities reading at grade level to 27 percent reading at grade level. One twenty-year-veteran teacher commented, "[Schools of promise] has been exciting and rejuvenating, I feel energized like I did when I was just starting my career."

Although much progress is still needed and these reform efforts are difficult, the results are promising. We believe that the success in creating schools where all students, with no exceptions, are full members of general education classrooms and where all groups of students are achieving at higher levels comes from the many ways professional learning is embedded into the SOP partnership.

REFERENCES

Causton-Theoharis, J., Theoharis, G., Bull, T. H., Cosier, M., & Dempf-Aldrich, K. (2010). Schools of Promise: A school district-university partnership centered on inclusive school reform. *Remedial and Special Education,* Online-First, March 30, 2010. DOI: 10.1177/0741932510366163.

Darling-Hammond, L. (Ed.). (1994). *Professional development schools: Schools for developing a profession.* New York: Teachers College Press.

Edmonds, R. (1979). Effective schools for the urban poor. *Educational Leadership, 37*(1), 15–23.

Fashola, O. S., & Slavin, R. E. (1998). Schoolwide reform models: What works? *Phi Delta Kappan, 79,* 370–379.

Frattura, E., & Capper, C. A. (2007). *Leading for social justice: Transforming schools for all learners.* Thousand Oaks, CA: Corwin Press.

Holmes Group. (1990). *Tomorrow's schools: Principles for the design of professional development schools.* East Lansing, MI: College of Education, Michigan State University.

Huefner, D. S. (2000). *Getting comfortable with special education law: A framework for working with children with disabilities.* Norwood, MA: Christopher-Gordon.

McLeskey, J., & Waldron, N. (2006). Comprehensive school reform and inclusive schools. *Theory into Practice, 45,* 269–278.

Peterson, M., & Hittie, M. M. (2003). *Inclusive teaching: Creating effective schools for all learners.* San Francisco: Allyn & Bacon.

Reese, W. J. (2005). *America's public schools: From the common school to "No Child Left Behind."* Baltimore, MD: Johns Hopkins University Press.

Teitel, L. (2004). *How professional development schools make a difference: A review of the research* (2nd ed.). Washington, DC: National Association for Accreditation of Teacher Education.

Theoharis, G. (2009). *The school leaders our children deserve: Seven keys to equity, social justice, and school reform.* New York: Teacher College Press.

11

Technology on the Frontier of Inservice Teacher Education

Diane Lapp, Thomas DeVere Wolsey,
Douglas Fisher, and Sharon Walpole

On the first night of class, Alana, a graduate student enrolled in a course for potential literacy coaches, had a set of expectations that reflected her experiences. She thought the class, *Leadership in Literacy*, would mirror others in her master's program—a traditional textbook and plenty of lectures by the instructors. Instead, what she found was a course designed to build on her experiences as a teacher of ten years to develop skills to prepare her to coach in her elementary school and to engage her in emerging conceptualizations about coaching shared through multiple seminal texts.

She also found a model that integrated both twenty-first-century technologies and more traditional face-to-face classroom experiences. Initially nervous about both the literacy coaching content and the use of technology as a learning tool, Alana embraced the opportunity. After the course introduction, she said, "This is why I came to graduate school. I'm going to learn something new."

DESIGNING THE LEADERSHIP IN LITERACY COURSE

A recent survey of colleges and universities (Parsad & Lewis, 2008) reported that 65 percent of degree-granting institutions in the United States offered instruction at a distance; the largest percentage of those distance-learning courses was taught online. Of those, 35 percent of courses were hybrid or blended learning environments combining both face-to-face and online instruction. Alana's course was one such hybrid environment, blending online and on-ground learning experiences. In past courses, Alana's professors had learned that students preferred blended learning. The students felt better connected to their professors and to their peers (Lapp, Frey, Fisher, Moore, & Cappello, 2008).

Student opportunities for blended learning are increasing rapidly at traditional, on-ground universities. Effective blended, or hybrid, learning occurs when the professor employs the best of both face-to-face classroom instruction and information and communication technologies (ICTs). In blended learning environments, attention to the needs of students, the demands of the curriculum, the strengths of ICTs (Wells, 2007), and traditional learning environments are featured.

The *Leadership in Literacy* course was guided by the premise that graduate students in literacy leadership should know the research describing the multiple roles and responsibilities of reading specialists and literacy coaches. Students would build the knowledge and competencies to:

1. Provide direct support for classroom teachers through staff development and inservice education they design; and
2. Design effective reading/language arts programs for their schools.

To support Alana and her K–12 colleagues in achieving these goals, this blended course offered both online and within-classroom experiences designed to build the knowledge base, facilitate a sense of shared purpose, foster a learning community, and promote professional learning outcomes. Six of the participants had never been in a course offering an online component. Ten others had experienced an online chat environment for discussion of articles from professional journals or children's literature.

Hybrid Learning

Effective learning environments designed for adults emphasize experiences, offer opportunities for personal applications of learning, and allow for self-direction. Effective environments also foster the notion that learners contribute to the learning community rather than simply taking factual and conceptual knowledge away from it. Schneider and Germann (1999) pointed out that these qualities may be promoted through thoughtful electronic mediation. This confidence with learning communities may be especially important to the work of literacy coaches.

Many schools recognize the general benefits of a coach or specialist who is able to work with teachers to improve instruction, but the role is often undefined, leaving the coach with little direction, pulled by competing demands from the school system (Lapp, Fisher, Flood, & Frey, 2003). As literacy coaches (and those who want to be literacy coaches) navigate these difficult circumstances, they require opportunities to collaborate with others to define their roles as coaches through conversation and reflection.

Breaking the Mold of the Traditional Classroom

In class, face-to-face, Alana and her colleagues developed critical strategies they would need as literacy leaders by practicing how to gently and artfully support teachers to improve their classroom practices or instructional routines. The environment was safe for practice. Working in small groups, they were provided with video scenarios simulating the range of requests they might receive when working with teachers. For example, one video was of a second-grade teacher who requested an observation by a coach to explore whether she was effectively modeling a read-aloud. Another video showed a high school science teacher who modeled how to read a science text. She had requested that the coach offer suggestions about her performance as well as her students' engagement.

With the video fresh in their minds, Alana and her colleagues, in pairs, wrote scripts for coaching sessions. They then participated in a "fish bowl," role-playing the scripted parts. This was followed by whole-class conversations about the coach's suggestions and the language used to convey the suggestions. Participants reported that these simulated practices provided insights about the delicate nuances of effective coaching. They extended this practice by observing each other's classroom instruction and applying the coaching skills they were learning through the classroom simulations. They agreed that the simulated interactions in class were very similar to ones they experienced as they coached each other. Additionally, students commented that the flexible presentation skills and careful language choices literacy coaches use when working with teachers are important considerations for their own success.

Technology Improves Collaboration

As noted, technology increases the possibility and potential for collaboration with others. In their book clubs, teachers were able to work with other members of the class. However, an essential quality of literacy leadership is to engage with others beyond the schoolhouse walls. Diverse and rich professional networks help teachers to solve problems that seem intractable at their schools and empower them to lend their own expertise to others.

PROFESSIONAL RESOURCES FOR LITERACY COACHES

Online Forums

- International Reading Association Forums on Facebook, http://www.facebook.com/pages/International-Reading-Association/81491751082#
- Literacy Coaching Clearinghouse, http://www.literacycoachingonline.org/forums.html

Book Club Selections

- Allen, J. (2006). *Becoming a literacy leader: Supporting learning and change.* York, ME: Stenhouse.
- Bean, R. M. (2004). *The reading specialist: Leadership for the classroom, school, and community.* New York: Guilford.
- Casey, K. (2006). *Literacy coaching: The essentials.* Portsmouth, NH: Heinemann.
- Rodgers, A., & Rodgers, E. M. (2007). *The effective literacy coach: Using inquiry to support teaching & learning.* New York: Teachers College Press.
- Walpole, S., & McKenna, M. C. (2004). *The literacy coach's handbook: A guide to research-based practice.* New York: Guilford.
- Wepner, S. B., & Strickland, D. S. (2008). *The administration and supervision of reading programs* (4th ed.). New York: Teachers College Press.

To illustrate this, students chose from a variety of national and international professional forums or blogs and contributed to the online communities there. They then provided links to their posts or printed them out for discussion. These online forums provided the teachers with venues to interact with people all over the world as they engaged in discussions about literacy coaching. The interactions also connected students with scholars, an experience they might not have considered possible. One of the students noted, "I posted a comment and a question on the coaching clearing house. I got my question answered within a few hours and I got a personal message from the author of one of the papers we read in class!"

Online Book Clubs

In addition, students collaboratively read, discussed, and shared insights about books on the topic of literacy coaching. These conversations occurred outside of class in online book clubs. They participated in these book clubs both to engage in the content of the books and to experience an alternative vehicle for professional development that they could use in their own coaching. The online book clubs provided concrete evidence that technology increases the potential for teacher collaboration in ways that cannot occur in a brick-and-mortar classroom or in a one-hour professional development session.

Online book clubs fit the students' needs as both readers and scholars because they could read on their own schedules and interact with others reading the same book. In this format, Alana was able to develop a sophisticated understanding of what it takes to be a literacy coach by not only reading a book but also sharing her own insights and learning from the experiences of others in her group (figure 11.1).

While students valued the opportunity to work with each other online and on ground, they recognized the need for expert guidance as well. The professors arranged an interactive video session with Dr. Sharon Walpole, the author of several books and other articles they had read (Blamey, Meyer, & Walpole, 2008; Walpole & McKenna, 2004). Again, technology made this connection and collaborative experience possible when it would have been very difficult otherwise. Webcams and Voice over Internet Protocol (VoIP) allowed Alana and the other teachers to see

Author: Alana

Post date: Thursday, February 29, 2009

Total Views: 43

Post: I just finished reading the entire book, and I must say that was very fulfilling. I would like to know what chapter you feel was most beneficial or inspiring to you as a future literacy leader?

I actually like the reading chapter 9-Scheduling and Budget because it gave me an idea of what a typical day may be like for me in the future. I appreciated reading about how she plans a typical day/week/month. The "Rhythm of a Year" on page 143, showed how she spends time supporting teachers and students, and how she budgets money to benefit both student and teacher literacy needs. I realize that although being a literacy leader seems a bit overwhelming, a lot can be accomplished with planning. I want to make sure that when I plan in the future, I include time to discuss and interact with colleagues, help students, budget money, attend and create workshops, and communicate with parents; among other things!

Figure 11.1.   A Graduate Student's Book Club Post

and talk with Sharon in real time. While students participated via VoIP software on the West Coast of the United States, Sharon sat in her home in Delaware.

The distance learning activity added richness to the traditional classroom as students asked questions and shared experiences with the author of the literature they had read. For Sharon, this experience was new and vastly more satisfying than an asynchronous interaction. She had often answered questions, sent by colleagues who were teaching coaching classes, about her work. Such interactions lacked context, however. She knew that the students' questions were real and that they were experiencing intense and scholarly attention to the immediate issues of coaching. She had the chance to ask questions and engage with them to be sure she understood the students' questions, and the students knew that her answers were authentic and not prepared carefully in advance.

Table 11.1 shows how the qualities of effective adult learning experiences were featured in Alana's *Leadership in Literacy* course using the hybrid model with some components online and others in a brick-and-mortar classroom.

Table 11.1. **Features of Effective Adult Learning Environments**

Adult Learning	Online	Face-to-Face
Emphasize adults' experience and existing expertise	Discussion online permitted adult learners to integrate their experience with what they were learning in class and from each other.	Demonstrations helped adult learners understand complex literacy coaching interactions.
Learning is personally applicable	Online discussion forums allowed teachers time to think about the books they read and compose thoughtful responses to the books and to the other teachers in the discussion groups.	Teachers practiced realistic encounters with colleagues in coaching situations and developed face-to-face presentation skills.
Learning emphasizes self-direction	Online book clubs were developed around teachers' choices that addressed their own needs as literacy leaders.	
Learning extends beyond the walls of the university classroom	Teachers engaged with colleagues nationally and internationally in professional forums. Teachers interviewed an expert on literacy coaching from another part of the country.	Teachers attended presentations and evaluated them. They observed each other in K–12 classrooms and practiced their coaching skills with each other.
Learners contribute to a community of learners and to the larger community in their schools and families	Online discussion fostered community, in part through the rigorous exploration of important self-chosen texts and through the sharing of experiences based on those readings.	Teachers contributed to, learned from, and shared insights to professional associations.

LEARNING TO BE A LITERACY COACH

As students read and thought about coaching, online discussion provided a space for them to reflect. Extensive interaction with colleagues may be especially important to the growth of literacy leaders and coaches. The online discussion was asynchronous in nature; thus, student participants were able to construct thoughtful responses to their colleagues' postings. Time to compose and think about what one is going to write in an online discussion is a hallmark of threaded discussions (Grisham & Wolsey,

2006). When we queried students about the effectiveness of the online book clubs, four themes emerged.

1. Students appreciated the interaction online book clubs afforded. One student wrote, "I enjoy bouncing ideas off of others. I also think people raised questions that I hadn't originally considered, and that was great."
2. Students saw these interactions as deep and took advantage of the chance to return to the text after reading their colleague's responses. As Carol explained, "I was able to process a person's opinion before responding."
3. Students appreciated the flexibility built into the online format for discussion. As adult learners who balance jobs, families, and other responsibilities, students liked the idea that they could read their texts on a schedule they developed with their colleagues and post responses during times convenient for them.
4. Students reported that the online discussion kept them on task, consistently reading both the professional texts and their colleagues' reflections. The peer interaction helped students to stay on task since individuals did not want to let their colleagues down by failing to participate. Andrea spoke for many when she told us that the online forum made visible their contributions to the discussion, which in turn helped them stay focused and on task.

IMPLICATIONS

Beyond convenience, flexibility, and cost factors (Parsad & Lewis, 2008), blended learning offers pedagogical advantages. Before beginning the hybrid course for literacy coaches, the professors asked several critical questions. The answers to those questions informed decisions about how best to make use of the hybrid environment.

1. What are the course outcomes or objectives?
2. Which activities are best suited for face-to-face interaction? For example, the coaching practice sessions with peers are well suited

to real-time interaction because these are the types of interactions literacy coaches encounter in their schools.

3. Which activities lend themselves well to asynchronous discussion online? Book clubs permit students to think about their reading and their experiences, and to respond thoughtfully after scholarly reflection.

4. How might others—who are not part of the course—contribute to the learning environment? The distance interview with Dr. Walpole helped students extend their learning by bringing a guest to the classroom. Further, the graduate students were able to interact with other literacy professionals all over the country by participating in online forums outside the course management system.

This blended instruction facilitated opportunities for teaching and learning: asynchronous online discussion, real-time online video discussion with a literacy coaching expert, and on-ground activities that simulated the literacy coaching environment in schools. All of these strategies used by aspiring coaches can also be used by actual coaches as they connect with their adult learners. When instructors match activities with instructional purposes, teacher inservice can result in increased participation, learning, and engagement.

NOTE

All graduate students' names are pseudonyms.

REFERENCES

Blamey, K. L., Meyer, C., & Walpole, S. (2008). Middle and high school literacy coaches: A national survey. *Journal of Adolescent & Adult Literacy, 52*, 310–323.

Grisham, D. L., & Wolsey, T. D. (2006). Recentering the middle school classroom as a vibrant learning community: Students, literacy and technology intersect. *Journal of Adolescent and Adult Literacy, 49*, 648–660.

Lapp, D., Fisher, D., Flood, J., & Frey, N. (2003). Dual role of the urban reading specialist. *Journal of Staff Development, 42*(2), 33–36.

Lapp, D., Frey, N., Fisher, D., Moore, K., & Cappello, M. (2008). Traditional vs. online literacy methods courses: Comparing student teachers' understandings and application. *Reading Professor, 30*(1), 34–38.

Parsad, B., & Lewis, L. (2008). *Distance education at degree-granting postsecondary institutions: 2006–07* (NCES 2009–044). National Center for Education Statistics, Institute of Education Sciences, U.S. Department of Education. Washington, DC. Retrieved July 2, 2010, from http://nces.ed.gov/pubs2009/2009044.pdf

Schneider, S., & Germann, C. (1999). Technical communication on the web: A profile of learners and learning environments. *Technical Communication Quarterly, 8*(1), 37–48.

Stern, B. S. (2004). A comparison of online and face-to-face instruction in an undergraduate Foundations of American Education course. *Contemporary Issues in Technology and Teacher Education, 4*, 196–213. Retrieved July 2, 2010, from http://www.citejournal.org/vol4/iss2/general/article1.cfm

Walpole, S., & McKenna, M. C. (2004). *The literacy coach's handbook: A guide to research-based practice.* New York: Guilford.

Wells, J. G. (2007). Key design factors in durable instructional technology professional development. *Journal of Technology and Teacher Education, 15*, 101–122.

12

Teaching Outside the Book:
Inservice Teacher Education for a New World

Susan K. Parry, Valerie B. Brown-Schild, Lisa B. Hibler,
Charles R. Coble, and Ruben G. Carbonell

Ms. Lisa Hibler represents a cohort of highly skilled STEM teachers (science, technology, engineering and mathematics) practicing in North Carolina. Colleagues describe her as someone who "inspires students and colleagues . . . someone who understands the benefits of taking risks in the classroom and modeling divergent, creative thinking." Yet North Carolina risked losing this successful teacher to burnout until she connected with the Kenan Fellows Program for Curriculum and Leadership Development (KFP). Because of her skills and the respect she had earned in the classroom, Ms. Hibler received the prestigious two-year fellowship that offered an opportunity to update her content knowledge while remaining an active teacher.

Ms. Hibler and her KFP colleagues are the teachers our students need today to respond to the challenges educators and policy makers have been debating since before the 1983 release of *A Nation at Risk* and beyond the 2007 publication of *Rising above the Gathering Storm*. Friedman (2005) summarized the concerns of preeminent scholars when he stated, "because it takes fifteen years to create a scientist or advanced engineer . . . we should be embarking on a crash program for science and engineering education immediately. The fact that we are not doing so is our quiet crisis" (p. 275).

CONNECTING THE BEST

Founded by the Kenan Institute for Engineering, Technology & Science at North Carolina State University in 2000, the Kenan Fellows Program for Curriculum and Leadership Development (KFP) is uniquely positioned to address this crisis by promoting effective teacher leadership, retaining skilled teachers, and connecting educators to professionals outside the classroom to make K–12 STEM education relevant to students. Each class of fellows includes approximately twenty-five select public school teachers from diverse disciplines. Working with mentors, fellows develop a curriculum project, pilot it in the classroom, and share it online with teachers across the country; topics range from interactive gaming to genetics/genomics. Fellows build leadership skills by providing staff development to colleagues, presenting at conferences, and engaging with policy leaders and elected officials. Participants receive laptops, $10,000 as a stipend, and six graduate credits, along with enhanced respect as teacher leaders.

Designed to tap resources in research universities and industry laboratories, the innovative KFP model cultivates a network of professional partnerships, pairing teachers with researchers in two monthlong summer externships involving hands-on research projects that are, as one KFP teacher described it, "so cutting edge it wouldn't even be in a book." Sustained professional development in Summer Institutes focuses on enhancing teaching and leadership skills and on inquiry-based instruction. Not only are fellows learning outside the book, they are encouraged to teach outside the book by actively engaging students in authentic problem-centered learning based on insights gained in research experiences—the use of microbeam technology in developing new materials or the effects of environmental agents on DNA, for example.

In addition to translating research experiences into instructional materials, fellows cultivate working relationships with professionals in critical environments that rarely intersect with the traditional public school classroom. Fellows develop partnerships with university, business, industry, and education leaders, providing experiences that equip fellows to serve as catalysts for higher-quality STEM education in their schools and districts.

NEW CENTURY, NEW CHALLENGES

KFP teachers serve as education leaders in a rapidly changing world. Against the backdrop of global development and technological progress, the KFP originated in North Carolina's Research Triangle region, including Duke University, North Carolina State University, and the University of North Carolina at Chapel Hill, where the need for well-prepared scientists and engineers was obvious. Rural parts of the state, where textile and manufacturing industries had dominated local economies for decades, were less obvious environments for scientists and engineers. But as outsourcing and automation displaced workers, transitioning to a more diversified economy created the demand for greater STEM skills.

Today, the KFP employs innovative strategies to help teachers prepare students for a world in which increased scientific literacy is an essential skill. Since 2000, the program has served more than 100 teachers statewide. But with nearly 100,000 teachers across North Carolina's 100 counties, much more needs to be done.

Student Performance Lacking in Science and Mathematics

U.S. high school students were outperformed by peers in sixteen of twenty-nine other countries of the Organization for Economic Cooperation and Development (OECD) on international assessments of science literacy, and scored lower than the OECD average in problem-solving ability; U.S. fifteen-year-olds scored below students in twenty-three other OECD countries in mathematics literacy (Baldi et al., 2007). National Assessment of Educational Progress (NAEP) results from 2005 showed that only 25 percent of North Carolina fourth graders and 22 percent of eighth graders were considered proficient or advanced in science.

The percentage of North Carolina students enrolling in advanced science courses has declined since 1996, with 24 percent of high schoolers in 2006 taking chemistry, physics, or advanced science, compared with 31 percent nationally. One fourth of North Carolina middle school science and math teachers were not certified in their content areas (Council of Chief State School Officers, 2007).

Teachers Need Support to Succeed

Teachers serve a critical role in addressing the enormous challenges of increasing student knowledge and skills. The more knowledgeable teachers are about scientific practice outside the classroom, the better equipped they are to leverage improvements in student performance. The KFP provides this link for teachers, one that is lacking in many districts. "As a system, we're playing roulette," said Dr. Charles Coble, former chair of the KFP Board of Advisors. "It's a dangerous game, when we're competing with the rest of the nations. . . . There's no systematic, planned intervention to ensure that America's teachers develop their content knowledge and pedagogical skills throughout their career. It may or may not happen, and that's no way to run a nation" (Kenan Fellows Program, 2009).

The Carnegie Corporation of New York's Institute for Advanced Study Commission on Mathematics and Science Education (Carnegie-IAS Commission, 2009) urged professional development for teachers that brings cutting-edge technology and hands-on pedagogy into the classroom: "To lead a revolution in math and science education, teachers need opportunities to experience powerful math and science learning. Motivating, relevant, inquiry-based science and math learning . . . should be built into teachers' initial preparation and ongoing professional development. Educators also need continuous contact with fresh content, especially in science and technology" (p. 39).

Studies show better student performance associated with teachers who have good laboratory skills and effectively promote higher-order thinking and hands-on learning (Wenglinsky, 2000). Providing access to this professional development is critical in order for the United States to compete with other countries where teacher learning is a priority, leading to increased student achievement, improved teacher retention, and greater teacher leadership (Darling-Hammond, Wei, Andree, Richardson, & Orphanos, 2009).

Schools Must Connect to the World

In order to achieve world-class success for teachers and students, American classrooms must align with rapid changes in STEM research. The Carnegie-IAS Commission (2009) recommended moving beyond the typical school setting to include resources "such as museums, universities, research laboratories, businesses, and trade and professional associations" (p. 8).

KFP teachers do exactly this, leveraging resources found in authentic research experiences in private, university, and government settings. Silverstein, Dubner, Miller, Glied, and Loike (2009) attributed the success of a research experience program to key elements in the laboratory experience: "What is common is that all teachers are treated as professionals, challenged to think independently and creatively, and engaged in studying an authentic contemporary scientific problem. This stretches teachers professionally and personally, sharpens their analytic and laboratory experiment–management skills, and enables them to better understand and communicate science concepts and practices" (p. 442).

CHANGING THE FUTURE OF STEM EDUCATION

The KFP addresses these challenges by applying an integrated approach to STEM education, making teachers and students more successful in STEM classes *and* in other areas as well. As the Carnegie-IAS Commission (2009) reported, "Learning math and science from textbooks is not enough: students must also learn by struggling with real-world problems, theorizing possible answers and testing solutions" (p. 13). Each teacher's unique experience in the program ultimately fosters students who are prepared to face the demands of the new world.

Retaining and Revitalizing Fine Teachers

The KFP recognizes the importance of retaining experienced, effective classroom teachers and supporting the inclusion of STEM in their instruction. In North Carolina, although graduate degrees or National Board certification bring salary increases, many teachers today find that advancing professionally requires moving out of the classroom. Particularly in the STEM fields, where good teachers are in short supply and talented professionals may be lured away by research and industry, employing strategies like KFP to nurture the talent we have is critical.

Lisa Hibler (shown in photo 12.1 in her in classroom) left a career in chemical engineering to share the excitement of science as a teacher, but her enthusiasm waned after five years of classroom stresses. Affecting change or offering input in her large urban district seemed difficult, if not impossible. She looked for new avenues to grow as a teacher but found few opportunities for growth within the busy context of classroom teaching.

Photo 12.1.   Lisa Hibler with her students

Throughout her fellowship, Ms. Hibler partnered with mentor Dr. David Ollis, a chemical engineering professor at N.C. State University. Dr. Ollis shares Ms. Hibler's vision of making science relevant to students. They worked to find hands-on examples that demonstrate the application of chemistry in students' daily lives. He visited her class monthly, helping students turn ordinary objects like hot packs and antacid tablets into experiments. Ms. Hibler's new connections opened the door for her Advanced Placement Chemistry classes to see science in action at research labs at N.C. State University and the University of North Carolina at Chapel Hill.

The KFP reinvigorated Ms. Hibler's desire to make a difference in and out of the classroom: "The time demanded by the program was significant, but the rewards were tremendous. I feel more confident as a leader at my school and about my teaching. I'm now looking for opportunities to mentor other teachers and help new teachers become more confident leaders" (L. Hibler, personal communication, January 5, 2010).

Retention of teachers like Ms. Hibler is a national problem; far too many talented teachers leave the profession. Today, 83 percent of all KFP alumni remain active teachers in the classroom, while 16 percent hold other leadership roles in schools or education policy organizations. Evaluations also show that, while many fellows enter the program with outstanding credentials (30 percent are National Board certified and nearly half hold an advanced degree in their field), participation in the program encourages further advancement within teaching. Since entering the program, 25 percent of fellows subsequently started National Boards or an advanced degree and 53 percent have received educational awards. These data suggest that the program is a cost-effective model to promote effective STEM teacher retention (Donley Educational Evaluation Consulting, 2009).

Research Opportunities Bring Relevance

Faced with the need to support the most competent science and math instruction, the KFP helps teachers and students access the rich capacity of innovative research labs. The absence of relevance in schoolwork is frequently cited as a cause of lackluster student engagement and high dropout rates. Because the scientists and engineers serving as mentors represent diverse areas—from nanotechnology and robotics to sustainable farming and the design and manufacture of fragrances—the KFP creates mutual awareness and synergy among teachers, researchers, and innovative industries to make STEM instruction relevant.

Biology teacher Ms. Rebecca Hite brought her summer externship into her Carrboro High School classroom in the form of a deadly plant pathogen. Based on Ms. Hite's work with mentor and N.C. State University plant pathologist Dr. Jean Ristaino, Ms. Hite's students became crime scene investigators, exploring the mysterious pathogen that caused Ireland's massive potato crop failure and resultant Great Famine.

In addition to providing equipment, materials, and training not readily available to most high school teachers, Ms. Hite's partnership with Dr. Ristaino also gave her firsthand knowledge of scientific evidence to share with her students. As a result, Ms. Hite's students are eagerly learning about advanced scientific techniques, as well as the historical significance of the Great Famine and the impact of plant pathogens on the global food supply.

In Ms. Sonja McKay's seventh-grade classroom, students are not learning about global consumerism from a textbook. Instead, they are holding a web conference with students in Hyderabad, India, discussing the science of package design. Ms. McKay's mentor, Bill Beck of MeadWestvaco, made this exciting interaction possible, connecting the students using voice threads, web conferences, and other technologies. The project permeates the school, with social studies and language arts teachers expanding the lesson on global consumerism to include information about India and persuasive writing projects to promote their products.

In program evaluations, fellows report greater awareness of STEM careers and more use of inquiry and technology by their students. Among the cohorts, 85 percent report they have established new contacts in the education community and 93 percent say the program has enhanced their teaching skills. Workshops presented by fellows are highly rated and fellows' online curricular resources have garnered more than 650,000 hits, extending the impact of the program to teachers around the world (Donley Educational Evaluation Consulting, 2009).

Teachers Lead and Learn from Each Other

The KFP cultivates leadership through ongoing opportunities based on national standards for staff development in addition to focusing on relevant and rigorous STEM curriculum. Mr. Jeff Milbourne teaches at his alma mater, the N.C. School of Science and Math, a residential school for gifted students. In addition to the physics curriculum Mr. Milbourne implemented as a fellow, he also credits the program with helping him gain confidence as a teacher leader. As a young teacher, he had been hesitant to discuss pedagogical and political topics with colleagues who had once been his teachers.

Since becoming a fellow, Mr. Milbourne has taken a more active leadership role on campus, serving on both the faculty senate and a twenty-first-century learning task force. These opportunities have given him an increased sense of ownership in the school's decision-making process and helped connect him with his colleagues as well.

In addition to linking fellows with business leaders, policy makers, and education scholars, the KFP also helps teachers connect with each other. "I am in awe of the passion, commitment and diligence shown by these talented Fellows towards teaching. Spending time with them certainly enhanced my commitment toward the profession," said Mr. Milbourne. "Interacting with this group was also an important reality check, reminding me of challenges faced by colleagues in other school settings" (J. Milbourne, personal communication, January 5, 2010).

In evaluations, fellows say that they have benefited from new leadership roles as a result of the program: 74 percent have made professional presentations or provided professional development; 80 percent report enhanced professional leadership, especially with educational leaders and policy makers; and 93 percent report that networking with other fellows enhances their own skills (Donley Educational Evaluation Consulting, 2009). These leadership roles may lead to greater teacher retention, as the biennial N.C. Teacher Working Conditions Survey reports that teachers who feel empowered in their schools are less likely to leave for other opportunities (Hirsch & Church, 2009).

EXPANDING OPPORTUNITIES
FOR SUCCESSFUL TEACHERS

Since 2000, the KFP has functioned as an action research project to design and implement a new model for the professional advancement of teachers—one that links them directly with research scientists and engineers. Program evaluations demonstrate that teachers thrive in such environments and can apply those experiences *outside the book* to create exciting learning opportunities with their students and teaching colleagues. Given the program's effect on teacher retention and professional growth, we are committed to reaching out across the state—perhaps even joining with national programs offering similar features—to expand KFP's impact while carefully maintaining quality.

REFERENCES

Baldi, S., Jin, Y., Skemer, M., Green, P. J., Herger, D., & Xie, H. (2007). *Highlights from PISA 2006: Performance of U.S. 15-year-old students in science and mathematics literacy in an international context.* Washington, DC: Institute of Education Science National Center for Education Statistics, U.S. Department of Education.

Carnegie Corporation of New York—Institute for Advanced Study Commission on Mathematics and Science Education (Carnegie-IAS Commission). (2009). *The opportunity equation: Transforming mathematics and science education for citizenship and the global economy.* New York: Author.

Committee on Science, Engineering, and Public Policy (COSEPUP) and Policy and Global Affairs (PGA). (2007). *Rising above the gathering storm: Energizing and employing America for a brighter economic future.* Washington, DC: The National Academies Press.

Council of Chief State School Officers. (2007). *State indicators of science and mathematics education 2007.* Retrieved January 6, 2010, from http://www.ccsso.org/content/pdfs/SM%2007%20tables%20and%20figures1st.pdf

Darling-Hammond, L., Wei, R. C., Andree, A., Richardson, N., & Orphanos, S. (2009). *Professional learning in the learning profession: A status report on teacher development in the United States and abroad.* Dallas, TX: National Staff Development Council.

Donley Educational Evaluation Consulting. (2009). *Kenan Fellows program evaluation 2008–2009.* Retrieved January 8, 2010, from http://www.ncsu.edu/kenanfellows/sites/default/files/2009eval_report.pdf

Friedman, T. (2005). *The world is flat: A brief history of the twenty-first century.* New York: Farrar, Straus and Giroux.

Hirsch, E., & Church, K. (2009). *North Carolina teacher working conditions survey brief: Working conditions influence teacher retention.* Santa Cruz, CA: New Teacher Center. Retrieved January 20, 2010, from http://ncteaching conditions.org/sites/default/files/attachments/NC_teacher_retention.pdf

Kenan Fellows Program for Curriculum and Leadership Development (Producer). (2009). *Teaching students to think outside the book* [Motion picture]. Available from the Kenan Fellows Program, Campus Box 7006, Raleigh, NC 27695.

National Assessment of Educational Progress. (2005). *State comparisons.* Retrieved January 8, 2010, from http://nationsreportcard.gov/science_2005/s0106.asp

National Commission on Excellence in Education. (1983). *A nation at risk.* Washington, DC: U.S. Department of Education.

National Governor's Association Center for Best Practices. (2007). *Building a science, technology, engineering and math agenda.* Washington, DC: Author.

Silverstein, S., Dubner, J., Miller, J., Glied, S., & Loike, J. D. (2009, October 16). Teachers' participation in research programs improves their students' achievement in science. *Science, 326,* 440–442.

U.S. Department of Education. (2009). *Race to the top program: Executive summary.* Retrieved January 27, 2010, from http://www2.ed.gov/programs/raceto thetop/executive-summary.pdf

Wenglinsky, H. (2000). *How teaching matters: Bringing the classroom back into discussions of teacher quality.* Princeton, NJ: Educational Testing Service.

13

Promoting Teachers' Social and Emotional Competencies to Support Performance and Reduce Burnout

Patricia A. Jennings

Teaching is more socially and emotionally demanding than it has ever been in the past. Growing numbers of children come to school unprepared and often at risk of mental health and behavioral problems (U.S. Department of Health and Human Services, 1999). Yet teachers are expected to provide emotionally responsive support to *all* students, cultivate a warm and nurturing classroom environment, model exemplary emotion regulation (sometimes in the midst of chaos), coach students through conflict situations with thoughtfulness and sensitivity, successfully (yet respectfully) manage the challenging behaviors of increasing numbers of disruptive students, and handle the growing demands imposed by standardized testing.

Given these high expectations and demands, it is surprising that teachers rarely receive training to address and successfully handle the social and emotional challenges of teaching. Since little, if any, professional development targets these important competencies, it is understandable that the rate of teacher burnout is increasing and that teachers are leaving the profession at an alarming rate. Indeed, teacher distress and its resulting attrition is a growing problem. In the United States, approximately half of all teachers leave the profession within their first five years of teaching, and teacher attrition costs U.S. public schools more than $7 billion per year (National Commission on Teaching and America's Future, 2007).

Research suggests that when teachers cannot manage the social and emotional pressure of teaching, the classroom climate deteriorates and their students demonstrate lower levels of performance and on-task behavior (Marzano, Marzano, & Pickering, 2003). Furthermore, as the classroom climate deteriorates, it can trigger in the teacher a "burnout cascade" (Jennings & Greenberg, 2009, p. 492). Teachers may become emotionally exhausted as they try to manage increasingly difficult student behaviors. Eventually, teachers may resort to reactive and excessively punitive responses that do not promote self-regulation and may reinforce a self-sustaining cycle of classroom disruption.

THE PROSOCIAL CLASSROOM MODEL

Social and emotional competence (SEC) is a broad construct viewed as an outcome of social and emotional learning (SEL). The widely accepted definition of SEC, developed by the Collaborative for Academic Social and Emotional Learning (CASEL), involves five major competencies: self-awareness, social awareness, responsible decision making, self-management, and relationship management (Zins, Weissberg, Wang, & Walberg, 2004).

According to the Prosocial Classroom Model (Jennings & Greenberg, 2009) (see figure 13.1), teachers' social and emotional competence (SEC)

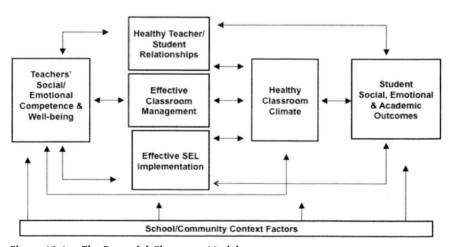

Figure 13.1. The Prosocial Classroom Model

and well-being play vital roles in their ability to cultivate a prosocial classroom climate linked to desired student social, emotional, and academic outcomes. SEC provides the necessary skill base and dispositions that help teachers form supportive relationships with their students, manage their classrooms effectively, and successfully implement social and emotional learning (SEL). These three factors are described with case vignettes that provide examples of their application in a classroom setting.

Teacher–Student Relationships

Supportive teacher–student relationships make a significant contribution to a healthy school and classroom climate, students' connectedness to school, and academic and social-emotional outcomes. When a teacher recognizes and understands students' emotions and the roles they play in the students' behavior, the teacher can more effectively respond to the students' needs and instill trust and respect. For example, because Mrs. Rivera understands that Joe's challenging behavior and difficulty with self-control result from emotions stemming from the troubles he faces at home, she can show empathy and concern for his situation. Her caring, yet firm response may be more effective in helping Joe learn self-control and on-task behavior than if she were to resort to punitive or coercive tactics that often provoke resentment and defensiveness.

Classroom Management

Decades of research on learning and behavior have supported a move toward more proactive and democratic intrinsically motivated approaches to classroom management. These approaches encourage cooperative and prosocial behavior through the establishment of warm and supportive learning communities, firm guidance, and limit setting, as well as preventative strategies that promote student autonomy rather than controlling negative behaviors through punitive measures (Brophy, 2006).

The successful implementation of these approaches requires a greater degree of social and emotional competence (SEC) than do more authoritarian approaches. Socially and emotionally competent teachers' keen understanding of classroom dynamics and conflict situations help them cultivate a caring, supportive community of learners collectively committed to maintaining a positive classroom climate. They proactively use their emotional expressions and support to engender enthusiasm and joy of learning. They are also able to guide and direct students while avoiding intractable power struggles.

For example, Joe has a history as the class scapegoat; sometimes his peers intentionally provoke him to see him overreact, causing a class disruption. Last year, Joe was quietly sitting at his desk in Mr. Martin's class when Susan stabbed him in the arm with her pencil. Reacting automatically, Joe swung out his arm, hitting Susan hard. Susan collapsed in a pile of tears, attracting Mr. Martin's sympathy. Because of his history with self-control problems, Mr. Martin assumed Joe was at fault. Applying an authoritarian approach, Mr. Martin reinforced Joe's scapegoat status and his peer's bad behavior by punishing Joe and rewarding Susan.

Mrs. Rivera is more socially and emotionally aware than Joe's previous teacher and she recognizes the social dynamic underlying such situations. When a similar incident occurred this year, she helped Joe communicate his feelings to Susan more appropriately while also identifying and responding to Susan's provocative behavior with firm limits. Joe's peers are now much less likely to intentionally provoke him; thus, the classroom climate is generally calmer and the students are more productive. Joe is also building more successful relationships with his peers and he is enjoying school more than he did in the past.

Social and Emotional Program Implementation

Teachers with high levels of social and emotional competence (SEC) are well prepared to effectively implement social and emotional learning (SEL) by modeling skills and behavior in naturally occurring everyday situations. For example, when Mrs. Rivera introduced skills to regulate strong emotions, she later demonstrated the technique when she was upset with disruptive classroom behavior.

"I am beginning to feel very frustrated by the talking because no one can hear me and I don't want to raise my voice," she calmly remarked. "I am going to take some deep breaths to calm myself down and wait for everyone to be quiet so I can continue." Not only did she show her students how to calm down in the midst of an emotionally heated situation, she also took full responsibility for her emotional state and gave her students the autonomy to take responsibility for their behavior so she could proceed with her lesson.

Three factors—teacher–student relationships, classroom management, and SEL program implementation—support the cultivation of a healthy classroom climate that is conducive to desirable social, emotional, and academic student outcomes. Furthermore, a healthy classroom climate may reinforce a teacher's enjoyment of teaching and his or her sense of efficacy and commitment to the teaching profession, resulting in a positive feedback loop that may prevent burnout and reduce costly attrition.

CULTIVATING AWARENESS AND RESILIENCE IN EDUCATION (CARE)

Building upon our most current understanding of the neuroscience of emotion and previous research applying mindfulness-based approaches to promoting well-being and reducing stress (Brown, Ryan, & Creswell, 2007), the Garrison Institute in Garrison, New York, began the development of a new intervention directed toward supporting teacher social and emotional competence (SEC) as a means of improving classroom climate and student outcomes. Cultivating Awareness and Resilience in Education™ (CARE) was designed by a team of educators and scientific advisors to help teachers manage stress and enliven their teaching and thereby promote improvements in relationships with students, classroom management, and social and emotional learning.

The CARE program involves a blend of instruction and experiential activities, including time for discussion and reflection. As field-based professional development, CARE is typically presented during the school year in four all-day sessions spread out over four to five weeks. It is also offered to the public every summer in the form of a five-day intensive retreat at the Garrison Institute. In the field, facilitators coach teachers by phone and e-mail between sessions to support them as they practice and apply the new skills they have learned. The Garrison Institute also works with schools to develop sustainability and ongoing support for teachers.

CARE Program Components

The CARE intervention utilizes three primary instructional components: (a) emotion skills instruction, (b) mindfulness and stress reduction practices, and (c) listening and compassion exercises.

Emotion Skills Instruction

Emotional exhaustion is a primary contributor to teacher burnout and can interfere with teachers' performance. To help teachers build emotional resilience, the CARE training introduces emotion knowledge and skills, combining direct instruction with experiential activities. This knowledge and experience helps teachers understand, recognize, and regulate emotional responses in themselves and in others with whom they work (students, colleagues, and parents).

Reflective practices and role-plays support teachers' recognition of emotional states and their exploration of their *emotional landscape*—their emotional habitual patterns, triggers, tendencies, and reactivity profile. These skills help teachers reappraise emotionally challenging situations and respond with greater clarity and sensitivity to their students' needs and the emotional climate of the classroom, resulting in more consistent, assertive, compassionate, and effective classroom management. It may also help teachers provide social and emotional support to their students through direct instruction, modeling, and practices such as coaching students through peer conflicts.

Mindfulness and Stress Reduction Practices

During the CARE program, teachers learn how to balance their work and personal lives to continually renew the inner strength they need to do their jobs well. To support emotion and attention regulation, to reduce stress, and to help teachers be more aware, fully present, and engaged with their teaching and students, CARE introduces a series of mindfulness activities. The sessions begin with short periods of silent reflection and extend to activities that bring mindfulness into everyday activities such as standing, walking, experiencing a quiet presence in front of a group, and in role-plays. Mindfulness-based physical activities drawn from the martial arts have been adapted and integrated to promote teachers' strong presence and self-confidence.

Listening and Compassion Exercises

To promote compassion and listening, CARE introduces *caring practice* and *mindful listening*. Caring practice is a guided reflection during which one mentally offers well-being, happiness, and peace—first to oneself, then to a loved one, a neutral colleague or acquaintance, and a person whom one finds challenging (such as a difficult student, parent, or colleague). Fredrickson, Cohn, Coffey, Pek, and Finkel (2008) found that this practice enhances well-being and strengthens one's personal resources, resulting in greater life satisfaction. Mindful listening practice involves listening with full attention, without the need to respond. A common tendency while listening is to think about how to respond in order to provide a helpful suggestion or answer. Through this practice, teachers learn that simply being present and listening fully is supportive in and of itself.

These integrated program components are developed across sessions augmented by individual reflection through writing and other forms of expression as well as group discussion. Teachers are provided with CDs of recorded guided practices for use at home, and a series of homework activities is suggested to help teachers apply and practice the program skills.

Program Evaluations

Since 2007, CARE has been piloted in the field with groups of teachers in Denver, San Francisco, and Philadelphia. The results of program evaluations suggest that CARE is attractive to teachers and has succeeded in helping them deal with the emotions of teaching. Between 2007 and 2009, CARE was offered as summer retreats at the Garrison Institute in New York and to teachers at a private school outside of Philadelphia. In April 2009, Wellspring Consulting conducted an evaluation of these CARE programs. The eighty-five participants with valid e-mail addresses (out of ninety-three total participants) were sent an e-mail with a link to the survey.

Most participants who responded found CARE to be valuable, and over 90 percent are highly likely or likely to recommend CARE to a colleague.

Eighty-four percent said that CARE was highly important or important for their professional development; 87 percent strongly agreed or agreed that all teachers should receive this training. Comments included the following:

- "I now have a calm and unshakable feeling that is deep within me, and this helps me to stay present, grounded, focused, creative, and thankful for each of the little miracles that I experience each and every day!"
- "I found the time to be some of the best spent time on training that I have had. I have implemented the strategies that I learned throughout a very difficult year and have offered some of the ideas to my colleagues and my student teachers."
- "The interpersonal (listening) work was very powerful. Most professional trainings lack this type of experiential component, which is the type of learning that stays with me."
- "I am much more present with my students throughout the day. I'm aware when emotions start to take over in a positive or negative way. This awareness helps me respond rather than react to a situation."

One teacher explained how CARE helped her be more responsive to a disruptive student:

CARE has given me the tools and skills to be more calm and centered. In a particular situation, I can act in response to what is needed in the moment, rather than reacting to it. Taking deep breaths, I can calm myself down and notice what feelings his comments are triggering in me. I can see beyond his behavior (shouting, swearing, and interrupting the class) into his feelings and the needs behind those feelings which triggered his reaction. This way of relating to myself and others is a more compassionate way that leads to open and honest communication. This provides a model to the student of how to relate to himself and to others with compassion. It creates an atmosphere of confidence, trust, and more joy in the classroom.

In 2009, the Prevention Research Center at Pennsylvania State University was awarded $932,361 from the U.S. Department of Education Institute for Educational Sciences with a subaward to the Garrison Institute to complete the development and evaluation of CARE in the context of urban and suburban districts in Pennsylvania. This two-year project is currently underway and CARE has been refined and modified in response to teachers' feedback, although the primary components have remained the same. The project will culminate in a randomized, controlled pilot study of this final version with elementary teachers. Outcome measures will include self-report measures of well-being, mindfulness, time urgency, burnout, and efficacy as well as observational measures of teachers' behavior and classroom climate.

CONCLUSION

Although teacher burnout and attrition is a growing problem, promoting well-being and social and emotional competence (SEC) may help teachers manage the daily stresses of teaching. As a result, they may successfully cultivate supportive and caring relationships with their students, establish and maintain classroom environments that are conducive to learning, and more effectively implement social and emotional learning curricula. Successfully creating and maintaining a classroom learning environment where students are happy and excited to learn reinforces teachers' efficacy and enjoyment of teaching, thereby preventing burnout and attrition.

Thus far, CARE appears to be a promising program to help teachers cultivate well-being and social and emotional competence (SEC) by teaching them about emotions and how they affect teaching and learning, and promoting mindfulness-based skills to reduce stress and promote self-awareness. However, this field is in its early stages of development and there is a need to articulate the constructs of well-being and SEC more clearly and to address how to measure these constructs in the context of an educational setting.

In the coming years, it will be important to explore more fully whether teachers' participation in CARE results in improved student outcomes. Furthermore, future work should explore the potential mediating effects of teachers' well-being and SEC on classroom and student outcomes. Preliminary research suggests that promoting teacher well-being and SEC— without explicitly applying these skills and dispositions to classroom practice—may have limited effects on classroom outcomes (Jennings, Foltz, Snowberg, Sim, & Kemeny, 2010).

This novel approach to supporting teachers' professional development has important educational policy implications. Teacher quality has come to the forefront in discussions of school reform. However, in previous research, neither years of education nor years of experience have predicted good teaching. Perhaps social and emotional competence (SEC) is a critical contributor to what makes a teacher highly successful. If so, promoting SEC in teacher professional development may improve teaching and, as an added benefit, promote efficacy and teachers' commitment to the profession.

REFERENCES

Brophy, J. (2006). History of research on classroom management. In C. M. Evertson & C. S. Weinstein (Eds.), *Handbook of classroom management: Research, practice, and contemporary issues* (pp. 17–43). Mahwah, NJ: Lawrence Erlbaum.

Brown, K. W., Ryan, R. M., & Creswell, J. D. (2007). Mindfulness: Theoretical foundations and evidence for its salutary effects. *Psychological Inquiry, 18,* 211–237.

Fredrickson, B. L., Cohn, M. A., Coffey, K. A., Pek, J., & Finkel, S. M. (2008). Open hearts build lives: Positive emotions, induced through loving-kindness meditation, build consequential personal resources. *Journal of Personality and Social Psychology, 95,* 1045–1062.

Jennings, P. A., Foltz, C., Snowberg, K. E., Sim, H., & Kemeny, M. E. (2010). *The influence of mindfulness and emotion skills training on teachers' classrooms: The effects of the Cultivating Emotional Balance Training.* Manuscript submitted for publication.

Jennings, P. A., & Greenberg, M. (2009). The prosocial classroom: Teacher social and emotional competence in relation to child and classroom outcomes. *Review of Educational Research, 79,* 491–525.

Marzano, R. J., Marzano, J. S., & Pickering, D. J. (2003). *Classroom management that works.* Alexandria, VA: ASCD.

National Commission on Teaching and America's Future. (2007). *Policy brief: The high cost of teacher turnover.* Retrieved March 15, 2010, from http://www.nctaf.org/resources/demonstration_projects/turnover/documents/CTTPolicyBrief6–19.pdf

U.S. Department of Health and Human Services. (1999). *Mental health: A report of the surgeon general*. Washington, DC: National Institutes of Health, National Institute of Mental Health.

Zins, J. E., Weissberg, R. P., Wang, M. C., & Walberg, H. J. (2004). *Building academic success on social and emotional learning*. New York: Teachers College Press.

14

From Muteness to Provocation: An Emerging Developmental Model of Teacher Leadership

Nita A. Paris, Harriet J. Bessette, Traci Redish, and Dawn Latta Kirby

Breaking the mold causes ripple effects. In this chapter, we document how designing an innovative, practice-oriented educational doctorate not only facilitated teacher leadership development but also challenged the existence of traditional doctoral programs in education—many of which remain wedded to an epistemology that privileges theory over practice and exclusivity over collaboration.

BREAKING THE MOLD OF CONFORMIST THINKING

Recent debate concerning expectations for school leadership has not been limited to discussions about P–12 principals, administrators, and the school systems in which they work. Faculties in higher education have also undertaken similar discussions about their programs' successes and weaknesses in preparing future school leaders. Although many faculty in educational leadership programs nationwide have heeded their critics (Murphy, 2005), others have not.

As Chomsky asserted, "If anyone at a university is teaching the same thing they were teaching five years ago, either the field is dead, or they haven't been thinking" (as cited in Solomon, 2003, para. 12). The historical knowledge base, content, and practices of yesterday's programs in higher education are, quite simply, no longer adequate for preparing educational leaders for tomorrow's schools. This vacuum offered us a unique opportunity to recast the paradigm of school leadership and to build a more distributed, inclusive, and sustainable preparation model within higher education.

We envisioned a program that would address the needs of our students, communities, and area schools' contexts, professional and content standards, and gaps in leadership preparation as noted both locally and by influential authors in the field (Levine, 2005; Murphy, 2005). We felt strongly that an appropriate new design would arise only from our collaborative, purposeful, transformative thinking; and, in turn, that a new design would help us and our doctoral students engage in the type of creative, constructive action needed to address the complex issues we observed in P–12 schools.

Our goals of collaboration and inclusion at all levels meant inviting faculty from other colleges within our university to assist in the doctorate's formation. We intentionally and thoughtfully sought to minimize power and control issues, which is not to say that disagreement and debate did not exist. Disagreement, we eventually found, pushed us to rethink and retool our efforts to develop a program that would surpass higher education's existing standards and operating procedures, in addition to our own expectations.

We reached many of our foundational decisions about the goals, mission, content, and structure of the program in one year's time. Levine (2005) and Shulman, Golde, Bueschel, and Garabedian (2006), who also articulated widespread problems with existing education doctorates and espoused strikingly similar programs, affirmed and authenticated our inclinations, processes, and essential program design elements.

Faculty reached consensus not only in their thinking about the kind of doctoral program that was needed to prepare teacher leaders but also agreed that we could model collaborative, distributed leadership and design the program and candidates' learning experiences in ways that would guide their development from one level of leadership functionality to the next. Our hope was that candidates would do the same for their colleagues in P–12 schools. Finally, we believed we could create a ripple effect of distributed leadership practices through teacher leaders who completed our program.

Framework and Lens

Understanding the social nature of *learning to learn* offers a window into the ways that learning to lead unfolds as a social act in schools. Vygotsky (1978) theorized that intellectual growth and knowledge reconstruction take place when individuals reach their intellectual capacity within the zone of proximal development (ZPD). Knowledge reconstruction takes place on two planes: the social, or *interpsychological*, plane, during which individuals socialize and mediate understanding with their peers and interact; and the individual, or *intrapsychological*, plane, within which the individual processes and mediates information as a result of social interaction. These two planes are relevant to distributive leadership as school and teacher leaders construct meaning as a social group.

When faculty are socialized in a collaborative mode, interpersonal relationships emerge and are further developed at the intrapersonal level when leaders work apart from their usual groups. The results are that the individual is intellectually altered: He or she has grown intellectually and has constructed new knowledge as a consequence of his or her social interaction.

A *distributed leadership* framework undergirds our doctoral program because it is an analytical tool or framework for *thinking about* and *reflecting upon* leadership practice in schools (Spillane & Diamond, 2007). A distributed lens allows educators to study how leadership activity is accomplished and how it links to instructional change and increased student learning. Further, effective school leadership practices must include multiple levels of teacher and specialist involvement that manifest as *distributed leadership practices and expertise* (Hargreaves & Fink, 2006), since transformative work is seldom accomplished exclusively by one group or person.

As Spillane (2006) pointed out, "Expecting one person to single-handedly lead efforts to improve instruction in a complex organization such as a school is impractical" (p. 26). We reasoned that if our doctoral program were to have a profound impact on teaching and leading in P–12 schools, then it was up to us to set the bar high.

Breaking Down the Walls of Traditional Structures

Our doctoral program in Leadership for Learning was designed as a post-master's professional practice doctorate in education with two strands—Educational Leadership and Teacher Leadership—and is composed of

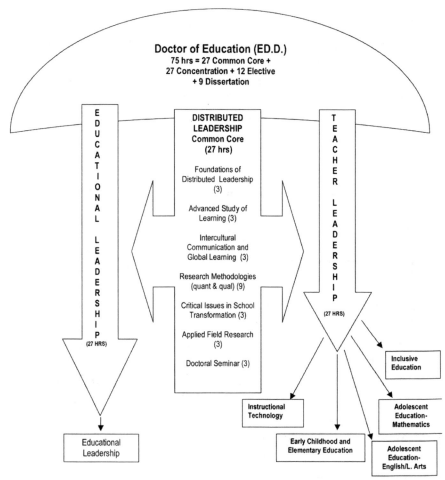

Figure 14.1.   Structure and Design of Kennesaw State University's EdD in Leadership for Learning Degree

many concentrations, such as elementary and early childhood education, adolescent education with a specialization in mathematics, adolescent education with a specialization in English/language arts (ELA), inclusive education, and instructional technology (figure 14.1).

The program derives unity through its central focus on distributed leadership for school improvement. Doctoral students complete a common core where they develop an understanding of the principles of distributed leadership—for example, recognizing distributed leadership practice in action, distinguishing between distributed leadership and other forms of leadership, identifying their own advances toward distributed leadership, and provoking others to actively pursue distributed leadership roles. Our students focus on developing shared leadership expertise and building networks of influence as collaborative teams for change and improvement.

Through collaborative case studies and problem-based learning experiences embedded in courses as well as in schools, cohorts of students—regardless of disciplinary concentration—work together to tackle tough, tectonic challenges prevalent in today's P–12 schools, some of which have been ingrained in our educational culture for years. The core unifies the cohort and allows doctoral students to explore their ideas around distributed leadership. Students also complete course work in a respective concentration, the focus of which is on deepening and broadening content and pedagogical knowledge, skills, and dispositions. This focus prepares teachers and leaders to serve as effective instructional leaders who empower others, support and sustain change within schools, and advance best practices in curriculum, instruction, and assessment.

Breaking the Silence of Isolation: Embracing a Cohort Model

The cohort design of this doctoral program is like few others nationally. Faculty were united in the decision to design a collaborative, cross-disciplinary cohort model within which students would align with one of six concentrations. The cohort model not only provides a setting conducive to collegial support and collaboration, but it also provides the infrastructure and fertile ground for students to form *communities of practice*—individuals bound together by shared expertise and passion for a joint enterprise (Wenger & Snyder, 2000).

As one of our doctoral students stated near the end of her second year, "The particular strengths of the program may lie in the cohort model itself. . . . We thrive on connections with each other to discover greater potential within the distributed (leadership) model." Doctoral programs designed as cohorts possess three fundamental elements that Wenger, McDermott, and Snyder (2002) identified as the structural foundation of communities of practice: (a) a *domain of knowledge* that defines a set of issues, (b) a *community of people* who care about the domain, and (c) the *shared practice* that they are developing to be effective in their domain.

In classes, we witnessed how social interaction and dialogue assist students' professional learning. In their cohorts, our students socialize and mediate understanding of distributed leadership practice with their peers. In the three years that we followed our students' development as teacher leaders, we noticed gradual changes in the way they approached discussions related to distributed leadership with their colleagues and faculty.

We found that students who once held a passive role in their schools became active in their local contexts, volunteering to lead book studies or forming a committee of colleagues interested in developing closer ties to formal leadership. In retellings of local situations and in discussions in classes, students demonstrated the extent to which they were honing their understanding of distributed leadership practice—intellectual growth and applied knowledge that appeared to be socially mediated by conversations, readings, reflections, and exchanges with cohort members, colleagues, and professors. We noted how their conceptualizations and insights morphed with every class, small group, or informal discussion. Clearly, their insights signaled a shift in how they were conceptualizing their own roles within their schools. Our students were breaking the silence.

Evidence of Impact: The Ripple Effects of Change

In the three-year journey we have taken with our students, we have observed and recorded evidence of their developmental understanding of distributed leadership practice. Using qualitative methods, we reviewed videotaped interviews, interview transcripts, self-assessments, and a range of written documents that yielded insights into the varied ways in which students internalized and conceptualized evidence of distributive leadership roles in their schools.

We asked questions such as:

- Has your doctoral course work contributed to your understanding of distributed leadership and if so, how?
- In terms of building collaborative relationships, teams, and community partnerships that communicate and reflect distributed leadership for learning, would you place yourself at the *novice*, *midrange*, or *enlightened* stage of development?

Additionally, we noted trends in formal and informal class conversations. As repeatable and consistent patterns began to take shape, we theorized that our students were operating on different developmental levels of understanding related to distributed leadership.

Levels of Understanding Derived from the Cohort Model

At first, the levels were not easily distinguishable. With each rereading of the evidence, however, the levels became more evident. We discovered that students' understanding of, recognition of, and experience with distributed leadership practice appeared to cluster around five hierarchical, descriptive levels that we labeled as *Muteness, Inductee, Initiator, Inviter,* and *Instigator* or *Provocateur*.

At the first level, *Muteness*, doctoral students' responses indicated a lack or a poor understanding of distributed leadership practice. Responses in this category suggested that students were unable to recognize and contribute to discussions relevant to distributed leadership practices. At the *Inductee* level, students demonstrated an evolving understanding of distributed leadership, could identify it in their schools, and apply it to their own learning but did not actively adopt a distributed leadership stance in bringing about change.

The third level, *Initiator*, was characterized by students' solid understanding of distributed leadership practice and their intent to adopt a distributed leadership role to effect change. It is at this level that adaptive expertise emerged. At the *Inviter* level, students were able to identify their distributive leadership roles, and they increasingly encouraged and invited others to participate in distributed leadership activities and conversations.

At the highest level, we concluded that *Instigators* or *Provocateurs* created mindfulness toward leveraging and sometimes provoking or challenging others to pursue actively distributed leadership practices and discussions; they were engaging in roles and actions causing the ripple effects we originally envisioned. For example, a student who reported that she "had not historically taken great strides to promote distributed leadership of others even though we talk about our book study club" differed from another who testified, "I am working with teacher leaders in schools for the whole year and I'm becoming part of their trusted outside capital. Inviting them to lead a discussion group is only a small piece of the puzzle."

While both understood distributed leadership practice and engaged others in conversations around goal setting in professional development (as evidenced by conversations, self-report inventories, and exam responses), only one discussed prompting others to go a step further and pursue a distributed leadership role. These students were rated as *Inviter* and *Instigator*, respectively.

The greatest shift between Year 1 and Year 3 occurred between the *Inductee* and *Initiator* levels. In the following statements, Maeve, a fifth-grade classroom teacher with a penchant for technology, operating at the *Inductee* level, debates the worth of distributed leadership practice. She states, "Many distributed leadership activities, such as common goal setting, positively correlate with student achievement. This suggests that distributed leadership is well worth exploring and may indeed have a positive impact on student achievement."

Chester, an eleventh-grade mathematics teacher who is becoming increasingly more involved in the organizational processes in his school, seeks to identify his distributive leadership role in *initiating* change. He admits, "My experiences in this program have introduced me to sustainable driven change theory, but I am struggling with my role in this aspect."

Although our five levels are hierarchical in nature, we discovered that the differences between them are not rigid. In fact, findings suggest that students' understandings and experiences with distributive leadership practice are fluid given the context and could be characterized by more than one level. Further, we noticed a trend with students moving toward more provocative levels of understanding and involvement in distributed leadership practice as they advance in their program (figure 14.2).

IMPLICATIONS AND CONCLUSIONS

Our research journey has confirmed our commitment to an interdisciplinary, collaborative doctoral program, the conceptual and theoretical frameworks of which are substantiated in students' own words and actions. We conclude that the identified developmental progression from *muteness* to *instigation* or *provocation* evidences a hierarchical construct that is applicable to a range of settings.

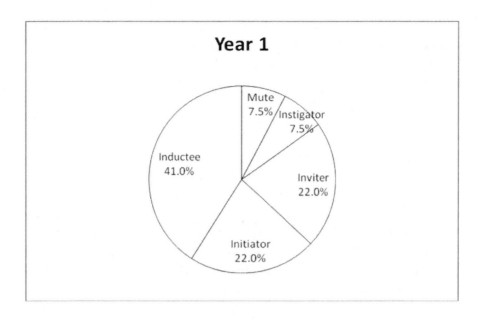

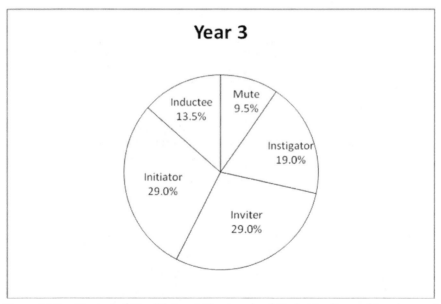

Figure 14.2. Percent of Candidates at Five Levels of Understanding and Involvement in Distributed Leadership Practice at Years 1 and 3

As our inductive analysis and constant comparison of their reflective narratives suggest, the majority of our students moved in the direction of developing deeper and broader understandings of both collaboration and distributed leadership practice. With understanding and knowledge come trust and acceptance of multiple perspectives and increased willingness to acknowledge the necessity of diversity in decision-making and learning contexts.

The desire and ability to scaffold this advancement for our students is one of our key findings. As we provide learning experiences for students that guide them from one level of leadership functionality to another, they are able to learn to do the same for their colleagues. Distributed leadership then becomes an *activity* rather than remaining a static textbook concept.

Activity is replicable, meaning that our model of constructing a doctoral program across diverse academic interests and fields can be accomplished in other academic settings, in part if not in totality. As our university develops additional doctoral programs in areas unrelated to teacher education, implicitly—if not directly—promoting transferrable leadership, faculty are considering our model as they construct their programs.

Long-standing academic silos are beginning to crumble, and we see our colleagues accepting leadership roles and developing as leaders themselves in ways they have not previously experienced. Just as our students develop distributed leadership practice in their work contexts, so do we, in higher education.

In short, one of the key implications is that this program, with its active modeling of faculty collaboration and distributed leadership across three colleges within our university, is influencing our university's culture as well as the work contexts and cultures in the schools and districts of our doctoral students. This expansion of distributed leadership to other settings and the accompanying transformations within our students allow them to bring their lived experiences from our program into their work settings and apply it to broader constituencies. Those who know how to negotiate diverse views critically collaborate to solve problems and promote distributed leadership development for themselves and others are the *instigators* needed to provoke change in twenty-first-century educational contexts.

Lest we sound as though we have created a utopia, we acknowledge that tensions continue to exist among our ongoing successes. We observe the tendency among those working within and beyond the program to drift toward siloed thinking and action. This propensity is counteracted by those among us who—spontaneously and individually—assume the role of leader at least long enough to focus on our shared programmatic purposes, goals, and mission. The very innovations of this model that have *broken the mold* of siloed and discreet interests threaten, themselves, to break the *model*. As leaders within our own program, we deliberately and consciously decide anew to divert degenerative chaos that such a wide range of stakeholders could engender. By grounding our own leadership and collaborative development in engagement, intentionality, and gravitational synergy, we professionally nurture and nourish both our students and ourselves.

REFERENCES

Hargreaves, A., & Fink, D. (2006). *Sustainable leadership.* San Francisco, CA: Jossey-Bass.

Levine, A. (2005). *Educating school leaders.* Washington, DC: Education Schools Project.

Murphy, J. (2005). *Connecting teacher leadership and school improvement.* Thousand Oaks, CA: Corwin.

Shulman, L. S., Golde, C. M., Bueschel, A. C., & Garabedian, K. J. (2006). Reclaiming education's doctorates: A critique and a proposal. *Educational Researcher, 35*(3), 25–32.

Solomon, D. (2003, November 3). The professorial provocateur. *New York Times Magazine.* Retrieved May 15, 2009, from http://www.nytimes.com/2003/11/02/magazine/02QUESTIONS.html?ex=1075093200&en=bf7731407efe6331&ei=5070

Spillane, J. P. (2006). *Distributed leadership.* Thousand Oaks, CA: Sage.

Spillane, J. P., & Diamond, J. B. (Eds.). (2007). *Distributed leadership in practice.* New York: Teachers College Press.

Vygotsky, L. S. (1978). *Mind in society: The development of higher psychological processes.* Cambridge, MA: Harvard University Press.

Wenger, E., McDermott, R., & Snyder, W. (2002). *Cultivating communities of practice.* Cambridge, MA: Harvard Business School Press.

Wenger, E., & Snyder, W. (2000, January–February). Communities of practice: The organizational frontier. *Harvard Business Review,* 139–145.

III

COLLABORATIVE TEACHER
EDUCATION PRACTICES

Summarizing twenty years of research on effective teacher development and professional learning, Darling-Hammond and Richardson (2009) examined what components of high-quality professional development practices contribute to successful teacher *and* student learning. Their conclusions were that teachers learn most effectively when

> (a) their content knowledge is addressed as well as how to best convey that knowledge to their students; (b) they understand how their students acquire specific content; (c) they have the opportunities for active, hands-on learning; (d) they are empowered to acquire new knowledge, apply it to their own practice, and reflect on the results; (e) their learning is an essential part of a reform effort that connects curriculum, assessment, and standards; (f) learning is collaborative and collegial; and (g) professional development is intensive and sustained over time. (p. 49)

Darling-Hammond and Richardson (2009) also noted that one of the most successful frameworks for teachers' professional learning is one based on teacher collaboration through professional learning communities. Recognizing the importance of collaborative practice, the following section of this volume offers examples of personal, professional, and organizational collaborations implemented both for the purposes of preservice and inservice teacher development.

In the first chapter of this section, Elizabeth A. Skinner takes us to Chicago, Illinois, where community-based recruitment of future teachers is actualized through the Grow Your Own Teachers movement. Twyla Salm and Lace Marie Brogden explore ways to develop successful inter-professional internships for preservice teachers, along with interns from social work, nursing, kinesiology and health studies, and justice studies at a Canadian university. Victoria Hasko and Soria Colomer present ways that social networking sites may serve as an innovative resource in foreign language teacher technology education. Jana Noel discusses how school-community-based urban teacher education offers a voice for the community. Miguel Zavala introduces the readers to the Association of Raza Educators (ARE), which is also a community-based teacher organization and serves as an alternative framework for teacher collaboration. In the section's closing chapter, Mary Ellen Freeley, Andrew Ferdinandi, and Paul Pedota invite us to a New York City public school to witness the implementation process and outcomes of school improvement efforts implemented through a successful university–school partnership.

REFERENCE

Darling-Hammond, L., & Richardson. N. (2009). Teacher learning: What matters? *Educational Leadership, 66*(5), 46–53.

15

Grow Your Own Teachers:
Community-Based Change in Teacher Education

Elizabeth A. Skinner

In an effort to change a downward educational spiral, a group of community leaders and parents from the Logan Square neighborhood in Chicago began taking college classes in preparation to become bilingual teachers in their neighborhood schools. From this local neighborhood initiative evolved the Grow Your Own (GYO) Teachers movement in Chicago and throughout the state of Illinois. In the Logan Square neighborhood, the original project was an effort to address the shortage of bilingual teachers, whereas throughout the city and state, the goal is to decrease teacher turnover at high-need schools and increase the number of Latino and African American teachers so as to better reflect the schools' student populations.

Through an examination of the original project in Logan Square, this chapter describes the evolution of the GYO Teachers initiative in Illinois and the efforts of organizing groups and colleges of education to meet the needs of local schools while at the same time transforming the traditional notion of teacher education.

COMMUNITY-BASED TEACHER EDUCATION

As colleges of education prepare their graduates to meet the needs of an increasingly diverse student population, one attempt at improving the cultural competency of their teacher candidates has been to provide opportunity for field placement and student teaching in unfamiliar and/ or diverse urban communities. Typically, this form of community-based teacher education means that elementary teacher candidates, who are largely white and female, are assigned to schools with primarily Latino and African American students at some point while completing their required field hours (Zumwalt & Craig, 2005).

Some universities, especially those that run Professional Development Schools (PDSs), intensify the experience by offering students the opportunity to not only complete required field hours and student teaching in a community but also the opportunity to live in that community. While both of these models of community-based teacher education have merit, they do not inherently provide the teacher candidate with an understanding of the complex nature of the relationship between the school and the community. There persists a need for teachers and teacher candidates to understand the importance of connecting with the communities where they work (Koerner & Abdul-Tawwab, 2006).

One viable, innovative, and complementary alternative to traditional community-based teacher education programs—as envisioned and executed in the state of Illinois—is the Grow Your Own (GYO) Teachers initiative. In addition to being an innovative example of community-based teacher education, the GYO movement is an example of a collaborative response to crucial issues of teacher recruitment and retention that schools face. The unique collaboration between community-based organizations, institutions of higher education, local school districts, and the Illinois State Board of Education (ISBE) supports parents, community members, and paraprofessionals in low-income communities to become fully certified classroom teachers.

THE LOGAN SQUARE NEIGHBORHOOD

In order to understand the evolution of GYO Teachers in Illinois and to begin to think about how it may be successfully replicated in other colleges of education, it is important to describe the context in which the statewide initiative began. Logan Square is one of a few Chicago neighborhoods that is multiclass and multiracial, although Chicagoans commonly identify it as a Latino neighborhood, in spite of recent gentrification.

Data from the 2000 census show that 65 percent of the residents of Logan Square are of Hispanic origin. However, within this Hispanic population there is a fair amount of diversity. Nearly 50 percent of the Hispanics are Mexican and the next largest group is Puerto Ricans at 35 percent (CensusScope, n.d.). Consideration of elementary school data also helps define the community: at six Logan Square elementary schools, the percentage of Hispanic students is between 78 percent and 92 percent at each school. The percentage of low-income students is between 88 percent and 97 percent for each school (Chicago Public Schools, n.d.).

A report on the status of Latinos in the Chicago Public Schools (CPS) indicated, among other things, that Latino students are attending the most overcrowded schools in the system and that the lack of Latino teachers and administrators is harming the students. In the CPS, 38 percent of the student population is Latino, while only 13 percent of teachers are Latino (Aviles, Capeheart, Davila, & Pérez Miller, 2004). The Logan Square elementary schools are representative of schools in the entire CPS district in that they face the challenge of overcrowded schools and a shortage of fully certified bilingual teachers.

THE LOGAN SQUARE NEIGHBORHOOD ASSOCIATION

The Logan Square Neighborhood Association (LSNA) is a multi-issue, community-based organization that began to work on education initiatives after Chicago's pathbreaking 1988 School Reform law took effect. One of LSNA's most visible efforts in the schools is the Parent Mentor Program, which began in 1995. Each year LSNA hires and trains about 120 parents to tutor for two hours a day in the schools. The mentors are paid stipends each semester and attend weekly workshops aimed at strengthening families and developing leaders within the community.

The philosophy guiding this and other LSNA education initiatives is the desire to create schools that are centers of community. This requires developing social capital among the mothers and also between the parents and professionals, namely teachers and principals (Stanton-Salazar, 2004). Ideally, the resultant networks reach across class, culture, and language. LSNA's efforts are also based on a strong belief in the value of the funds of knowledge the parents bring with them into the school (Moll, Amanti, Neff, & Gonzalez, 1992).

After working as parent mentors, some of the community members, mostly women, expressed an interest in continuing their own education in order to become bilingual teachers in their local schools. They approached the education organizer at LSNA with their idea. Most of those interested were mothers who worked (either in or out of the home) and had many family responsibilities, so a traditional four-year university program was not an option for the community members. College was also out of the question financially.

The lead education organizer at LSNA listened, and after approaching several local universities with the idea, finally partnered with the bilingual education program at Chicago State University to create Project Nueva Generación. The project was initially funded in August 2000 as a federal Title VII grant for five years. Presently, Project Nueva Generación continues with funding from the State of Illinois as part of the Grow Your Own Teachers initiative.

THE COLLEGE OF EDUCATION

Defining the role of the college of education is critical in clarifying the true collaborative nature of the project. In order to meet the needs of the non-traditional-age Latina/o students in Project Nueva Generación, the adaptations at the university level began with the admissions process. The community-based organization recruited potential students from their pool of parent mentors, school volunteers, and local leaders and then helped them through the application process. Applicants often needed help obtaining foreign transcripts, translations of those transcripts, and community college transcripts. Once the application materials were gathered, the university-based coordinator of the project accepted the applications, reviewed them with an admissions officer at the university, and personally contacted students regarding completion of their files. Upon being admitted to the program, the students were eligible for full financial support, originally provided by a federal Title VII grant. The funds covered all expenses, including tuition, books, and child care.

During the first two years of the program in Logan Square, the students took all of their classes at the community center at Monroe Elementary School. The university coordinator ordered the necessary textbooks from the university bookstore and then passed them out to students on the first night of each class. Classes were held in the evenings and childcare was available on site. University professors—thoughtfully selected based on their experience working with non-traditional-aged college students and their experience working with students who speak English as a second language—commuted to Logan Square to teach.

The students had virtually no contact with the bureaucracy of the university during the first two years of the program. If the students needed to take care of something at the university, they called the university-based program coordinator. The coordinator also met with each student individually to discuss academic progress and serve as an advisor. This initial very high level of support meant that the students could adjust to being in college in the comfort of their community.

Being able to stay in their geographic community eased the transition into college for the students, but the sense of community created by the cohort model was just as significant. In addition to the institutional support, the students in the program created their own informal network that provided support for emotional and academic struggles. The entire cohort took classes together the first year and got to know each other and at the same time got to know the university personnel. Group activities and presentations in class during the first semester of the program allowed the students to develop rapport with one another in a comfortable environment.

As the program evolved and the students progressed and began to travel to the university, located on the far south side of the city, they began to rely heavily upon each other for academic and social support. They shared transportation and parking expenses or took public transportation together. Moral support on campus and outside of classes was also important. One student described the support mechanism in this way: "We are like a huge family that if one falls down, we all help them to get up. I have learned so much from all of them. We all have one thing in common, wanting to be educated; we all have children, we all have problems, and we are so similar and then again, we are so different."

THE EVOLUTION OF GYO TEACHERS IN ILLINOIS

While the Logan Square Neighborhood Association and the bilingual education program at Chicago State University were collaborating on Project Nueva Generación, other community-based organizations in Chicago were also organizing around education issues. One such organization was ACORN (Association of Community Organizations for Reform Now). ACORN had conducted research in their neighborhood schools and documented the fact that 40 percent of new teachers leave each year (Frost, 2005). Alarmed by these data, the organization began to look for possible solutions and learned about Project Nueva Generación.

Grow Your Own Illinois was formed when ACORN, LSNA, and three additional community-based organizations began to collaborate in order to address their common educational concerns. Using Project Nueva Generación as the model, the group organized in Chicago and throughout the state to draft legislation, lobby, and ultimately get GYO Teachers Illinois into law. Initially, revenue was not appropriated, but in 2005 the Illinois state legislature approved a $1.5 million appropriation for statewide GYO Teachers planning and development.

During the planning and development year, GYO Teachers Illinois identified low-income schools with high rates of teacher turnover and helped to develop partnerships among these schools districts, community-based organizations, and institutions of higher education. There are now eleven GYO consortia in the state of Illinois, all working to replicate the success of Project Nueva Generación. Each consortium consists of a community-based organization, an institution of higher education, and a school district. In total, the consortia have recruited around 500 potential teacher candidates, 80 percent of whom are people of color.

THE IMPLICATIONS OF SUCCESS FOR PROJECT NUEVA GENERACIÓN AND GYO TEACHERS

In December of 2006, the first two Project Nueva Generación students graduated. The number of graduates who have completed all teacher certification requirements continues to grow. As teachers, they are culturally connected with the lives and realities of the families with whom they work. Because of their own experiences, they understand the inherent barriers to academic and personal success for members of the community. Just as important as understanding the barriers, though, is the belief in the potential present in the communities where they work.

As faculty at colleges of education rethink the traditional notion of community-based teacher education programs, they might consider following the example of Project Nueva Generación and GYO Teachers Illinois. Although not an immediate response to the problems plaguing urban schools, nor a solution that will result in large numbers of graduates, GYO Teacher programs have the potential to complement and enrich community-based programs and traditional student teaching programs already in place in colleges of education.

For communities, the goal of such programs is to recruit and retain highly qualified teachers for hard-to-staff schools and hard-to-fill positions. However, the community-based and collaborative nature of the program indicates that there is more at stake than filling teacher vacancies. An additional motivation for the GYO Teachers movement is to challenge the existing social structure of schools and colleges of education and prepare teachers from the community who will serve as leaders and agents of change in these schools (Schultz, Gillette, & Hill, 2008).

To this end, colleges of education must adapt their own practices so as to foster the success of GYO Teacher candidates. Exemplified by Nueva Generación, this adaptation does not mean lowering entrance requirements, creating a path of alternative certification, or acceptance of substandard academic performance. Rather, it calls for creative measures that tap the enormous assets that the students bring into the program and provides additional support mechanisms when and where they need them. At the same time, colleges of education must view the urban communities and residents as genuine assets, not simply locations to place traditional student teachers for diverse field experiences.

REFERENCES

Aviles, A., Capeheart, L., Davila, E., & Pérez Miller, A. (2004). *Dando un paso ¿pa'lante o pa'tras? Latinos in the Chicago Public Schools*. Chicago: 2nd Legislative Education Advisory Committee, Senator Miguel del Valle.

CensusScope. (n.d.). *Race and ethnicity selections, 1980–2000*. Retrieved May 14, 2005, from http://www.censusscope.org/us/print_chart_race.html

Chicago Public Schools. (n.d.). *School test scores and demographic reports*. Retrieved February 9, 2008, from http://research.cps.k12.il.us/resweb/School Profile?unit=3520

Frost, S. (2005). *Here one year, gone the next: Summarizing the teacher turnover data for 64 ACORN neighborhood schools, 2002–2003 to 2003–2004*. Chicago: Illinois ACORN.

Koerner , M., & Abdul-Tawwab, N. (2006). Using community as a resource for teacher education: A case study. *Equity & Excellence in Education, 39*, 37–46.

Moll, L., Amanti, C., Neff, D., & Gonzalez, N. (1992). Funds of knowledge for teaching: Using a qualitative approach to connect homes and classrooms. *Theory into Practice, 31*, 132–141.

Schultz, B., Gillette, M., & Hill, D. (2008). A theoretical framework for understanding Grow Your Own teachers. *Sophist's Bane, 4*(1 & 2), 69–80.

Stanton-Salazar, R. (2004). Social capital among working-class minority students. In M. A. Gibson, P. Gándara, & J. P. Koyama (Eds.), *School connections: U.S. Mexican youth, peers, and school achievement* (pp. 18–38). New York: Teachers College Press.

Zumwalt, A., & Craig, E. (2005). Teachers' characteristics: Research on the demographic profile. In M. Cochran-Smith & K. M. Zeichner (Eds.), *Studying teacher education: The report of the AERA panel on research and teacher education* (pp. 111–156). New York: Routledge.

16

Cooking "Hickory Soup" and Other Ways to Develop Successful Interprofessional Internships for Preservice Teachers

Twyla Salm and Lace Marie Brogden

BURNING THE SOUP

Three weeks into a fourteen-week practicum, tasked with the sacred ritual of preparing Friday's soup for the entire school staff, five interprofessional university interns stared blankly at one another after the first official taste test. There was no denying the soup had burned on the bottom—the charred taste permeated the entire pot. "How," muttered one, "could five such capable women overlook stirring the soup?"

Having collaborated earlier that morning, all had agreed to return to the kitchen periodically to check on the soup. It didn't seem like a daunting task. Nevertheless, after the soup was simmering, the interns parted ways for a few hours . . . the nursing intern was teaching hand-washing, the education intern was conducting reading tests, the justice intern worked in the staff room preparing for conflict resolution group, the social work intern was developing a genogram, and the kinesiology intern was meeting with the school's special education teacher. During this productive time, the soup was left to bubble for just a little too long.

EDUCATIONAL CONTEXT

The project that brought these interns from multiple disciplines together is part of an initiative to facilitate collaboration between human service students from the faculties of Education, Social Work, Nursing, Kinesiology and Health Studies, and Justice Studies at a Canadian university. The project was designed to facilitate Interprofessional Education (IPE), which is defined as learning with, from, and about each other during field placement internships (CAIPE, 2002).

CHALLENGES OF INTERPROFESSIONAL COLLABORATION FOR TEACHER EDUCATION

This chapter focuses on the challenges and benefits of preservice student involvement in interprofessional collaboration (IPC). In this context, IPC can be understood as a synergistic process through which professionals from two or more human service sectors work together to achieve outcomes that would not be possible to achieve in isolation. Although interprofessional education is now becoming commonplace in other human service faculties, teachers are often the least prepared profession to work on IPC teams, and limited information exists to guide interprofessional education in schools (Tourse, Mooney, Kline, & Davoren, 2005).

Working toward interdependence involves more than connecting or coordinating. It requires skills particular to interprofessional collaboration. In this teacher education program, interprofessional internships were designed to provide opportunities for education students to achieve the following collaborative competencies, based on the work of Barr, Koppel, Reeves, Hammick, and Freeth (2005):

- Describe one's roles and responsibilities to others in relation to other professions;
- Recognize the roles and competencies of other professionals;
- Work with other professions to implement change and solve problems effectively;
- Analyze differences and resolve conflict related to misunderstandings among the professions; and
- Facilitate interprofessional team meetings.

In the remainder of this chapter, key ingredients of an effective interprofessional education design for teacher education interns are discussed, and we propose strategies and ideas for turning an ordinary internship into a coveted interprofessional option for education students.

FRAMING THE INTERPROFESSIONAL FIELD

The field of interprofessional collaboration has evolved from integrated services, a field of study dating back over 100 years (Tyack, 1992). Although integrated services offered a way for human services professionals to connect or coordinate, it did not promote complex, higher-order IPC goals. Consequently, IPC has evolved from linking human services with schools into developing skills for collaboration in interprofessional contexts that seek to transform and disrupt conventional power relationships and social practices and to use linguistic tools to work together in new ways (Engestrom, Brown, Christopher, & Gregory, 1997).

Prompted by Canadian government policy direction (Romanow, 2002), current national and international health-care literature (President's Advisory Commission on Health Consumer Protection and Quality in the Health Care Industry, 1998) is burgeoning with research to guide health-care faculties as they incorporate interprofessional learning opportunities for students in a wide array of health-care programs. In contrast, IPC contributions to education literature are present but sparse, reflecting the limited interprofessional educational opportunities available for students in faculties of education (Palmer, McCorkle, Durbin, & O'Neill, 2001).

Despite the dearth of research related to interprofessional education in teacher education, there is reason to be hopeful that quality, interprofessional education opportunities will improve collaboration and, subsequently, the outcomes for both students and teachers. The benefits of complex partnerships between sectors include increased engagement with learning, improved academic outcomes, improved trust and support for families, and several improvements to administrative structures, including improved assessment and referral procedures, shortened wait lists, and improved recruitment and retention (Salm, 2010).

NEW WAYS TO MAKE SOUP:
IPC INNOVATION IN TEACHER EDUCATION

Stirring the Pot

Designing interprofessional internships for education students demands new ways of thinking about field placement design. Although, in our context, the interprofessional internship deviated from traditional teacher education requirements, education interns were still required to fulfill their obligations as teacher candidates for certification purposes. Consequently, they were assigned to cooperating teachers and classrooms in their area of concentration, and responsible for instruction and evaluation. Instead of being an *add-on*, IPC offers a different way of designing internship experiences for education interns.

Although faculties in other disciplines recruited student interns quite easily, education students were reluctant to alter their internship experience. For education students, becoming a teacher often meant reinscribing traditional social norms and practices associated with their image of the *teacher*. As a result, it was initially a challenge to convince the education interns that working collaboratively on an interprofessional team was integral to becoming and being a teacher.

One useful approach to disrupting the tightly defined preconceptions of *teacher* held by many of the education interns was to discuss notions of dominant culture and marginalization during group meetings (Warren, 2003). Education interns were encouraged to deconstruct the role of the teacher in relation to other professionals within schools, in both sheer number and prevailing social norms.

What was interesting about breaking the mold of a traditional internship was that those involved in the project, faculty members and interns alike, were able to understand and to question the rigid structure that had shaped previous practices. Revealing old molds of dominance and the ways they had shaped perceptions (Foucault, 1983) was key to helping education interns become more generous toward other professionals in the group and more open to meaningful collaboration and new ways of constructing professional practice.

Setting the Table

Several design structures were put in place to support the interprofessional internship initiative. Supports included one- or two-day inservice for interns and faculty, information sessions for school staff members, weekly meetings for IPC cohorts, and site-based coordinators. During the orientation workshop, participants received a manual outlining the general goals, roles, and responsibilities of each individual. A faculty advisor and an IPC coordinator, usually a social worker, were assigned to each cohort. The IPC coordinator played a crucial role in organizing daily demands of the project while the faculty advisor facilitated reflection and analysis.

COOKING UP SUCCESS: INTERNS IN ACTION

While many stories emerged from the experiences of the intern cohorts, two stand out as rich evidence of ways in which education interns developed the IPC interprofessional competencies the project sought to foster. These vignettes also illustrate the role of interprofessional education in enhancing the quality of teacher education and contributing to increased understandings between and among emerging professionals.

Education Interns as Leaders for Anti-Oppressive Education

One cohort worked with newcomer elementary students recently immigrated to Canada. The interns wanted to engage parents and thought it would be good to bring the parents to the school for an event. Using a middle-class paradigm, interns sent notes, made home visits, and prompted the children to encourage their parents' attendance at an event celebrating cultures and student achievement. Despite their efforts, few parents responded to the invitations or showed interest in school events. Subsequently, there was a sentiment held by some interns that immigrant parents did not value school or care about their children's education.

One day, however, the interns were prompted to revisit their previously held assumptions. Upon hearing the noise of a snow grader in the school parking lot, some of the children dived under their desks to protect themselves from what they perceived to be an army tank. As the interns confronted the children's reactions to the snow grader, they became acutely aware how their perceptions of *normal* were filtered through a particular lens. For some of the interns, it was the first time they recognized that they even had a lens.

Subsequently, the drama of the snow-grader event opened up a space for faculty to ask the students how their assumptions had influenced they ways in which they had judged parents, including how they understood immigrant parents' involvement in school events. Open to the fact that their perceptions might have been limited, if not faulty, the interns were able to use various professional competencies to reflect on their previously held assumptions and deconstruct the white, middle-class approach they had used when communicating with immigrant families (Warren, 2003).

The education intern in this cohort, who was well versed in antiracist theory, challenged the other group members to recognize racist and oppressive assumptions and how they were being played out in their activities with the immigrant children and parents. Debriefing, she noted, "I wondered if I would ever get to use all that anti-racist theory we were learning at the university. I thought it was interesting but I didn't know how I might act on it." Thus, it was the education intern in this cohort who showed leadership in anti-oppressive education, a theory-to-practice initiative we hope to build on in future interprofessional internships.

Preservice Teachers as Learners: Special Education Gaps

This second vignette emerged from one cohort's observations of a child with fetal alcohol spectrum disorder (FASD). In the weekly debriefing, the social work and nursing interns wondered why the teacher created an environment that was highly stimulating with bright colors, hanging mobiles, and visuals on the walls with a child with FASD in the room. In addition, the social worker and nursing interns did not have access to the child's cumulative file and found it particularly odd that they could not read his charts.

The social work and nursing interns concluded the teacher probably did not care very much about the child until the education intern spoke up, raising pedagogical questions related to visual cues for learning. All of the interns discovered they had correct yet limited knowledge of FASD, and also learned how their own professional lenses interfered with decisions affecting the child's health, learning, and social care. After a long, difficult conversation, they discovered how false assumptions can be made when there is limited understanding of others' perspectives. They agreed upon a new plan for action that was integrated and holistic.

Using an interprofessional approach involving the child, the parents, and the child's cumulative file, the interns constructed a plan for the child with FASD that respected the diverse learning needs of the entire class.

They suggested the teacher could wear a microphone to amplify her voice, create a "calm" space in the classroom that was free of bright colors and other environmental stimuli, and offer wobble boards or elastic foot bands to the student when he was fidgeting. Switching the discourse from blaming to problem solving became a conscious and intentional effort for all of the interns.

In the case of the education intern, what was most revealing was her limited understanding of the needs of special education students and the quality and abundance of suggestions coming from the interns from other faculties. These deficits were not unique to the intern; rather, they revealed gaps in the teacher education program that should be better addressed. These kinds of discussions led to epiphanies during debriefings, as described by one intern this way: "I am not sure how you would learn about all these different perspectives unless you had the opportunity to learn together from the start. As teachers, we make the best decisions that we can given the information we have at the time but I feel much differently now, because I know we will do a better job together."

Benefits of Interprofessional Internships

As these vignettes help illustrate, IPC teams enable rich professional engagement and sharing unlike collaboration available in uniprofessional conversations. Whether addressing oppressive practices or understanding special education, interns discovered how their professional lenses influenced their individual approaches to professional situations. Subsequently, they learned to value their own professional strengths and be open to the perspectives and scope of practice of their colleagues from other professions.

CONCLUSION

Back in the kitchen, the five interns stood around the burnt pot, but agreed to taste the soup. It wasn't inedible, but did have a slightly charred taste, leading one to exclaim, "Looks like we've just invented something new—hickory soup!"

The interns concluded that when working individually, their *soup* was not as good as it could have been because they had *gaps in the stirring.* Although they initially laughed and passed off their burnt attempt as *hickory-flavored soup,* the hickory-soup shenanigan became a euphemism within the cohort for the need to learn how to work together rather than assume professionals inherently know how to become interdependent collaborators.

Teacher education programs can benefit tremendously from collaborating with other human services faculties. They also have much to offer. Developing collaborative competencies in education interns and other human service professionals is a crucial step in ensuring that teachers and schools are part of interprofessional teams that support health, learning, and holistic, social-emotional development for children and their families.

REFERENCES

Barr, H., Koppel, I., Reeves, S., Hammick, M., & Freeth, D. (2005). *Effective interprofessional education: Argument, assumption and evidence.* Oxford: Blackwell.

Centre for the Advancement of Interprofessional Education (CAIPE). (2002). *Defining IPE* [Online]. Retrieved January 19, 2010, from http://www.caipe.org.uk/about-us/defining-ipe/

Engestrom, Y., Brown, K., Christopher, C., & Gregory, J. (1997). Coordination, cooperation and communication in the courts: Expansive transitions in legal work. In M. Cole, Y. Engestrom, & O. Vasquez (Eds.), *Mind, culture, and activity: Seminal papers from the Laboratory of Comparative Human Cognition* (pp. 369–386). Cambridge: Cambridge University Press.

Foucault, M. (1983). Afterword: The subject and power. In H. L. Dreyfus & P. Rubinow (Eds.), *Beyond structuralism and hermeneutics* (pp. 208–226). Chicago: University of Chicago Press.

Palmer, D. J., McCorkle, L., Durbin, S. B., & O'Neill, K. (2001). Preparation and experience of elementary teachers to work with community services for at-risk children, *Education, 121,* 554–565.

President's Advisory Commission on Health Consumer Protection and Quality in the Health Care Industry. (1998). *Quality first: Better health care for all Americans.* Washington, DC: U.S. Government Printing Office.

Romanow, R. J. (2002). *Building on values: The future of health care in Canada—Final report.* Ottawa, ON: Romanow Commission Report.

Salm, T. (2010). Measuring outcomes: A review of interprofessional collaboration in schools. *Physical and Health Education Journal, 76*(2), 6–11.

Tourse, R., Mooney, J., Kline, P., & Davoren, J. (2005). A collaboration model of clinical preparation: A move toward interprofessional field experience. *Journal of Social Work Education, 41*, 457–478.

Tyack, D. (1992). Health and social services in public schools: Historical perspectives. In R. E. Behrman (Ed.), *The future of children: School-linked services* (pp. 19–31). Los Altos, CA: Center for the Future of Children.

Warren, J. T. (2003). *Performing purity: Whiteness, pedagogy, and the reconstitution of power*. New York: Peter Lang.

17

Foreign Language Teacher Technology Education: Innovation through Social Networking

Victoria Hasko and Soria E. Colomer

"It was paralyzing, it was terrible. I was panicking." (Nati)

"Definitely [it's] been very, very exciting. I've loved it and I think it's been very positive as well." (Karen)

These above two quotes (cited in Sánchez-Serrano, 2008, pp. 160–161) evoke vividly dissimilar images, but in fact they refer to the same set of circumstances. Although bungee jumping and a rollercoaster ride come to mind, both of the narrators, Nati and Karen, were in fact describing their first encounters with instructional technology when they started teaching foreign language courses online. Why are their stories so diametrically opposed?

Considering the pervasiveness of computer-mediated communication in our lives, the tantalizing array of emerging technologies for computer-assisted language learning, the richness of available resources in foreign languages available at our fingertips, and the prevailing discourse of enthusiasm surrounding the topic of technological innovation for educational purposes, it is tempting to conclude that Nati's terrifyingly miserable experience of using computer technology for teaching must be an exception. But is it? And how can teacher education programs ensure that all preservice teachers will undergo the same professionally uplifting experience that Karen enjoyed in her first computer-assisted course?

PRESERVICE TEACHERS AS DIGITAL NATIVES

A cartoon in a recent issue of the *New Yorker* (2010, March 15) features a baby in a hospital nursery texting on a cell phone, "OMG! I just got born!" representing a pictorial parody not only of the ubiquity of technology in our lives but also of its expansion into the lives of increasingly younger users.

While earlier publications on teacher education used to lament the digital divide between students (*digital natives*) and teachers (*digital immigrants*) (Prensky, 2001), preservice teachers graduating today certainly qualify for digital citizenship as members of the demographic cohort referred to as the *Global* or *Net Generation* (McCrindle & Wolfinger, 2009), who grew up during the rise of computer communication technologies and the overwhelming majority of whom are avid, functional users of computer tools and the World Wide Web.

This shift in teacher demographics has significant implications for teacher education programs; it is becoming more and more apparent that we must shift the focus of the technology training we provide from instructing student teachers *how to operate* the technology to showing them *how to utilize it for pedagogical purposes*, that is, for improving learning outcomes and improving the effectiveness of their instruction.

The National Education Technology Standards developed by the International Society for Teacher Education (ISTE, 2008) no longer specify that technological fluency is a modern-day requirement for teachers—it is an implicit requirement. Instead, the technology standards communicate a set of benchmarks designed to foster *thoughtful pedagogical applications* of technology in the classroom by guiding teachers to do the following:

- Facilitate and inspire student learning and creativity;
- Design and develop digital-age learning experiences and assessments;
- Model digital-age work and learning;
- Promote and model digital citizenship and responsibility; and
- Engage in professional growth and leadership.

As helpful as the ISTE (2008) standards are, what is still lacking and needs articulation are benchmarks outlining *teacher technology train-*

ing standards. The goal of such standards would steer teacher education programs toward preparing novice instructors to choose apt pedagogical tools and to capitalize on them in the classroom for successful integration of technology and achievement of discipline-specific academic standards. As a result, the quality of teacher technology training in many disciplines would no longer be lagging behind the standards.

URGENT NEED FOR CHANGE

Recent studies suggest that teacher trainees will resist implementation of learning technologies if they believe that the tools they are apprenticed to use during teacher training are *outdated* or *irrelevant* to their everyday personal use practices (Kessler, 2006; Moe & Chubb, 2009). Therefore, to stay relevant and to ensure long-term effectiveness of the technology training that they provide, teacher education programs should create room for innovation and flexibility in their curriculum by refocusing instruction on tools that are well known, ubiquitously used, supported, and accepted by teachers. Failure to revisit professional development in light of new technologies could render teacher training programs obsolete.

What we know about the majority of preservice teacher trainees today is that, as citizens of the Net Generation, they are voracious users of network-based technology. They are accustomed to being surrounded by different interactive media-sharing technologies, which they rely on to stay in touch and to exchange information with their friends, families, extended acquaintances, and the whole global community of Internet users. We also know that they overwhelmingly prefer to do so through virtual social networking.

What are *social networks?* They are websites that allow their users to construct a public or semipublic profile, to articulate a list of other users with whom they share a connection, and to seek out new connections and/ or maintain communication with people who are already part of their extended social network. Facebook (www.facebook.com), MySpace (www .myspace.com), LiveJournal (www.livejournal.com), and Twitter (www .twitter.com) are examples of wide-appeal, global, social networks of sweeping popularity, on which 80–90 percent of the Net Generation have profiles (McBride, 2009).

It is only logical to argue that it behooves teacher education programs to capitalize on preservice teacher trainees' prevailing socializing patterns in the process of educating them about meaningful integration of social networking sites for pedagogical purposes. Of course, the innovative nature and ubiquity of social networking sites do not automatically guarantee their pedagogical worth and may not emerge as optimal tools for delivery of discipline-specific instruction in *all* academic fields. In the rest of the chapter, we focus on how social networking sites can boost excitement, creativity, and efficacy of instruction in the field of foreign language education, and outline steps for effective integration of social networking into foreign language teacher technology training.

COINS: A PROMISING CURRENCY

Given that social networks are presently the most common location for communication and community-building via the Internet, social networking holds rich promise for a communicatively oriented field of foreign language education. A particularly exciting technological innovation for language teachers and learners includes the latest global trend, which is the launching of social networks specifically designed as learning and teaching spaces for multilingual communities and whose members are united by the common goal of foreign language mastery.

Such websites, which we refer to as Collaborative Online International Networking Sites (COINS), include LiveMocha (www.livemocha.com), Mixxer (www.language-exchanges.org), My Happy Planet (www.my happyplanet.com), Busuu (www.busuu.com), Babbel (www.babbel.com), Voxswap (www.voxswap.com), and Xlingo (www.languageexchange .org). These and other COINS are offering content in multiple languages (thirty-five on Livemocha alone) and have amassed millions of registered members from around the globe.

The revolutionary idea behind the creation of COINS is rather simple. It is the acknowledgment that foreign language competence resides within foreign language communities and communication with their members. It also validates that speakers of different languages, motivated by their desire to learn more about new languages and cultures, can serve as sources of mutual development and support for each other. Hence, COINS's unique niche is in providing opportunities for virtual multilingual communication based on peer tutoring.

The design of COINS purposefully encourages members to learn languages by connecting with native speakers in the network and offering feedback on each other's speaking or writing performance. When creating a profile on COINS, users are asked to input information about the languages they speak and want to learn, levels of proficiency, as well as optional personal information, such as age, gender, and reasons for learning languages.

After joining COINS, users can select *friends* who best match their linguistic interests and choose to communicate synchronously (in real-time via chat or Skype options) or asynchronously (via profile-to-profile e-mails) with them. Users can also submit various assignments as text and/or audio files that are then corrected, commented on, and rated in terms of accuracy by other members, also in both modalities. COINS offer a variety of web-based audiovisual lessons for autonomous learning, but it is the social networking component and opportunities for interlingual and intercultural friendships that attract millions of users who are eagerly supplying volunteer tutoring in exchange for help with their own language skills.

In terms of their potential for immersion-like, interactive, and spontaneous interactions with native speakers, COINS serve as an exciting modern-day substitute for international sojourns, which have been traditionally viewed as a pinnacle of foreign language learning experience. Only a small percentage of U.S. learners get an opportunity to visit a country where the language they are studying is spoken, but for many students across the world, Internet-mediated communication with foreign language communities is becoming more customary than face-to-face and nondigital forms of communication.

COINS enable learners to reach out and establish virtual friendships with native speakers of foreign languages whose profile appeals to them, look through the culturally rich artifacts in foreign languages on the network (pictures, videos, songs, and messages), initiate instant discussions with a click of a mouse, complete numerous learning modules, and receive peer feedback. Traditional textbook-based snippets of readings on culture and occasional classroom role-plays cannot but seem contrived and dull in comparison to the wealth of exciting new communication opportunities that COINS offer.

IMPLICATIONS FOR FOREIGN LANGUAGE
TECHNOLOGY EDUCATION

COINS's promise for increasing the efficacy of foreign language instruction is intriguing, but novice instructors might find it challenging to recognize and utilize the educational potential of these tools. We propose the U.S. National Standards for Foreign Language Education (ACTFL, 1996) as a starting point for preservice teacher training on pedagogical integration of COINS. The standards, referred to as the 5Cs, include the following five goal areas:

- Communication: To engage in authentic communication in foreign languages;
- Cultures: To gain knowledge and understanding of other cultures;
- Connections: To connect with other disciplines and acquire information;
- Comparisons: To develop insight into the nature of language and culture; and
- Communities: To participate in multilingual communities at home and around the world.

Reaching the 5Cs and consequently leading learners to advanced proficiency levels has been a persistent challenge for the U.S. foreign language programs (Springer & Collins, 2008). COINS hold the promise for promoting standards-appropriate activities in foreign language classrooms by facilitating authentic, multimodal *communication* with academic *communities* of foreign language learners and multilingual exploration of *culture*, *comparisons*, and *connections* via social networking. The unique overarching characteristic of COINS-supported activities is that of *collaboration*, or, more precisely, *telecollaboration* (where *tele-*, Greek, stands for "distance"), which fuels the 5Cs with its inherent dialogic and interactional qualities.

Telecollaboration is a pedagogical model that has emerged as the hallmark of innovation and success in language education over the past two decades (Guth & Helm, 2010), but educational outcomes of virtual collaborative projects have been shown to depend to a large extent on the online behavior of the instructor, which includes *pedagogical*, *social*, and *managerial* functions (Meskill & Anthony, 2010; Palloff & Pratt, 2007). In light of these findings, we propose aligning COINS-oriented teacher technology preparation with the development of the aforementioned functions.

The *managerial* function of COINS-based instruction concerns the topics of design, implementation, and maintenance of telecollaborative projects—which are presently not part of mainstream teacher technology education curricula. Therefore, programs integrating training in the area of COINS-based telecollaboration should focus on preparing novice teachers to seek out and connect with interested foreign language educators abroad via COINS with the goal of establishing and maintaining interinstitutional collaborations with foreign schools. Novice teachers will need guidance with negotiating the conditions of and schedule for the telecollaborative exchanges with their foreign partners, setting up objectives for virtual communicative activities, developing rubrics for these activities, and maintaining interest and commitment of all parties (learners and partnering instructors) via COINS.

From a *pedagogical* standpoint, telecollaborative language learning projects have been proven effective in developing participants' linguistic skills in terms of grammar, lexis, phraseology, spelling, and pragmatics as well as intercultural awareness (Guth & Helm, 2010). Therefore, teacher candidates would benefit from activities that provide practice opportunities for them to design and facilitate COINS-based teaching activities, which would lead language learners to do the following:

- Negotiate (through discussion or debate);
- Co-construct (through collaborative authoring); and
- Share information in various modalities (text, graphics, audio, and video) on the topics of culture, customs, history, social events, mass media, or entertainment.

The skills of gauging learner participation and offering tailored forms of assistance are as critical in the virtual environment as they are during face-to-face lessons. Particularly important strategies for novice instructors preparing to teach within online learning communities via COINS would include:

- Calling learners' attention to grammar forms and lexis used in online communication;

- Corralling learners' attention to specific language and cultural content;
- Modeling linguistic forms for learners to appropriate and use; and
- Providing explicit and implicit feedback on mistakes or misunderstandings (Meskill & Anthony, 2010).

With regard to the *social* function of COINS-based teacher preparation, novice educators will also need training in issues of resolving intercultural communication misunderstandings and conflicts that might emerge during social networking, as well as the promotion of friendly, fair, and secure social environments essential to the success of foreign language learning, which is always fraught with high anxiety for learners.

Finally, to master and implement the pedagogical, social, and managerial functions of foreign language education through social networking, teacher education programs should allocate time for teacher trainees to become comfortable and proficient users of all technical features/functionalities of COINS, such as creation of profiles and academic groups, uploading and downloading multimedia files, providing multimodal peer feedback, and completing COINS-based learning modules.

EXPLORING THE VALUE

At the University of Georgia Foreign Language Education Program, we are exploring the educational potential of COINS with the goals of improving the quality of preparation provided to our preservice teachers and enabling them to achieve the ACTFL (1996) standards. Over the last two years, our preservice student teachers enrolled in the Foreign Language Curriculum and Methods, Grades 7–12 seminar carefully documented their use, practices, and critical evaluation of social networking sites as digital spaces for teaching and learning foreign languages in reflective journals.

The review of the journal entries revealed that the preservice teachers grew to appreciate the opportunity to experiment with COINS and recognized the instructional potential of COINS-based activities. Thus, they positively assessed their experiences of practicing foreign languages in a communicative setting, exploring COINS-based learning modules that incorporated multiple modalities to engage learners, learning cultural trivia firsthand from the native speakers, and discovering pedagogically useful linguistic resources through social networking that otherwise would have remained unknown to them.

Creation and maintenance of collaborative contacts via COINS was not a smooth process for all teacher trainees. The use of technology and implementation of social networking projects indeed requires patience, dedication, and consideration of issues of cyber security, but the dividends of using COINS for promoting the efficacy of foreign language promise to be bountiful. Preservice teachers' journals offer rich testimonies of how the COINS training contributed to the increase of their pedagogical content knowledge and informed their teaching philosophies. As one preservice teacher shares:

> [By exploring COINS], I have learned much that will be incorporated into my own teaching style. I have learned the importance of creating lessons that integrate all aspects of language learning. It is only when students gain exposure to language in a variety of forms that we can expect them to become proficient. I have learned the value of collaborative work. I shall implement such practices into my classroom by creating mixed-ability groups. In these groups, the target goal would be for my students to learn from one another and work together to decipher meaning. This teaching strategy, as I have learned, will ultimately nurture independent thinkers.

Participation in COINS also led our teacher trainees to discover—sometimes much to their chagrin—that they also needed to strengthen their language skills, not just their instructional knowledge, to participate in and facilitate conversations with native speakers. They reported being exposed to advanced concepts in grammar as well as colloquial expressions not commonly taught in traditional language classes during interactions with native speakers of foreign languages via COINS. This finding left us hopeful that the educational value of COINS-based activities will extend beyond the methodology seminar and will promote lifelong learning among the participants.

CONCLUSION

Our examination of preservice teachers' longitudinal interaction with COINS revealed a number of important insights that need to be taken into consideration by teacher technology educators. The fact that participating student teachers engaged with COINS independently and without any overt difficulties with creating profiles, using different website features, or accessing content is quite telling. This confirms our earlier conclusion that teaching preservice teachers of the Net Generation only *about* technology is not sufficient and may even be irrelevant in some cases. While the concept of *teachers-as-learners-of-technology* still has an important role in shaping teacher technology training (after all, changes in the world of technologies are dizzyingly swift), perhaps even more relevant today are such concepts as *teachers-as-learners-of-teaching*, *teachers-as-learners-of-their-subjects*, and *teachers-as-learners-of-profession*, all in the context of educational technology integration.

On the other hand, preservice teachers' reflective engagement with COINS illuminated the need for a participatory basis of teacher technology training programs that include structured opportunities for preservice teachers to experiment with, integrate, assess, and reflect on the pedagogical potential of existing and emerging technological tools in light of their instructional goals and learners' needs. Only if these conditions are met can we reasonably anticipate that novice teachers will be able to meet the ISTE (2008) benchmarks and to use technological tools successfully for purposes of curricular innovation, effective delivery of content, student engagement, and their own maintenance of professional passion, vigor, facility, and satisfaction. Then, perhaps they will be spared the frustration of Nati's experience and will embark on their journeys toward becoming technologically savvy and effective educators with confidence and enthusiasm.

REFERENCES

American Council on the Teaching of Foreign Languages (ACTFL). (1996). *Standards in foreign language learning: Preparing for the twenty-first century.* Lincolnwood, IL: National Textbook Company.

Guth, S., & Helm, F. (Eds.). (2010). *Telecollaboration 2.0: Language, literacies and intercultural learning in the 21st century.* Bern, Switzerland: Peter Lang.

International Society for Technology in Education (ISTE). (2008). *National educational technology standards for teachers.* Retrieved June 16, 2010, from http://www.iste.org/AM/Template.cfm?Section=NETS

Kessler, G. (2006). Assessing CALL teacher training: What are we doing and what could we do better? In P. Hubbard & M. Levy (Eds.), *Teacher education in CALL* (pp. 23–44). Amsterdam, Netherlands: John Benjamins.

McBride, K. (2009). Social-networking sites in foreign language classes: Opportunities for re-creation. In L. Lomicka & G. Lord (Eds.), *The next generation: Social networking and online collaboration in foreign language learning* (pp. 35–58). San Marcos, CA: CALICO.

McCrindle, M., & Wolfinger, E. (2009). *The ABC of XYZ: Understanding the global generations*. Sydney, Australia: UNSW Press.

Meskill, C., & Anthony, N. (2010). *Teaching languages online*. Bristol, UK: Multilingual Matters.

Moe, T. M., & Chubb, J. E. (2009). *Liberating learning: Technology, politics, and the future of American education*. San Francisco: Jossey-Bass.

Palloff, R., & Pratt, K. (2007). *Building online learning communities: Effective strategies for the virtual classroom*. San Francisco: Jossey-Bass.

Prensky, M. (2001). Digital natives, digital immigrants. *On the Horizon, 9*(5). Retrieved June 16, 2010, from http://www.marcprensky.com/writing/

Sánchez-Serrano, L. (2008). Initiation by fire: Training teachers for distance learning. In S. Goertler & P. Winke (Eds.), *Opening doors through distance language education: Principles, perspectives, and practices* (pp. 175–202). San Marcos, CA: CALICO.

Springer, S., & Collins, L. (2008). Interacting inside and outside of the language classroom. *Language Teaching Research, 12*, 39–60.

18

School-Community-Based Urban Teacher Education as a Voice for the Community

Jana Noel

Responding to the critique that teacher education is removed from the realities of K–12 schools, in 2004, Sacramento State University created the Urban Teacher Education Center (UTEC) that moved teacher preparation off of the university campus and into Broadway Circle Elementary School (pseudonym). A key principle driving the creation of the Urban Teacher Education Center was that by moving teacher education into urban schools and communities, preservice teachers and faculty would better understand the realities of urban education, including the social, political, and economic conditions affecting the lives and education of urban children and their families (Noel, 2006).

UTEC operates under the concept that in order to effectively educate children in urban settings, teachers must learn about and engage in the communities of their students. In recognition of its strong community connections, UTEC won the 2008 California Quality Education Partnership Award for Distinguished Service to Children and the Preparation of Teachers.

Broadway Circle School is a very low-income, culturally and linguistically diverse elementary school in a large Northern California city that serves children from two neighborhood public housing projects. Every family in the projects receives some form of federal assistance and 100 percent of students in the school receive free or reduced lunch, a federal measurement of poverty. The school's student demographics are

59 percent African American and 94 percent children of color. English language learners (ELLs) make up 23 percent of the school's population, with the main home languages being Spanish, Vietnamese, Cantonese, Marshallese, and Mien. Both Broadway Circle School and the school district in which it is located are in Program Improvement status, indicating that student test scores have not met the target set by the No Child Left Behind standards.

As outsiders coming into Broadway Circle School and its neighborhood community, the Sacramento State Urban Teacher Education Center (UTEC) needed to be very aware of trust issues. As clearly illustrated by Reed (2004), "Low-income neighborhoods are jaded by the comings and goings of organizations . . . weary of seeing new initiatives come and go" (p. 81). In the case of this particular community, the need for more stable school–community connections was overwhelmingly evident during one year when the principal and assistant principal both resigned just before the school year began.

The school district's response was to rotate four retired principals through the school on alternating days. The result of an inconsistent administration was a breakdown in communication and a lessening of trust from the parents and neighboring community. An unexpected consequence of the Urban Teacher Education Center moving into this school was that the community turned to UTEC for some stability as another voice to represent them at the school, and for both structural and spontaneous joining of efforts to both create and strengthen efforts to educate children.

THE CHALLENGES

Leadership Turnover

The principal and assistant principal of Broadway Circle School resigned just prior to the beginning of the 2005 school year. With no time to hire a qualified full-time principal, the district assigned four retired principals to rotate through the school year. Since retirees are only allowed to work for a set number of days during the year, each principal needed to determine how best to utilize those days. While one of the principals served mostly

as the solo principal, the remaining principals overlapped their days of responsibility and also sometimes served as co-principals. For the latter part
of the year, one principal served on Monday-Wednesday-Friday, while
the other served on Tuesday-Thursday. Needless to say, communication
broke down. Agreements made with one principal were not always communicated to the alternating principal. Both the teachers and the community lost trust in the school to effectively serve their children.

Outsider Status

Within the UTEC–Broadway Circle School and community collaboration,
there was the all-too-common cultural mismatch between the preservice
teachers, who were 75 percent white and 100 percent monolingual, and the
school's students, who were 94 percent children of color and 23 percent
ELLs. Issues of race, class, privilege, and community dynamics come into
play in all interactions. UTEC needed to carefully consider how people in
the neighborhoods might take a racially, economically, and educationally
marked view of its preservice teachers and faculty (Noel, 2010).

THEORETICAL FRAMEWORK

UTEC's work has been framed by two theoretical frameworks: (a) theories of presence and (b) trust.

Theories of Presence

Theories of *presence* in urban schools point out that becoming accepted
and integrated into a community requires time spent in the community.
Murrell (2001) discusses the idea of *being there*, of being physically
present in schools in order to learn, to show commitment, and to build
trust with community members. Rosenberg's (1997) concept of *dwelling*
provides another way to think of being there. As Rosenberg describes,
"We need to think about what it means for us to *dwell* in the institution
. . . to fasten our attention, to tarry, to look again. We take root, day after
day" (p. 88).

This physical presence must be supplemented with a certain attitude, or *humility of practice* as defined by Murrell (2001). In this concept, educators "have to avoid the fatal assumption that they know all they need to know about the culture, values, traditions, and heritages of the people they purportedly serve" (Murrell, 2001, p. 31). Rather, "The measure of our success as agents for change is not the *expertise* we bring as university people, but rather our *capacity to learn in the company of others . . . working* with them on *their* enterprises of change" (p. 33). Community members need to realize that school-community-based teacher education is there, learning in and with the community, for the long term.

Development of Trust

Hoy and Tschannen-Moran (1999) identified five facets involved in developing, establishing, and maintaining trust: benevolence, honesty, openness, reliability, and competence. However, collaborative relationships do not begin with all five facets of trust already in place. Rather, trust is a dynamic phenomenon that takes on a different character at different stages of a relationship. First, when partners do not have a professional or personal relationship, they will make a calculation about the worthiness of a potential collaborative partner based on factors such as the amount of risk connected with the collaboration. In the example of the UTEC–Broadway Circle School collaboration, both constituencies needed to establish a trust relationship so that the preservice teachers and the student learners would benefit.

Second, as the collaboration begins and activities commence, partners can gauge the repeated activities and level of commitment of their partners, and a trust develops based on knowledge of the individuals' work, commitment, and trustworthiness (Bottery, 2003). Third, as partners spend time working together, and repeated collaborative activities have been effective, partners come to recognize that they have developed relationships based on shared goals, procedures, and beliefs.

Finally, flexibility is a hallmark of the mature partnership that has gone through this process of trust development (Hands, 2005).With an enhanced authentic partnership, one can expect partners to be able to act with flexibility, to enact change when needed, and to incorporate new community needs and institutional demands.

PERSONAL STORIES AND STRUCTURAL CHANGES

What follows here are some of the author's journal entries, preservice teacher reflective journal writings, and newly developed structural components fostering the community's trust in UTEC to serve as a voice for them in school matters.

Coordinator's Journal Entry #1

I finally got to meet the matriarch of the neighborhood. Apparently if anything gets done in [housing project #1], it goes through Ms. F. Danced with Ms. F at the Jazz assembly. We were terrible! But we laughed so hard, and all the teachers and other parents laughed so hard at us, that I think we now have that connection I have desired. Ms. F told me that I could visit her neighborhood anytime.

Structural Change #1: Center Tutoring/Mentoring Program

This after-school program, initially operated within the center's public housing complex, was created and is operated by two men who grew up in the neighborhood, moved out to get their college degrees, and now give back to their former community by running this center. UTEC preservice teachers assist as tutors/mentors, and the program has now become a formalized community–university partnership.

Coordinator's Journal Entry #2

After arriving at the school and learning about UTEC's focus on community, two of the rotating principals asked for my help in learning more about the community. I led the two principals on a walking tour of the housing complex, introducing them to the neighborhood's matriarchal family and showing them the neighborhood's tutoring/mentoring center.

Coordinator's Journal Entry #3

Since there are no buses at this school, all children must walk to school. One of the principals and I initiated the practice of serving coffee to parents outside the cafeteria as they arrived at the school with their children. The principal even decided to do a "drive through" coffee delivery, for parents who dropped their children off at school by car.

Preservice Teacher's Story

A UTEC preservice teacher observed a Broadway Circle School student climbing the fence between the housing projects and the road. She stopped her car to talk with the student, and got permission to serve as an unofficial crosswalk guard. A parent who had seen this preservice teacher acting as crosswalk guard asked if she could help him get information on community colleges for himself. She did some research on her own and interviewed two staff members of the school who live in the neighborhood, and prepared a packet for the parent and for the community overall.

Structural Change #2: Family Resource Center

In collaboration with Broadway Circle School's assistant principal, the preservice teachers and the UTEC coordinator created the Family Resource Center. UTEC preservice teachers served coffee to parents, assisted with computer access, and operated the children's book give-away section and the parent book exchange. This center later became a classroom for a parenting workshop offered by the university and a G.E.D. course offered by the school district.

Coordinator's Journal Entry #4

[While getting ready to walk home with her child after school, a parent called out,] "Hey Dr. Noel, our church is holding a bar-b-q this weekend in the projects. Do you and your students want to come?"

Structural Change #3: Broadway Circle School
Community Outreach Committee

With permission of one of the four rotating principals, the UTEC coordinator initiated and chaired a Community Outreach Committee at the school. Originally comprised of the UTEC coordinator and three teachers, the intent was to eventually include community members on the committee. However, when a new principal was assigned to the school, the committee was disbanded.

Coordinator's Journal Entry #5

Went to Broadway Circle School for the Monday morning assembly. I sat on the bench by the office next to Ms. G., a mom who is very vocal about her views. When it came time for the National Anthem she looked at me and said, "You know, those kids aren't singing. . . . Maybe one of those leadership roles could be doing the National Anthem with the microphone." I said "That's a great idea. Maybe you should tell Ms. [principal], or I could." She said, "Oh you should, because you have more pull with her."

ASSESSING THE IMPACT

The personal and structural examples given above offer anecdotal evidence of the success of UTEC's efforts to become accepted and integrated into Broadway Circle School and its community. Additionally, however, an evaluation of the UTEC collaboration with school and community was undertaken after the fifth year of the program, utilizing Likert scales and interviews with teachers, administrators, and support staff, and a focus group with three community leaders.

Benefits and Perceived Level of Equality in the Program

When asked about the benefits of UTEC's activities, 95 percent of all respondents agreed that having UTEC at the school and community benefits both the school's children and UTEC preservice teachers. A further set of questions attempted to determine the perception of equality in decision making on the part of the various partners, asking whether the participants felt that their voices were heard in the planning and delivery of UTEC's activities. While 63 percent of Likert scale respondents agreed or strongly agreed that they "have a say," 45 percent of these respondents marked either disagree or strongly disagree. Interestingly, more teachers perceived a lack of voice in these matters (50 percent) than did support staff (20 percent). This is consistent with the administrator interviewed, who described herself as not having much say in the program. The community members in the focus group, however, felt very empowered to make decisions regarding the activities that involve UTEC/community collaboration. This provides an indication of the important role of UTEC in providing a space for community voices to be heard.

Trust and Outsider Status

One hundred percent of survey respondents either agreed or strongly agreed with the notion that "I feel that I can trust UTEC faculty and students," while 91 percent agreed with the statement that "I feel that UTEC faculty and students trust me." Community leaders in the focus group expressed an initial concern, now alleviated, related to outsiders. They were sure that UTEC would not *stick around* (Reed, 2004). The community leaders expressed that they are *amazed* that UTEC is still active in their community after five years.

Impact on Confidence

One member of the focus group indicated that with the community's partnership with UTEC, he finally feels like he is able to have an impact on the children of the neighborhood at the full spectrum of their lives. Previously, he felt he had to work only with the elementary children, and his impact might end as they entered middle school. Now he feels able to *give up* the tutoring/mentoring program he ran at the public housing site in order to run a similar program at the high school, because he knew his mother, the community's matriarch, in combination with UTEC, could run the elementary school program on their own.

CONCLUSION:
BECOMING A VOICE FOR THE COMMUNITY

In the effort to create a more authentic teacher education program for Sacramento State preservice teachers, the Urban Teacher Education Center moved off of the university campus and into Broadway Circle School. By *being there* every day, members of the community have begun to see the program representatives and preservice teachers as fully committed to their neighborhood. We have been invited into neighborhood gatherings and have been trusted to serve as tutors/mentors in community-led programs. The school has allowed us to initiate or help facilitate efforts that would connect the school more closely with the parents and the community. Due to the instability of leadership during our time at the school, UTEC has become the more stable force at the school. Despite our outsider status, UTEC has been afforded the personal and structural opportunities to connect with community members. We have become a voice for the community.

REFERENCES

Bottery, M. (2003). The management and mismanagement of trust. *Educational Management Administration & Leadership, 32,* 245–261.

Hands, C. (2005). It's who you know and what you know: The process of creating partnerships between schools and communities. *School Community Journal, 15*(2), 63–84.

Hoy, W. K., & Tschannen-Moran, M. (1999). Five facets of trust: An empirical confirmation in urban elementary schools. *Journal of School Leadership, 9,* 184–208.

Murrell, P. C., Jr. (2001). *The community teacher: A new framework for effective urban teaching.* New York: Teachers College Press.

Noel, J. (2006). Integrating a new teacher education center into a school and its community. *Journal of Urban Learning, Teaching, and Research, 2,* 197–205.

Noel, J. (2010). A critical interrogation of privilege, race, class, and power in a university faculty-urban community relationship. *Urban Review.* DOI 10.1007/s11256-009-0131-4.

Reed, W. A. (2004). A tree grows in Brooklyn: Schools of education as brokers of social capital in low-income neighborhoods. In J. L. Kincheloe, A. Bursztyn, & S. R. Steinberg (Eds.), *Teaching teachers: Building a quality school of urban education* (pp. 65–90). New York: Peter Lang.

Rosenberg, P. M. (1997). Underground discourses: Exploring Whiteness in teacher education. In M. Fine, L. Weis, L. C. Powell, & L. M. Wong (Eds.), *Off White: Readings on race, power, and society* (pp. 79–89). New York: Routledge.

19

The Association of Raza Educators: Community-Based Teacher Organizing and the Development of Alternative Forms of Teacher Collaboration

Miguel Zavala

Limited by the exigencies and regulations of university teacher-education programs, urban teacher educators often struggle with providing and sustaining spaces that further both the educational and political development of their students. Usually, there is little follow-up with these future teachers once they leave teacher education programs or once they become absorbed into the bureaucracy of large urban school districts. Not subject to the social norms and regulations of teacher education programs, the Association of Raza Educators (ARE) can be characterized as an experiment in participatory democracy where educators, driven by the goals of social justice, come together to build communities of struggle with students and parents. This chapter documents some of the teacher-led projects in ARE and the lessons learned, and makes an argument for supporting the mediation of teacher collaboration through teacher-led community-based organizations.

THE IMPORTANCE OF TEACHER COLLABORATION

Educational researchers and practitioners have recognized the value of teacher collaboration as a general strategy for promoting the fertilization of pedagogical ideas, diffusion of knowledge, and cross-curricular implementation among teachers who often find themselves disconnected from each other in what has been amply documented as an isolationist teaching culture (Hobson, 2001). Several researchers have identified key positive aspects of teacher collaboration, such as peer mentorship (Cornu, 2005; Duncan-Andrade, 2007), pedagogical reflection (Burbank & Kauchak, 2002), and personal support (Hargreaves, 1992). Others studies suggest that teacher collaboration is linked to a broader strategy for teacher retention (Smith & Ingersoll, 2004) and student achievement (Goddard, Goddard, & Tschannen-Moran, 2007).

CULTURAL, HISTORICAL, AND INSTITUTIONAL CHALLENGES

Creating the conditions necessary for the development of teacher collaboration will require a significant restructuring of state-sponsored teacher education programs and the organization of public schools, which have historically overburdened teachers by providing little time and resources for cross-dialogue around questions of teaching and learning, peer mentorship, and the building of school–community relations. Nevertheless, alongside the institutional support for teacher collaboration is a requisite change in the profession from an isolationist culture into a collaborative culture (Nias, Southworth, & Yeomans, 1989).

Attempts have been made by universities and school districts to foster teacher collaboration practices via institution-based teacher inquiry groups, peer mentorship, and ongoing professional development. The need, however, for teachers themselves to address questions of pedagogy, curriculum design, and social support has led them to develop teacher networks independent of the formal institutions for which they work. This has enabled them to break away from the isolationist culture present in those institutions and better address local needs while simultaneously engaging in bottom-up forms of collaboration and mentorship.

A fundamental challenge remains for teacher-educators, principals, and other stakeholders interested in the formation and institutional diffusion of teacher collaboration: the formation of *deliberate structures* (Snow-Gerono, 2004) that would enable the development of collaborative practices and cultures. As Burbank and Kauchak (2002) iterated, "the challenge for teacher educators is to create structures both within their programs and within school to provide opportunities for this professional development strategy to develop and grow" (p. 513).

THE ASSOCIATION OF RAZA EDUCATORS (ARE) AS A MODEL OF TEACHER COLLABORATION

Characterized as a community-based organization, ARE was founded in 1994 in response to California's Proposition 187, which sought to deny undocumented immigrants access to public services such as health and education.

FROM THE AUTHOR'S REFLECTIONS

I first met ARE members in 2006 at a scholarship fund-raiser for undocumented students. I began attending their biweekly meetings and was fascinated by the discussions ARE teachers were having about education, social justice, and the role of educators as community organizers. Since then, I have assumed various leadership positions and am currently cochair of the Los Angeles chapter and a representative in the State *Concilio*, which is a secondary leadership structure that addresses cross-chapter work. Immersed in community work through ARE, I have gained a better understanding of the value of community-based organizing while my views of education as social transformation have broadened. Having taught for five years as a middle school teacher in one of the most densely populated areas of urban Los Angeles, I noted that the collaborative experiments other teachers and I had undertaken in developing cross-curricular social justice units were small steps in comparison with the strides being made by ARE teachers.

This project uses an ethnographic approach to documenting the kinds of practices that mediate teacher collaboration within ARE. In this case, ethnography is a useful method of inquiry for exploring the formation of cultural processes over extended periods of time. Ethnographic in its intent, this documentary account uses a diverse set of tools, such as observation, archival documents, interviews, and so forth, as resources for understanding teacher collaboration.

THE ASSOCIATION OF RAZA EDUCATORS:
LEADING ACTIVITIES

With chapters in San Diego, Los Angeles, and Oakland, ARE has initiated a series of teacher-led projects. The diagram presented in figure 19.1 is a visual representation of the evolving relation between four leading activities within ARE: political education, pedagogical development, participatory action research, and community activism.

Although each leading activity encompasses a set of practices, these practices do not grow in isolation and must be viewed in the context of broader ARE goals and organizational structures. For example, whether interviewing parent organizers, attending community forums, reviewing studies, writing position statements, or developing informational brochures for parents, all of these research-specific tasks are undertaken as part of a campaign to ensure that 107th Street Elementary survives. Already on a list of low-performing schools, ARE is concerned that the community school is not appropriated by an outside agency. One of our aims is to educate the local community about privatization generally and the district alternatives specifically, and to organize with the teachers and parents at 107th St. Elementary to ensure that their voices are heard and that they are able to take community control of their school.

In sum, the leading activities and their corresponding practices that take form within ARE are developed in chapter standing committees, which are at the base or heart of ARE work and projects. Thus, any given prac-

• Position Statements   • Policy & Issues Briefs
• Studying Up Research   • ARE Journal, *Regeneración*
                        Participatory
                        Action Research

• Curriculum   • Campaign Development
  Exchange   • Parent and Student Organizing
• Conference   **Pedagogical**   **Community**   • Coalition Building
presentations **Development**   **Activism**   • Community Forums
• Human Rights   • Scholarship Fundraising
  Curriculum
                        Political
                        Education
        • Education Segments   • Noche de Cine
        • ARE Annual Conference   • Reading Circle

Figure 19.1.   Association of Raza Educators (ARE) Leading Activities

tice emerges organically—that is, through the organizational structures of ARE—and is intricately woven with other components, in many instances campaigns and community forums

THE MEDIATION OF POLITICAL EDUCATION IN ARE

The activity of political education will be highlighted in this chapter since it has emerged as a salient concern among ARE members, especially in light of the need to increase awareness of teachers' movements around the world and their responses to assaults on public education.

The significance of mentoring new members by allowing them a space to participate in campaign work and community activism cannot be underestimated. Political education, and any other leading activities within ARE, must be understood as intricately tied to other activities and practices. Many times, the most powerful vehicle for educating ARE teachers about teachers' movements and community activism is achieved through informal discussions with other experienced members and through direct participation in organized struggle.

Political Education Segment

"We must be aware of the political and theoretical underpinnings that inform our teaching," said one ARE member, after our collective reading and discussion of Yeshitela's (2005) "The Right Kind of Medicine." Planned within the Education and Membership Committee, political education segments are designed to address issues of teaching and pedagogy alongside what has been termed *political education*. Broadly, political education entails a critical awareness of historical and political events as they relate to education. Recognizing the shortcomings of teacher education programs that often limit courses to technical aspects such as teaching and learning, ARE has sought to create a space where critical political and social consciousness of historical and geopolitical events is developed and shapes what ARE educators do inside and outside the classroom. Within ARE, political education is mediated by four distinct projects: Political Education Segments, *Noches de Cine* [Movie Nights], Reading Circles, and the ARE Annual Conference (see table 19.1).

Table 19.1.   Association of Raza Educators (ARE), Los Angeles, Political Education Projects

Project	Description
Annual Conference	**Themes** Colonialism and Urban Education (2007) The Struggle for Social Justice in Education (2008) Rethinking Social Justice in Education (2009) Striving for True Praxis in Urban Education (2010)
Reading Circle	**Readings** "Toward a Decolonizing Pedagogy" by Carlos Tejeda "Ideology and Ideological State Apparatuses" by Louis Althusser "The Intellectuals" by Antonio Gramsci "The Right Kind of Medicine" by Omali Yeshitela *Pedagogy of Indignation* by Paulo Freire "Imagining Justice in a Culture of Terror" by Antonia Darder *The Wretched of the Earth* by Frantz Fanon
Noche de Cine	**Films** *The Guerrilla and the Hope: Lucio Cabañas* *El Violin* *La Otra Conquista* *Che, the Movie* *Bastards of the Party*
Meeting Segment	**Topics** Privatization and Corporate Charter Schools The Condition of Undocumented Students Teacher Movements in Latin America, Canada, and the United States

What does political education look like within ARE general meetings? For the most part, political education is mediated by teacher-led presentations and dialogue. The themes are generated out of the context of ARE members' realities and the communities in which they teach. Some of the presentation themes have included the privatization of education, colonialism and education, and teacher movements (see table 19.1). Text from a reading circle may be revisited. Not all presentations, however, are led by ARE teachers. In one instance, a student organizer, who is herself an undocumented immigrant, came to speak on the struggles of undocumented students.

Noche de Cine

Noche de Cine is patterned after the 1950s and 1960s Latin American *revolutionary cinema*, which raised political consciousness by bringing film to the people, making it both accessible and educational. In March of 2009, ARE began the Noche de Cine film series with *The Guerrilla and the Hope: Lucio Cabañas* (see table 19.1). The film depicts the life of Lucio Cabañas, an Oaxacan teacher turned revolutionary whose quote "*Ser Pueblo, Hacer Pueblo, y Estar Con el Pueblo*" [Be the Community, Build Community, and Be with the Community] was used for the 2009 annual conference theme.

Organized by ARE teachers, the film screenings are widely attended by high school students and the local community. Most recently, the Education and Membership Committee has planned the screening of three films, *La Otra Conquista*, *Che: The Movie*, and *Bastards of the Party*, under the theme of Colonialism. These screenings include film viewing and post-film discussion, with historical analysis and context provided by ARE members.

Reading Circles

The first wave of reading circles created an arena for teachers to deepen their understanding of critical social theory, history, and politics by introducing them to critical texts, providing the occasion for in-depth analysis, and for some, a chance to revisit texts as educators rather than college students. Readings are selected because each brings to the fore a discussion of social justice, neocolonialism, and the concept of a decolonizing pedagogy.

Each reading circle is, by design, set up to elicit dialogue and critical analysis among the participants. Because teachers come to the circle having read the text, the space is used to break down the readings in an effort to generate discussion, read against the grain of the text, critique, and pose further questions. Often, teachers begin to outline ways in which the readings can be used to inform their teaching, and lead teachers to question their role as teachers, education as an institution, and what each participant can do to change the realities of their students.

Annual Conference

ARE annual conferences bring together students, teachers, organizers, and community members for an all-day event that involves presentations, performances, keynote speeches, and film screenings. Conference themes have centered on colonialism and urban education, social justice education, and community activism. Each conference has brought together over 500 participants and has included well-known scholars such as Carlos Tejeda, Jeffrey Duncan-Andrade, Donaldo Macedo, Antonia Darder, and Rodolfo Acuña, with community activists such as Mzuri Pambelli, Omali Yeshitela, Sakeenah Shabaaz, and Rosa Clemente.

Like most teacher-led conferences, the diverse set of presentations has addressed curriculum development and pedagogy. The theme of community activism in ARE conferences, however, is more prominent. For example, community-based organizations have enriched the dialogue by presenting their work against military recruiters on high school campuses, police brutality, corporate media and youth culture, immigration policies, the rights of undocumented students, and teacher resistance.

SUCCESSES AND ENDURING STRUGGLES

Constituting *deliberate structures* or organizational spaces in the mediation of teacher collaboration practices is critical. Absent attention to the development of deliberate structures, existing forms of teacher collaboration will most likely disappear once institutions pull their resources or once the local conditions that have led to teachers working together on a particular project are gone. At the heart of this challenge is the question: How do we constitute and sustain organic structures, from the bottom up, especially within or against the tide of reforms, policies, and ideologies that seek to de-professionalize teaching? Political education initiatives are one example of efforts to provide such a structure to ARE members.

The success of ARE projects can be measured by the effect they have on their participants and by the degree to which they obtain ARE-specific goals. More important, the constitution of deliberate structures is primary in the development of alternative forms of teacher collaboration. One can argue that the growth of ARE, with the recent founding of the Los Angeles and Oakland chapters, and the constitution of a California statewide leadership body, the State *Concilio*, as well as the increased membership in all chapters—from 20 to over 100 active members in the past six years—ARE is a flourishing example of a deliberate structure that encourages alternative forms of teacher collaboration.

IMPLICATIONS FOR TEACHERS AND TEACHER EDUCATORS

ARE is an experiment in participatory democracy that seeks to develop alternative forms of teacher collaboration through community organizing for social justice. ARE political education projects provide insight into how teacher-led community organizing can enable other collaborative practices. Thus, teacher educators need to study the ways in which community-based teacher organizing fosters the cultural, curricular, and pedagogical knowledge required of educators working in urban contexts.

REFERENCES

Burbank, M. D., & Kauchak, D. (2002). An alternative model for professional development: Investigations into effective collaboration. *Teaching and Teacher Education, 19*, 499–514.

Cornu, R. L. (2005). Peer mentoring: Engaging pre-service teachers in mentoring one another. *Mentoring & Tutoring: Partnership in Learning, 13*, 355–366.

Duncan-Andrade, J. (2007). Urban teacher development that changes classrooms, curriculum, and achievement. In P. J. Finn & M. E. Finn (Eds.), *Teacher education with an attitude: Preparing teachers to educate working-class students in their collective self-interest* (pp. 173–190). Albany: State University of New York Press.

Goddard, Y. L., Goddard, R. D., & Tschannen-Moran, M. (2007). A theoretical and empirical investigation of teacher collaboration for school improvement and student achievement in public elementary schools. *Teachers College Record, 109*, 877–896.

Hargreaves, A. (1992). Cultures of teaching: A focus for change. In A. Hargreaves & M. G. Fullan (Eds.), *Understanding teacher development* (pp. 216–240). New York: Teachers College Press.

Hobson, D. (2001). Learning with each other: Collaboration in teacher research. In G. Burnaford, J. Fischer, & D. Hobson (Eds.), *Teachers doing research: The power of action through inquiry* (pp. 173–191). Mahwah, NJ: Lawrence Erlbaum.

Nias, J., Southworth, G., & Yeomans, R. (1989). *Staff relationships in primary schools: A study of organizational cultures.* London: Cassell.

Smith, T. M., & Ingersoll, R. M. (2004). What are the effects of induction and mentoring on beginning teacher turnover? *American Educational Research Journal, 41*, 681–714.

Snow-Gerono, J. L. (2004). Professional development in a culture of inquiry: PDS teachers identify the benefits of professional learning communities. *Teaching and Teacher Education, 21*, 241–256.

Yeshitela, O. (2005). The right kind of medicine. In O. Yeshitela (Ed.), *Omali Yeshitela speaks* (pp. 21–54). St. Petersburg, FL: Burning Spear Uhuru Publications.

20

School Improvement: Collaboration for Success

Mary Ellen Freeley, Andrew Ferdinandi, and Paul Pedota

OVERVIEW OF THE PROJECT

In 2007, the St. John's University School of Education and a New York City vocational high school entered into a collaborative effort to change the direction of a persistently struggling school to a school that would successfully meet the academic standards mandated by the No Child Left Behind legislation (NCLB, 2001). The high school—an inner-city school with a population of approximately 1,500 students—did not meet Adequate Yearly Progress (AYP). The student body is 70 percent black or African American and 80 percent male. Twenty percent are identified as students with special needs, 75 percent are at or below the poverty level, and 90 percent meet eligibility for the free or reduced lunch program.

The recently appointed principal of the school reached out to St. John's in an effort to help him (a) bring about positive change in the areas of teaching and learning, (b) improve how teachers and students interact with each other, and (c) clarify the role of the school guidance counselors. To ascertain the needs of the school effectively and successfully, a retreat was planned for all participants. The university faculty who would be the consultation team (CT) were former successful administrators and teachers in New York City who had the expert knowledge and hands-on experience to understand the school's needs and to guide and support change.

The primary purpose of this retreat was to open a conversation where ideas could be expressed in an open and safe environment. This exchange of ideas allowed the CT to better understand the issues, to see how the school leadership viewed the issues and each other, and to establish trust among all participants. Trust alone cannot guarantee success—but in any environment where individuals do not trust one another, there is no chance to improve (Bryk & Schneider, 2003).

The CT did a great deal of listening at the initial meeting to gain an understanding of what the school's needs were. In addition, the individual presenters from the university exhibited consistency, integrity, and concern; fostered an environment for open communication; and presented a willingness to share ideas, which promoted trust among all the participants (Tschannen-Moran, Uline, Hoy, & Mackley, 2000). At the conclusion of the two-day meeting, school staff understood that establishing and maintaining trust was important if the school was to change from failing to succeeding (Bryk & Schneider, 2003), and the CT had an understanding of the issues and expressed genuine concern and a willingness to work with the school leadership. It was also clear that the quality and duration of the CT's professional development program would be an important factor in improving teaching practices as well as having a positive impact on student learning (Hirsch, Koppich, & Knapp, 2001).

DEVELOPMENT AND IMPLEMENTATION OF A PLAN

During the first few visits to the school, through informal observations and conversations, it was apparent that there was a need to change the way teachers viewed students both as individuals and academically, as well as raise the teachers' respect for student ability and by extension raise the expectation of students' performance (Elmore, 1996). In an attempt to accomplish this, the CT began to work with the departmental assistant principals, who are responsible for supervision, in reviewing classroom observation practices and procedures.

A workshop was conducted by the CT on the pre- and postobservation processes to review procedures that would support change in professional practices and would increase the quality of classroom instruction and student learning. For example, we discussed and modeled the use of prior teacher observations (a) to build skills in a professional development approach, and (b) to document areas in continued need of improvement for marginal teachers. Additionally, university faculty emphasized that a positive climate among the staff would help to ensure that people would work in their departments to identify and solve problems (Blasé & Blasé, 2001). Furthermore, individual meetings were conducted with supervisors who requested support from the consultants or whom the principal identified as needing direct CT intervention.

In particular, one assistant principal of a major subject area sought additional consultation time. She was eager to improve her supervisory practices and invited the CT to join her in a classroom observation (with the teacher's agreement) and then to observe her conducting a postobservation conference. Based on those experiences, it was recommended that she utilize an observational rubric with her teachers to ensure that the expectations of the lesson were clearly communicated and aligned to standards and to foster teacher reflection.

One area of the rubric—student engagement—became the focus of her future work with her department. Since the assistant principal identified this as a need common to her teaching staff, the CT created a PowerPoint presentation that the assistant principal could use at a subsequent departmental meeting. The CT suggested that at a future department meeting she ask one teacher who was demonstrating success with student engagement to present some strategies he had found to be successful.

As with all other building supervisors, the assistant principal was encouraged to think of the department meeting as a vehicle for teacher growth and learning. For example, the CT provided also a PowerPoint presentation on differentiated instruction with the suggestion that the teachers include a demonstration of a strategy at one meeting and then solicit feedback from those who utilized it at the next meeting. The CT recommended having staff share their thoughts on how the strategy might be adapted, tweaked, or enhanced to meet the specific needs of their students. The supervisors agreed that this approach would lead to hands-on experiences with differentiated instruction and provide teachers with ownership of the instructional strategies.

Subsequent visits centered on observing the interactions between students and staff as they entered the building, traffic flow, behavior in the hallways prior to class and after the late bell, disruptions to the instructional program, bell-to-bell instruction, and the rapport between students and teachers in their subject classrooms. The CT met frequently with the principal regarding concerns as they emerged and brainstormed with him to seek solutions that he was comfortable with and that would be viable within the culture of his building.

Another area for development was centered on the principal's view of himself as the authority figure in the school, and building confidence in his roles as instructional leader, manager, change agent, communicator, and team leader for program assessment and implementation (Fullan, 2002; Glickman, 2002).

Evidence of the CT's success in the area of principal development was realized at the wrap-up meeting at the conclusion of the school year. Most obvious to the CT was the much-improved level of cleanliness of the building, the quiet and sense of order that pervaded the hallways, and the principal's confidence in himself as the building leader. The principal was emerging as a thoughtful, reflective, and inquisitive professional. His priorities shifted from focusing on a school in need of restructuring to one that was now completing a comprehensive education plan for the following year. Of particular note was the way the principal handled a specific situation upon the CT's arrival and then used that situation as a teachable moment with his assistant principal. Not only was the resolution student focused but also the principal modeled an important lesson for his protégé.

NEXT STEPS

The principal presented four key questions that he hoped to use to move the school further forward:

1. What should our students learn?
2. How will we know they have learned it?
3. What do we do if they did learn it?
4. What do we do if they did not learn it?

He realized that these questions led directly to the issues of measurement and accountability. Thus, a number of suggestions that could be assessed were made by the CT as planning for the next school year got underway:

- Develop student leaders and give them the opportunity to take owner-ship of their school.
- Motivate students to want more from their school experience. This starts with the teachers; teachers must raise the bar; teachers must own the mission and the vision.
- Schoolwide, have all stakeholders identify one specific goal that they would hold themselves accountable for accomplishing.
- Encourage teachers to use a huge K/W/L chart on the side of a class-room wall to demonstrate clearly to the students what they *Know*, *Want to learn*, and record when they *Learned it* (with evidence).
- Develop a syllabus or a calendar of lessons for teachers to ensure continuity and consistency across courses and within a department.
- Have each assistant principal identify one teacher with whom they would work with closely for improvement over a year, and give new teachers a buddy teacher.
- Create a school-oriented visual that could be duplicated, distributed, and prominently displayed to document *where we were*, *what we've accomplished*, and *where do we go next*.
- Enhance outreach and recruitment of students by bringing guidance counselors from feeder schools in for lunch, sending parents and stu-dents to the feeder schools, having the Spotlight students and honors students visit the schools, and hosting community events. All agreed that there were many ways to rebuild the reputation of the school by using small, focused positive steps.
- Introduce a new schoolwide initiative called *Win the Day*. The Guid-ance Department will identify a cohort of students who will receive personalized mentoring in order to help "win their day" by attending all of their classes (including the first and last periods of the day), coming to school daily on time, completing all assignments, and monitoring their own classroom behavior. Through a partnership with the Guidance Department, all staff members will be challenged to set personal goals to win their day as well.

EMPHASIS ON THE ROLE OF THE SCHOOL COUNSELORS

In order to address the principal's concern regarding the school counsel-ing program, a St. John's University professor from the Department of

School Counseling joined the CT team. From the initial meeting with the principal and then with the school counselors, it was clear the principal and the counselors did not see the counselors' work in the same way. The principal was looking for the counselors to take their work to a higher level—that is, to exceed the standard. The counselors felt they were drowning in paperwork and underappreciated by the principal.

After numerous meetings with the consultant, it became clear that there were some positives to build on and some obstacles to overcome. The positives included counselors admitting that things could be better, viewing the consultant as a positive change agent, and respecting the leadership of the assistant principal of guidance who showed a willingness to work on improving school experiences. The three primary obstacles included a lack of authentic enthusiasm for making change, the perception that the counselors were not appreciated, and—most disturbing to the counselors—the belief that decisions were top-down and arbitrary.

The consultant worked with the counselors in a number of venues:

1. Helping them identify problems and own the solutions;
2. Creating a project and working with a buddy counselor to reach out to students;
3. Attending an overnight retreat to learn from other experts in the field;
4. Doubling their efforts to change the school climate by committing to two positive phone calls each week to parents; and
5. Establishing closer relationships with their teacher colleagues through visibility in the building.

IMPACT OF THE SCHOOL–UNIVERSITY COLLABORATION

As a result of the collaboration, the school's yearly Quality Review from the New York City Department of Education cited the following findings regarding what the school does well:

- Students assessed to be in greatest need are first to receive support to improve their progress and performance.

- Staffing and scheduling decisions are based on strong evaluations of individual students' performance and the nature of the program and intervention that they are most likely to require.
- Systems and structures are being implemented that enable the school to function effectively on a day-to-day basis.
- The principal's high expectations are raising the expectations of the entire school community so that goals established are challenging but achievable.
- There are effective and consistently applied procedures in place to encourage and monitor student attendance and tardiness.
- The entire administrative team has a clear vision for procedures and systems to effect change.
- School leaders track the outcome of periodic assessments and other diagnostic measures and use the results to make strategic decisions to modify practices to improve student outcomes.
- There is support and professional development from a university to help meet the needs of teachers and students.

The annual Quality Review also cited a few areas in need of improvement, which included: (a) further develop a schoolwide approach to the objective collecting and interpreting of data; (b) ensure that teachers use data to plan and provide differentiated instruction; (c) further develop effective partnerships with outside entities to support the academic and personal growth of students; and (d) improve the consistency with which teachers record information about individual students and their classes as a whole, as well as evaluate their progress against targets set for improvement.

CONCLUSION

As a result of these findings, the CT plans to focus on the major area in need of improvement—the use and interpretation of data—as we continue our work with the school's staff into the next school year. A professional development program is planned for the entire staff during the summer to increase understanding as to why data are important and how they can be used to drive instruction and support student achievement. All collaborators are committed to the school's motto, *Failure is not an option*, and eager to see continued improvement for the benefit of the students.

REFERENCES

Blasé, J., & Blasé, J. R. (2001). *Empowering teachers: What successful principals do* (2nd ed.). Thousand Oaks, CA: Corwin Press.

Bryk, A. S., & Schneider, B. (2003). Trust in schools: A core resource for school reform. *Educational Leadership, 60*(6), 40–45.

Elmore, R. F. (1996). Getting to scale with good education practice. *Harvard Educational Review, 60,* 1–26.

Fullan, M. (2002). The change leader. *Educational Leadership, 59*(8), 16–20.

Glickman, C. D. (2002). The courage to lead. *Educational Leadership, 59*(8), 41–44.

Hirsch, E., Koppich, J. E., & Knapp, M. S. (2001). *Revisiting what states are doing to improve the quality of teaching: An update on patterns and trends.* (Working Paper). Seattle: Center for the Study of Teaching and Policy, University of Washington, in conjunction with the National Conference of State Legislatures.

No Child Left Behind Act of 2001, Pub. L. No. 107–110.

Tschannen-Moran, M., Uline, C., Hoy, A. W., & Mackley, T. (2000). Creating smarter schools through collaboration. *Journal of Educational Administration, 28,* 247–271.

IV

GLOBAL PERSPECTIVES ON
TEACHER EDUCATION

Among many others whose research focuses on global trends, Baker and LeTendre (2005) explored recent changes in globalization from an educational perspective. They claimed that national differences and global similarities coexist as the future of schools and schooling take on a more global characteristic. Their analysis continued with the following statement.

> In spite of the fact that nations (and their subunits, provinces, and states) have immediate political and fiduciary control over schooling, education as an institution has become a global enterprise. . . . Ideas and demands and expectations for what schools can, and should, do for a society have developed well beyond any particular national context. (p. 3)

In our effort to present innovative preservice and inservice teacher educational practices, we have also decided to look beyond one particular national context and feature initiatives from around the globe. Three chapters in section IV represent Canadian programs. Geoffrey B. Soloway, Patricia A. Poulin, and Corey S. Mackenzie discuss successful ways of integrating mindfulness training into initial teacher education programs at the University of Toronto and at the University of Manitoba. Next, Anne Chodakowski and Kieran Egan of Simon Fraser University, Vancouver, outline the role of imaginations and emotions in preservice teacher education. Later in the section, Lorenzo Cherubini of Brock University describes an innovative model of community-based collaborative teacher development practices to enhance aboriginal student learning and to heal open wounds caused by previous, less culturally responsive practices.

Additionally, Ian Matheson, Mairi McAra, and Thomas Hamilton invite us to witness the transformation of teacher induction practices in Scotland, which, as they noted, was once little short of scandalous and is now world class. Tasha Bleistein and Tao Rui take the readers to a Chinese minority region where cross-cultural cooperation leads to enhanced professional development for inservice teachers. Last but not least, Liz Barber along with her colleagues Tom Smith, Alexander Erwin, Vanessa Duren-Winfield, Tenika Walker, Brian Mosleley, and James Worsley from North Carolina A&T State University as well as the collaborating teachers from the Domasi Demonstration Primary School, in Zomba, Malawi, offer a powerful account of the participatory action research they developed collaboratively to support teacher development.

REFERENCE

Baker, D., & LeTendre, G. (2005). *National differences, global similarities: World culture and the future of schooling.* Stanford, CA: Stanford University Press.

21

Preparing New Teachers for the Full Catastrophe of the Twenty-First-Century Classroom: Integrating Mindfulness Training into Initial Teacher Education

Geoffrey B. Soloway, Patricia A. Poulin, and
Corey S. Mackenzie

It is 8:30 on Wednesday morning. Thirty-five teacher candidates are sitting in a circle and the bell rings. This bell is different from the regular school bell. The chime is rung three times to signal the beginning of a group mindfulness practice, which is the way each class starts. Teacher candidates are invited to settle into their chairs and to notice thoughts, emotions, and sensations in the body. They are instructed to cultivate acceptance in response to whatever they notice, moment by moment, by maintaining the focus of their attention on the breath.

Sitting in a classroom without desks is already a foreign experience for many. Now they are intentionally entering stillness and silence in the company of their peers and instructors. Dubiousness arises; mind waves come to shore repeatedly: "Why are we sitting in a circle? What's the point of this exercise? What does it have to do with education? I can't stay focused on the breath. I am not very good at this."

As their mindfulness practices build, these teacher candidates learn that during stressful times it is possible to connect with a slow, still awareness that lies beneath the surface of moment-to-moment experiences; an awareness that remains undisturbed, able to witness the regular flow of thoughts, sensations, and emotions—and then let them go. The chime rings again, signaling the end of the practice and the beginning of a discussion about what was noticed and how this relates to teaching and learning.

BEGINNINGS AND BACKGROUND

It was a spark of synchronicity that brought together an assistant professor and two graduate students. A new elective course was being designed within the initial teacher education program at the Ontario Institute for Studies in Education of the University of Toronto (OISE/UT) entitled Stress and Burnout: Teacher and Student Applications. This new class intended to address the problems of burnout and attrition among beginning teachers, many of whom decide to leave the profession early in their career due to their inability to cope with the increasing complexity and emotional demands of the classroom (Montgomery & Rupp, 2005).

The program goal was to develop a curriculum of study that would help teacher candidates cultivate competencies for thriving and coping with the modern demands of being a teacher. A program of study was created with mindfulness at its core. Mindfulness-based interventions are increasingly available in North American and European health-care institutions. Mindfulness training strengthens one's capacity to pay attention, nonjudgmentally, to one's thoughts, feelings, and body sensations, thereby enabling a more skillful response to life's challenges. Kabat-Zinn (1990) developed and evaluated the first structured mindfulness-based program (Mindfulness-Based Stress Reduction, MBSR). Since then, a growing body of empirical evidence has emerged supporting the efficacy of MBSR programs in reducing stress and improving physical and mental health outcomes (Grossman, Niemann, Schmidt, & Walach, 2004).

Under the umbrella of education, there was a need for and opportunity to translate this work for teacher candidates. Rather than simply providing teacher candidates with a traditional MBSR program, the program was adapted in two ways. First, a formal wellness component was added to emphasize not only the need to reduce stress but also to enhance well-being. Second, methods of practicing mindfulness in the classroom were incorporated. In this way, working with teachers candidates also introduces the potential of providing them with strategies for infusing mindful wellness into their classrooms for their students' benefit. The core curriculum created for the Stress and Burnout course is called Mindfulness-Based Wellness Education (MBWE).

MINDFULNESS-BASED WELLNESS
EDUCATION IN PRACTICE

The three authors taught MBWE for the first time within the framework of a nine-week (thirty-six-hour) elective course in an initial teacher education program at OISE/UT. Since then, the course has evolved to being offered twice each year. Furthermore, the MBWE course has been continually evaluated using both quantitative and qualitative methods in order to better understand its impact and to support its evolution.

The primary objectives of the course are to help teacher candidates do the following:

1. Enhance their ability to respond (versus react) to stressful situations both within and outside of the classroom in order to reduce their levels of stress and improve their health;
2. Explore their understanding and experience of various aspects of wellness; and
3. Learn teaching strategies for bringing mindfulness and wellness into their classrooms.

The first objective is met through the introduction of mindfulness via both formal and informal practices. Formal mindfulness practices are twenty minutes in length and are similar to those used in MBSR programs, including the body scan, mindful yoga, and mindful sitting meditations focusing on the breath. Teacher candidates participate in formal mindfulness practices in class and also at home four days per week for twenty minutes, and receive a guided version of each practice on a CD to support their homework practice. Teacher candidates are also encouraged to *bring mindfulness to life* by integrating present-moment awareness into everyday common activities such as eating, speaking, listening, and by paying particular attention to emotions and common thought patterns.

The second objective is met by introducing teacher candidates to a wellness wheel. As shown in figure 21.1, the wellness wheel has mindfulness in the center surrounded by seven dimensions of wellness, including physical, emotional, social, mental, ecological, vocational, and spiritual.

Figure 21.1.   Wellness Wheel

The wellness wheel serves as a framework to explore a new dimension of wellness each week, through the lens of mindfulness. Teacher candidates use arts-based methods to create a piece of their wellness wheel to illustrate their learning through collage, painting, or drawing. At the end of the course they have a whole wheel, representing their personal multidimensional wellness.

Finally, the third objective is met by introducing, each week, discussion of a mindful teaching strategy for the classroom. For example, teacher candidates role-play challenging communications with parents using skills learned in the course. They also learn to use the wellness wheel for classroom planning and to develop an integrative curriculum.

EXPERIENTIAL CURRICULUM

To complement in-class and at-home formal and informal mindfulness practices, teacher candidates receive a set of readings consisting of key theoretical articles on mindfulness, wellness, and teaching from books such as Kabat-Zinn's (1990) *Full Catastrophe Living*, Palmer's (1998) *The Courage to Teach*, and Miller's (1996) *The Holistic Curriculum*. Teacher candidates also receive a wellness workbook that is color coded to the theme of wellness being explored that week and includes a space for teacher candidates to record their observations and insights from the week in relation to mindfulness, wellness, and teaching.

MBWE differs from a regular academic course as it is not lecture based. Rather than solely reading about stress and strategies for reducing it, the course is highly experiential, which helps create a practice-based body of experience for teacher candidates to use both within the classroom and throughout their lives. Experiential and practice-based learning is now emphasized within teacher education (Ball & Forzani, 2009) because it addresses the problem of enactment that arises in the space between theory and practice, "Learning how to think and act in ways that achieve one's intentions is difficult, particularly if knowledge is embedded in the practice itself" (Darling-Hammond, 2006, p. 37). Cultivating capacities for mindfulness and wellness during their training, teacher candidates will be better able to transfer this knowledge into their practicum experiences and future professional endeavors. The following quote from a teacher candidate's workbook illustrates this point:

> I really do think practicing mindfulness aided me in this practicum. There were times when I felt I was getting upset and I went to my breathing. This became like a natural reaction because of me practicing breathing each day. Because of this "tool" my stress levels feel as if they have lowered significantly, and allowed me to be a more mindful teacher.

Many other teacher candidates also commented on the practicality of the course and suggested that it be a required rather than elective part of the initial teacher education curriculum.

WHAT WE DISCOVERED

Elsewhere we fully discuss the results of our qualitative and quantitative evaluations of the program (Poulin, Mackenzie, Soloway, & Karaoylas, 2008). Here, we highlight its effectiveness. After the first year of implementation, the initial results of our research demonstrated that in comparison to teacher trainees in control classrooms, those taking the Stress and Burnout course exhibited significantly greater increases in mindfulness, life satisfaction, and teaching self-efficacy. A replication study with a longer follow-up assessment and a qualitative component not only provided additional support of our earlier findings, but it also demonstrated that improvements in mindfulness predicted improved teaching self-efficacy and physical health ratings (Poulin, 2009).

IMPLICATIONS

The introduction of mindfulness-based strategies into teacher education and K–12 education is in motion and, in turn, the MBWE program continues to evolve. The initial intention for the course and research was centered on reducing stress and enhancing wellness in order to reduce the risk of burn-out and attrition among beginning teachers. However, after teaching the course a number of times, new insights have revealed wider implications for mindfulness training within initial teacher education. For example, after returning from practicum, teacher candidates are reporting an important link between their learning in MBWE and their experience in the classroom:

> My attitude and mind-set can be picked up by the students and when I present myself as a balanced and mindful teacher, the students will respond in a calmer manner. The basics of this course can be used to approach classroom management from an entirely different perspective.

Jennings and Greenberg (2009) identified social and emotional competence (SEC) and well-being of the teacher as an integral part of cultivating a healthy teacher–student relationship and effective classroom management skills. Further, the growing research investigating the impact of mindfulness practice with children and youth (Burke, 2010) suggested that mindfulness training for preservice teachers will extend beyond a preventive approach to teacher stress and burnout. Mindful teachers will also bring knowledge, skills, and strategies into the classroom for students. Graduates from our program have already begun doing so and have found it helpful as a best practice (Poulin, 2009).

MOVING FORWARD MINDFULLY

Over the years, the impact of bringing mindful wellness into initial teacher education has become more complex and meaningful in ways we did not originally foresee. For example, an emerging theme is that teacher candidates completing MBWE go through a deeper personal transformation that informs their overall pedagogy and teacher identity:

> Often people say "practice makes perfect." In this course we have learned that "practice allows us not to be perfect." From this course and its practices and concepts I have been able to understand that [by] being mindful throughout my life, I can embrace both the positive and negative events that happen. This allows me to continually learn, a concept that summarizes education in its simplest form.

MBWE prepares teacher candidates for thriving within stressful classrooms as well as providing them with new pedagogical perspectives, strategies, and practices for creating and supporting an inclusive and calm classroom community. To conclude, in 1890, James stated in the *Principles of Psychology*, "The faculty of voluntarily bringing back a wandering attention, over and over again, is the very root of judgment, character and will. . . . An education which should improve this faculty would be an education par excellence. But it is easier to define this ideal then to give practical directions for bringing it about" (p. 424).

Current neuroscience research suggests that mindfulness training may be a practical direction to build the faculty of attention (Jha, Krompinger, & Baime, 2007), which would not only support learning within curricular content areas but would also serve the expanding curricular objectives related to social and emotional learning, character education, healthy schools, global citizenship education, and environmental education. As the overall demands of teaching continue to increase, we see that mindfulness training for teachers will no longer be a program that breaks the mold of teacher education but one that contributes to creating a new mold of educating teachers.

FINAL REFLECTIONS

Cycles of harmful stress reactivity perpetuate themselves in the minds and bodies within our schools and systems of education. MBWE provides an opportunity to break this cycle by providing teacher candidates with the skills they need to become mindful teachers and to create mindful classrooms. Mindfulness does not necessarily bring immediate change to challenging circumstances in our lives and classrooms; however, it does provide us with the freedom to choose the way we respond to whatever comes our way, and that is incredibly powerful and liberating—for teachers, for students, for all of us.

> Wednesday morning arrives again and a chime signals the beginning of the group silent practice, the beginning of learning to greet each moment with fresh eyes. These moments of stillness invite everyone in the circle to a greater awareness of automatic reactions, judgments, and biases that typically go unnoticed. As instructors, we sit as part of the circle, engaged in the same learning process of calming the mind and opening the heart, gaining insight into our authentic selves. As the formal practice concludes, the informal practice of relating to ourselves and each other with patience and kindness continues.

REFERENCES

Ball, D. L., & Forzani, F. (2009). The work of teaching and the challenge for teacher education. *Journal of Teacher Education, 60*, 497–511.

Burke, C. A. (2010). Mindfulness-based approaches with children and adolescents: A preliminary review of current research in an emergent field. *Journal of Child and Family Studies, 19*, 133–144.

Darling-Hammond, L. (2006). *Powerful teacher education: Lessons from exemplary programs.* San Francisco: Jossey-Bass.

Grossman, P., Niemann, L., Schmidt, S., & Walach, H. (2004). Mindfulness-based stress reduction and health benefits: A meta-analysis. *Journal of Psychosomatic Research, 57*, 35–43.

James, W. (1890). *Principles of psychology.* New York: Dover.

Jennings, P. A., & Greenberg, M. T. (2009). The prosocial classroom: Teacher social and emotional competence in relation to student and classroom outcomes. *Review of Educational Research, 79*, 491–525.

Jha, A. P., Krompinger J., & Baime, M. J. (2007). Mindfulness training modifies subsystems of attention. *Cognitive, Affective & Behavioural Neuroscience, 7*, 109–119.

Kabat-Zinn, J. (1990). *Full catastrophe living: Using the wisdom of your body and mind to face stress, pain, and illness.* New York: Dell.

Miller, J. P. (1996). *The holistic curriculum.* Toronto, ON, Canada: OISE Press.

Montgomery, C., & Rupp, A. A. (2005). A meta-analysis for exploring the diverse causes and effects of stress in teachers. *Canadian Journal of Education, 28*, 458–486.

Palmer, P. J. (1998). *The courage to teach: Exploring the inner landscape of a teacher's life*. San Francisco: Jossey-Bass.

Poulin, P. A. (2009). *Mindfulness-based wellness education: A longitudinal evaluation with students in initial teacher education*. PhD diss., University of Toronto, ON, Canada.

Poulin, P. A., Mackenzie, C. S., Soloway, G., & Karaoylas, E. C. (2008). Mindfulness training as an evidence-based approach to reducing stress and promoting well-being among human services professionals. *International Journal of Health Promotion and Education, 46*, 72–80.

22

Engaging Imaginations and Emotions in Preservice Teacher Education

Anne Chodakowski and Kieran Egan

THE EDUCATIONAL CHALLENGE

What if there were a way to make most students, most of the time, really care about what they were learning, while also improving their academic achievement? What if teacher education could offer preservice teachers tangible ways in which they could help bring about these educational outcomes, while also routinely stimulating their own understanding of and engagement with content they are to teach? There is indeed a way in which these educational *what ifs* can be achieved: The key is to regularly engage and stimulate the imaginations and emotions of learners.

According to numerous educational researchers, most current teacher education programs are doing less than an exemplary job of helping preservice teachers develop a deep understanding of the three cornerstones of teacher education: subject matter, pedagogy, and contexts (Cochran-Smith & Zeichner, 2005; Education Commission of the States, 2003; Wilson & Floden, 2003; Wilson, Floden, & Ferrini-Mundy, 2001).

The goal of our research and our innovative programs is to describe some of the ways in which one teacher education program has been successful in increasing teachers' subject matter understanding and pedagogical success by emphasizing the role of the imagination and emotions in learning, for both students in schools as well as for preservice teachers in teacher education programs. A review of the teacher education literature suggests that students' imaginations have not generally been the focus of teacher education programs (Richardson, 2001; Sikula, Buttery, & Guyton, 1996). Our educational challenge is to envision and forge a new mold for a teacher education curriculum: one in which the imaginations and emotions of students and preservice teachers is made central, so that their learning is both richer and more satisfying.

THE EDUCATIONAL CONTEXT

The Imaginative Education Research Group (IERG), based at Simon Fraser University (SFU) in Vancouver, Canada, was established in 2001. It is an umbrella organization for educational research, publication, international conferences, workshops and lectures, collaborative educational projects, web pages (www.ierg.net), visiting scholars, graduate students, and the creation and dissemination of imaginative educational resources.

The IERG is also regularly involved in numerous inservice teacher development projects, ranging from one-day workshops to long-term relationships with schools that aim to make students' imaginative engagement central to their education. (See www.ierg.net/LUCID/ and www.ierg.net/LiD for descriptions of two of IERG's more comprehensive projects.)

More recently, the IERG has also been concerned with how teacher education, at both the undergraduate and graduate levels, might be transformed so that the imaginative engagement of learners is made central to the educational process. The recommendations we make about how teacher education might be transformed to make the imagination of students and preservice teachers central to their learning are based on evidence gained from these contexts.

THE THEORY OF IMAGINATIVE EDUCATION (IE)

Imagination is conceptualized as the capacity to think of the possible, rather than simply the actual (White, 1990). The imagination seems also necessarily tied to emotions (Warnock, 1976); acts of imagination evoke some degree of emotional engagement. But this is an obviously limited explanation; the imagination does not satisfyingly lend itself to pithy definitions. At least at some level, then, we must also recognize the messiness inherent in the imagination (but, for a focused attempt to add clarity to the concept for educational purposes, see *A Very Short History of Imagination*, n.d.).

While current educational practice tends to assume that young children's understanding is based—at least initially—on the immediate, the concrete, and the actual, imaginative education draws attention to the fact that the things that most stimulate young students' emotional and imaginative engagement include, rather, the strange, exotic, distant, and wonderful. Talking animals, pirates, and star warriors are more evident in students' imaginative lives than are the structure of their neighborhoods. Such simple observations lead proponents of IE to recognize different ways of engaging students in learning from those currently dominant.

Our work is based largely, but not exclusively, on the conceptual research published in Egan (1997), in part built upon Vygotsky's work (1987–1999). It makes general recommendations about the imagination and emotions and also specifies pedagogical strategies that allow for students' increased imaginative and emotional engagement with the curriculum.

Like Vygotsky (1987–1999), we recognize that children's understanding changes in important ways as they are exposed to and adopt the various kinds of meaning-making that are a part of the larger culture in which they participate. Following Vygotsky, we call these *cognitive tools*. For example, one cognitive tool that is used by people in oral cultures worldwide is the story: Stories, fictional and nonfictional, allow us to encode events in ways that are both vivid and memorable. The cognitive tools one uses are culturally mediated, which means that given a culture that uses a wide variety of cognitive tools, any individual in that culture has access to and has the opportunity to acquire those particular cognitive tools.

Another key feature of IE theory is that sets of cognitive tools accumulate to develop somewhat distinct *kinds of understanding*. This means that one develops new kinds of understanding as part of the process of gaining mastery of his or her constituent cognitive tools. For example, with *somatic* understanding, we make meaning primarily by way of our bodies and emotions, humor, musicality (rhythm and pattern), and intentional gesturing. As children come to understand and use oral language consistently, they develop *mythic* understanding and its associated cognitive tools, such as story, binary opposites, metaphor, image, rhyme and rhythm, role-play, and jokes.

Older children develop, along with literacy, *romantic* understanding, and so begin to gain mastery of its cognitive tools including narrative, association with heroes, extremes and limits, as well as collecting and organizing. The use of theoretic thinking, commonly associated with the disciplines, characterizes *philosophic* understanding and its cognitive tools of using metanarrative, anomalies, and alternative schemes. Finally, we use *ironic* understanding with its reflexive focus on language and meaning when we can understand that each of these kinds of understanding is appropriate in various contexts but also know that meaning itself is never complete (Egan, 1997).

IE IN TEACHER EDUCATION

Imaginative teacher education, then, has two main goals: (a) preservice teachers' understanding of various ways in which they might best engage their students imaginatively (by using a range of cognitive tools to help students develop various kinds of understanding), and (b) their own continued imaginative development. Clearly, the achievement of the second goal is, at least to some degree, implicated in the achievement of the first. But because most preservice teachers in such a program are unlikely to have had much, if any, experience of education that has deliberately attempted to foster their own imaginative development, it is unlikely that most preservice teachers will have kept each kind of understanding as "alive" or vibrant as might be ideal.

The IERG's teacher education work, including both teacher education program involvement and teacher development, has tended to focus on teachers' understanding of various ways in which they might best engage their students imaginatively, and some degree of pedagogical mastery in doing so. Curriculum documents and the instructional approaches used by more typical teacher education programs do not tend to draw preservice teachers' attention to the importance of students' imaginative and emotional engagement with the content they are to learn or to give teachers examples or experiences of how they might best do so.

Our approach is unique. Certainly, our preservice teachers in British Columbia must be familiar with the documents that outline the provincially mandated curriculum and specific understandings and abilities that students are expected to achieve. However, in their planning and teaching, we ask them to consider curricular questions and engage in pedagogical experimentation that differs significantly from those of more typical programs. Preservice teachers' first pedagogical challenge is to identify the imaginative and emotional importance of the topic, for both themselves and their students.

Engaging Imaginatively

With a fifth-grade unit on human body systems, for example, we begin by asking preservice teachers to identify the significance of the topic. Why should we care about human circulation? What is amazing about digestion? How is the skeletal system a thing of wonder? To this end, we might ask them to investigate how a particular system compares with those of other mammals, or to imagine shrinking down to experience the complexity of noises, movements, transformations in color, texture, and function, as the system carries out its tasks.

We also ask preservice teachers to evoke an image or metaphor that best captures the marvelous aspect of the system, locate puzzles and mysteries about our bodies' functioning, and find patterns between it and other animals' functions, and so on. Activities such as these help preservice teachers imaginatively engage with a topic and identify particular cognitive tools that can lead to students' increased imaginative engagement.

Most fifth-grade students will also have at least some familiarity with and confidence using the cognitive tools of romantic understanding as well. We expect preservice teachers preparing to teach an imaginative unit on body systems to be familiar with various romantic cognitive tools they could use to engage students imaginatively. We therefore ask preservice teachers to identify heroic qualities within the topic. What historical figures—such as William Harvey (1578–1657)—or contemporary heroes are associated with particular systems of the body?

What aspect of the system could students study in exhaustive detail? For example, when teaching human digestion, we may explore what the actual length of the colon is when stretched out. What are the extremes and limits of each system that students might find exciting, troubling, inspiring, and so on? Student learners could research who the first person was to survive a heart transplant or what was the greatest amount of food consumed by an individual in one sitting. Preservice teachers also practice using other *romantic* cognitive tools, such as collecting and organizing, revolt and idealism, and human strengths and emotions, and consider how they might be effectively used to engage students' imaginations.

Story Structuring

The second essential aspect of imaginative planning is curriculum selection. In order to imaginatively engage students, teachers do not simply use various cognitive tools randomly, as a grab bag of activities. Rather, an imaginative unit should be organized so that it is a coherent whole: the initial tension or wonder of the unit should be developed by way of particular cognitive tools meant to advance the unit's narrative structure and eventually resolved by the unit's conclusion.

Preservice teachers must also practice thinking about the topics they will teach as stories and consider which particular activities help their students engage with a unit's story. This necessarily means that teachers should include in their planning only those activities that will build an engaging story and discard those that may be distracting. We have found that developing a unit as a story can be challenging for some inexperienced teachers; however, it seems that imaginative education is more effective when it allows for rich engagement over a sustained period of time. Many preservice teachers take to it like ducks to water, saying this approach allows them to teach in ways they have always thought most interesting.

Our general approach to imaginative planning is summarized in our planning frameworks, which we have developed for each of *mythic*, *romantic*, and *philosophic* understanding. Each framework is organized around five teacher tasks, with explanatory questions. A basic framework for mythic understanding is as follows:

1. Locating importance
   What is emotionally engaging about this topic? How can it evoke wonder? Why should it matter to us?

2. Shaping the lesson or unit

Teaching shares some features with news reporting. Just as the reporter's aim is to select and shape events to bring out clearly their meaning and emotional importance for readers or listeners, so your aim as a teacher is to present your topic in a way that engages the emotions and imaginations of your students. To do so, consider which of the following dimensions of your students' imaginative and emotional lives can be used to shape your lesson or unit—all related to the skills good reporters work with:

2.1. Finding the story:

What is the story on the topic? How can you shape the content to reveal its emotional significance?

2.2. Finding binary opposites:

What abstract and affective binary concepts best capture the wonder and emotion of the topic? What are the opposing forces in your story?

2.3. Finding images:

What parts of the topic most dramatically embody the binary concepts? What image best captures that dramatic contrast?

2.4. Employing additional cognitive tools of mythic understanding:

What kinds of activities might employ other cognitive tools in your students' toolkits? Consider:

- Puzzles and mystery: How could students explore some aspects of the mystery attached to the topic? What puzzles might they wonder about?
- Metaphor: How might students employ metaphor in deepening their understanding of the topic?
- Jokes and humor: Could students learn—and create their own—jokes about the topic? How might they expand their understanding through play with what is humorous about it?
- Rhyme, rhythm, and pattern: Are there patterns in the topic students could play with? What activities might draw attention to rhyme, rhythm, and pattern?
- Games, drama, and play: How can students engage in games, drama, and play in learning about the topic?
- Embryonic tools of romantic understanding: Consider ways to engage students with the heroic and human dimensions of the topic. What kinds of activities might reveal the extremes? How

can these aspects draw students forward in their thinking about the topic?

2.5. Drawing on the tools of somatic understanding: How might students use some of the toolkit of somatic understanding in learning about the topic? How might their senses, emotions, musicality, and so on be deployed?

3. Resources

What resources can you use to learn more about the topic and to shape your story? What resources are useful in creating activities?

4. Concluding

How does the story end? How can the conflict set up between binary opposites be resolved in a satisfying way? Alternatively, what new questions emerge as students make sense of these opposing forces? What aspect of the topic might draw students forward in wonder?

5. Evaluating

How can one know whether the topic has been understood, its importance grasped, and the content learned?

More-detailed versions of our planning frameworks, including both original and revised versions, and accompanying curricular examples are also available (www.ierg.net/teaching/plan-frameworks/index.html).

Effective planning is a necessary but not a sufficient component of imaginative teaching. We also attempt to foster our preservice teacher's imaginative consideration of education, themselves as teachers, their students, and the curriculum in many other ways. For example, we aim to give them ample opportunities to witness, experience, discuss, and critique a wide variety of imaginative educational contexts. We challenge them and ourselves to consider the teacher education curriculum imaginatively by viewing a variety of educational theories and debates using the tools of various kinds of understanding. We also try to use cognitive tools from different kinds of understanding as regularly as possible in our own teaching practice.

EDUCATIONAL OUTCOMES

While students' imaginations have not generally been the focus of teacher education programs (Richardson, 2001; Sikula et al., 1996), a growing body of research indicates the educational potential of this approach. Teachers using procedures that engage students' imaginations document the effectiveness of structuring lessons around cognitive tools and employing story structure in shaping lessons and units of study. This is evidenced by both increased student engagement and improved academic achievement. While this is obviously educationally beneficial to all students, teachers often note the dramatic responses of those students who have been more disengaged from their academics, as Fettes (in press) reported with students participating in an imaginative and culturally inclusive approach to oral language development:

> Students who were normally disengaged from classroom activities began to show signs of genuine interest, willingly participating in group discussions and games, and often displaying insights and abilities that went well beyond the expectations of their teachers. We also heard from parents who commented on the unusual level of enthusiasm expressed by their children for what was happening in school. (p. 26)

Similar results have been reported by teachers using imaginative principles and practices in a wide range of educational contexts, including those working with at-risk youth, in classrooms with a significant population of First Nations students, in private school settings, and in online science lessons (Judson, 2008).

Clearly teacher reports of students' increased engagement and improved academic achievement provide only one picture of the educational whole. However, it is worth noting some commonalities in the claims of teachers who are exploring the potential of imaginative education in their classrooms. Teachers regularly report that they are "amazed at the success" they have experienced after experimenting with various aspects of the principles and practices of imaginative education (Pamela Hagen, personal communication, January 20, 2010); they also commonly feel some sense of professional renewal about experimenting further with imaginative education's ability to bring about increased student engagement and academic achievement.

Additional research points to the potential of imaginative teacher education to both improve the depth and breadth of preservice teachers' content understanding of the P–12 curriculum as well as bring about pedagogical action that can make student learning richer and more emotionally satisfying. Fettes (2005), for example, suggested that preservice teachers in his imaginative education cohort—while needing significant support in the development of their own imaginative capacities as teachers—responded enthusiastically to the notions of making curricula more imaginatively and emotionally engaging. Compton (2006) described supporting preservice teachers' development of their own somatic and mythic understanding and their experimentation with imaginative planning as successful and highly satisfying. She also noted that preservice teachers created achievable cross-curricular units that were *exciting and inspiring* for both the preservice teachers and their cooperating teachers.

CONCLUSIONS

We continue to develop our program in an attempt to improve efficacy and respond to changing contextual needs. We aim to conduct rigorous long-term research that seeks to answer these, as well as additional, questions: How effectively can we assess a clear relationship between imaginative teaching and improved student achievement? How might our program and approaches be limited or actually anti-imaginative? What kind of support can we provide to program graduates who have become teachers and to faculty who aim to reach their own imaginative teaching potential? How can we use knowledge from other disciplines and paradigms to keep us thinking about and imaginatively experimenting with education in general, and teacher education in particular?

From what our preliminary work with preservice teachers indicates, and what practicing teachers continue to tell us about imaginative education's potential, the future looks, at once, challenging and tremendously exciting.

REFERENCES

A very short history of imagination. (n.d.). Retrieved March 10, 2010, from http://www.ierg.net/assets/documents/ideas/History-of-Imagination.pdf

Cochran-Smith, M., & Zeichner, K. M. (Eds.). (2005). *Studying teacher education: The report of the AERA panel on research and teacher education.* Washington, DC: American Educational Research Association.

Compton, V. (2006, July). *Perched on the outside of the box, clinging to threads of familiarity: Incubating imagination through meditation practice in teacher education.* Paper presented at the fourth International Conference on Imagination and Education, Vancouver, BC. Retrieved November 1, 2008, from http://dev.papers.ierg.net/index.php?-table=papers&conference_id=2&-action=browse&-cursor=69&-skip=60&-limit=30&-mode=list

Education Commission of the States (ECS). (2003). *Eight questions on teacher preparation: What does the research say? A summary of the findings.* Denver, CO: Author.

Egan, K. (1997). *The educated mind: How cognitive tools shape our understanding.* Chicago, IL: University of Chicago Press.

Fettes, M. (2005). Imaginative transformation in teacher education. *Teaching Education, 16*(1), 3–11.

Fettes, M. (in press). Imagination and cultural inclusion in oral language development. *Language Awareness.*

Judson, G. (Ed). (2008). *Teaching 360°: Effective learning through the imagination.* Rotterdam, Netherlands: Sense Publishing.

Richardson, V. (Ed.). (2001). *Handbook of research on teaching* (4th ed.). Washington, DC: American Educational Research Association.

Sikula, J., Buttery, T. J., & Guyton, E. (Eds.). (1996). *Handbook of research on teacher education* (2nd ed.). New York: Macmillan.

Vygotsky, L. (1987–1999). *The collected works of L. S. Vygotsky.* New York: Plenum.

Warnock, M. (1976). *Imagination.* London: Faber.

White, A. R. (1990). *The language of imagination.* Oxford, UK: Blackwell.

Wilson, S., & Floden, R. (2003). *Creating effective teachers: Concise answers to hard questions: An addendum to the report "Teacher preparation research: Current knowledge, gaps, and recommendations."* Washington, DC: ERIC Clearinghouse on Teaching and Teacher Education.

Wilson, S., Floden, R. E., & Ferrini-Mundy, J. (2001). *Teacher preparation research: Current knowledge, gaps, and recommendations.* Seattle, WA: Centre for the Study of Teaching and Policy.

23

Teacher Induction in Scotland: Once Little Short of Scandalous, Now World Class

Ian Matheson, Mairi McAra, and Thomas Hamilton

Scotland's approach to the induction of newly qualified teachers (NQTs) was described as *world class* in its 2007 report by the Organisation for Economic Co-operation and Development (OECD) (Scottish Executive Education Department, 2007). Yet only seven years earlier the McCrone Committee, set up by the Scottish government (known at the time as the Scottish Executive) to investigate conditions of service for teachers, called the previous arrangements for teachers' probationary service "little short of scandalous." What had changed to merit such contrasting judgments?

After completing their university program of Initial Teacher Education (ITE), newly qualified teachers become provisionally registered with the General Teaching Council for Scotland (GTCS) and then serve a probationary period before becoming eligible for full registration. During this period, they must demonstrate that they have progressed from meeting the Standard for Initial Teacher Education (SITE) to attaining the Standard for Full Registration (SFR), which sets out the competencies expected of a fully registered teacher. These are defined in terms of Professional Knowledge and Understanding, Professional Skills and Abilities and, in an ambitious innovation not found in many such standards elsewhere, Professional Values and Personal Commitment.

WHERE WE WERE

Before 2002, there was no formalized induction scheme for NQTs in Scotland. New teachers simply applied for posts on the open market, and when fortunate enough to obtain one, served a two-year probationary period, at the end of which the head teacher either recommended the teacher for full registration, or otherwise if performance was felt to be unsatisfactory. During the 1990s, with full-time, permanent posts hard to obtain, the result was an unpredictable experience, often with short-term contracts in multiple schools, no structured support, and indeed no support of any kind unless the teacher were appointed to a school with able and helpful colleagues. This was the system condemned by the McCrone Committee in its report in 2000 (SEED, 2000).

WHERE WE ARE NOW

It was transformed, even revolutionized, by the introduction of the Teacher Induction Scheme (TIS) as part of the "Teachers' Agreement: A Teaching Profession for the 21st Century" (TP21) (SEED, 2001). This was a remarkable tripartite agreement between the Scottish Executive (now known as the Scottish Government), the local authorities as the main employers of teachers, and the teaching unions.

THE TEACHER INDUCTION SCHEME

What is unique about the Scottish Teacher Induction Scheme? It is designed to guarantee a training post in a school for one year to each eligible probationer, who benefits from the scheme in three important ways:

- Teaching a restricted timetable of 15.75 hours, representing 0.7 full-time equivalent (FTE) of the commitment of a fully registered teacher;
- Using the balance of this time for Continuing Professional Development (CPD);
- Having a designated supporter, with whom the probationary teacher meets weekly to discuss progress, and who carries out approximately

monthly classroom observations, both of these exercises focused on one specific aspect of the Standard for Full Registration.

Schools are funded to give supporters 0.1 FTE remission from class contact to carry out these duties (effectively half a day per week). While this can sometimes be difficult to arrange, the supporter tends to honor this agreement by working with the probationer outside normal hours, indicative of the supporter's own professional commitment.

At the end of the year, if the probationer has reached the Standard for Full Registration, the head teacher recommends to the General Teaching Council for Scotland that the teacher be given full registration. If not, but in the head teacher's opinion it is likely that the teacher has the potential to reach the standard, the recommendation will be for an extension of the probationary period. The final option available to the head teacher, where it is clear that there is no realistic prospect of reaching the standard, is to recommend cancellation of registration.

However, this system does not operate in isolation. Also part of "A Teaching Profession for the 21st Century" (SEED, 2000) was a review of the Scottish system of Initial Teacher Education (ITE) programs, all of which are delivered within the university system and which are now much better focused than they had been previously. As a result of this, most probationers reach the Teacher Induction Scheme better prepared and, with the support in place during the year, most do reach the standard. Since 2002, on average 98 percent of probationers have gained full registration at the end of the year, making the TIS a remarkable success story, which has attracted international interest from other European countries, the United States, and Australia.

Evaluating the Scheme

The General Teaching Council for Scotland (GTCS), as the regulatory body for the teaching profession in Scotland, has a key role in monitoring the implementation of the TIS. As part of that function, it has both undertaken and commissioned—in partnership with the Scottish Government— research into the experiences of probationers, into models of support provided to probationers and schools across the thirty-two local authorities, and into professional culture among new entrants to the profession.

This research has taken place amid a growing international interest in the influence of the impact of induction on the professional development of beginning teachers. This interest has focused on two areas: the experiences of teachers on induction programs and the effects of these programs on issues such as teacher effectiveness, learner achievement, and teacher retention.

Researchers in England and in Canada have found that critical elements contributing to the success of teacher induction programs included a reduced teaching demand in the first year, careful selection of mentors, and district-sponsored support. These elements are key features of the Teacher Induction Scheme in Scotland, which perhaps helps to explain the high satisfaction rates among probationer teachers in an early evaluative study of the scheme.

The General Teaching Council for Scotland has conducted a number of inquiries into aspects of the TIS. In 2005, a survey of all those who had gained full registration in the first two years of the scheme ($N = 3,908$) found that over 90 percent of the teachers believed that their supporter meetings and observed sessions had been well structured, focused, and, crucially, had helped in their development as teachers. They also believed that in general their Continuing Professional Development activities had been worthwhile, though there were concerns about duplication between some of the provision offered by local authorities (which was often compulsory to attend) and that at school level.

The teachers were almost unanimous that the TIS encouraged and provided opportunities for reflective practice and that it improved their classroom management skills; a large majority (81.5 percent) thought it was encouraging changes in school culture. This was an early sign of something very significant. Would the induction scheme and the other elements of TP21 do more than provide a good support to beginning teachers? Would they change the way in which schools worked? Would they make them more effective? Would they lead to gains in pupil learning?

These were among the questions posed by research commissioned by GTCS and the Scottish Government. The report by Hulme, Elliot, McPhee, and Patrick (2008) followed an extensive research process, including (a) an electronic survey to which 2,216 teachers responded, (b) six regional focus groups, (c) a survey of local authority officers followed by telephone interviews with eight of them, and (d) six case studies of individual schools, including interviews with senior and unpromoted teachers and workshops with pupils.

The research provided evidence of different attitudes among newer entrants to the profession than their more experienced colleagues in key areas with the potential to affect teacher professionalism and performance:

- They were more likely to believe that TP21 had enhanced the professional standing of teachers;
- They showed a more positive commitment to CPD as a professional obligation for teachers;
- They were more open to the practice of peer observation; and
- They were more confident of being able to identify their own development needs.

Additionally, they also expressed strong career aspirations, with 61 percent of those still serving as probationers showing interest in attaining the new status of Chartered Teacher (a status reserved for teachers who have completed a demanding master's level program that looks particularly at accomplished teaching and brings with it substantial salary increases) once they became eligible, though as with other teachers, there were relatively low levels of aspiration toward becoming senior managers.

Hulme et al. (2008) also found evidence that—although early career teachers had the greatest impact on classroom practice—senior promoted staff and other experienced teachers believed that the enthusiasm of the teachers who had entered the profession through the TIS had brought new enthusiasm to their schools. Some also believed that they were *revitalizing the profession.*

Early career teachers showed their commitment to wider teacher professionalism through their willingness to lead extracurricular activities as well as through their involvement in school committees and in working parties in areas such as curriculum development and assessment. While these views represent opinion rather than hard evidence, they do provide a strong indicator of the impact of the reforms in initial teacher education and of the TIS on the professional formation of beginning teachers in Scotland.

Evolving Support

As well as surveying the probationers, the General Teaching Council for Scotland has investigated the experiences of those who work with them during their induction year. Following the survey of probationers, GTCS issued questionnaires to head teachers and supporters, receiving substantial responses in both cases. The responses, summarized in quantitative and qualitative reports to the council, revealed that, while most believed that the TIS prepared the probationer well for future life as a fully registered teacher, they raised some issues with aspects of the scheme, including the persistence of the 0.7 FTE teaching timetable for the whole year, some feeling that this did not provide adequate experience of the practical issues that would confront the probationers once they were employed full time.

Both head teachers and supporters also had reservations about the adequacy of the 0.1 full-time equivalent allocation of time to supporters to cover the additional workload in taking on this task, especially in cases where the probationer was struggling to meet the requirements of the SFR. Perhaps not surprisingly, supporters' views were stronger than those of head teachers on this aspect. Responses also reinforced the point made in the probationer survey that there needed to be more coherence in planning to ensure that school and local authority CPD opportunities complemented each other to meet individual probationers' needs.

Partly to develop these themes further, and partly to monitor whether progress had been made, in 2008 GTCS conducted focus groups with head teachers and supporters in seven local authorities throughout Scotland, selecting the authorities to ensure they were representative in terms of geography, and providing a comparison between urban, rural, and island experiences. These showed that there had indeed been substantial progress over the issue of CPD, with better planning to ensure that most local authority provision provided generic CPD to cover issues common to all, school-level CPD focusing more on local needs, and supporters working effectively with probationers to identify opportunities to meet specific individual needs.

Schools gave evidence of many ways in which they have involved probationers in peer observation, in working with colleagues within the school and from neighboring schools, and in some cases interprofessional learning with external agencies such as social work, psychological services, or the police. Clearly, development opportunities are there to be exploited, sufficiently so that one head teacher felt the need to comment, "because there is such a comprehensive range of courses, in some ways with the very keen probationer you're actually just pulling back a little from overcommitting."

Matheson and Hulme (2009) revealed that, for the most part, the TIS is as much a success story as it is generally perceived to be. However, there remain some issues, especially in the small proportion of cases where the school becomes concerned that the probationer will not meet the Standard for Full Registration. The impact of such cases on the supporter, the head teacher, and sometimes the wider school community can be traumatic; participants used emotive language like "horrific," "devastating," and "damaging" to describe the experience. The negative experiences can be particularly stressful for supporters, most of whom are deeply committed and take such issues very personally. Often, it becomes essential for the head teacher, and if necessary the local authority, to support not only the probationer but also those responsible for guiding the probationer. However, with a success rate typically of 98 percent, such instances are mercifully rare in the TIS.

REFLECTIONS

The Teacher Induction Scheme has had a dramatic impact on the preparation of newly qualified teachers to accept their future full professional responsibilities as class teachers. With an average annual cohort over the first seven years of the scheme of approximately 3,000 teachers, it has produced the basis of a more skilled, more reflective, and more enthusiastic teaching profession for Scotland.

In recent years, two influential official reports have assessed progress. The Audit Scotland report (Pollock, Whyte, & Peak, 2006) concluded that the TIS is one of the most successful elements of the TP21 agreement, having "helped to ensure a seamless transition from university to teaching" (p. 24) and being well regarded by teaching professionals. A report by Her Majesty's Inspectorate of Education (HMIE, 2007) commented that the improved probation arrangements had produced newly qualified teachers with enthusiasm and skills, offering *a sound basis for future improvement.*

The inspectorate report acknowledged the TIS as "a major success" and that it had had "a positive impact on the overall ethos of self-evaluation in schools" (p. 27). It pointed to the benefits in professional development to the supporters and to those for other teachers in sharing the "positive and energising impact" of probationers (HMIE, 2007). The Teacher Induction Scheme had changed practice in some schools by encouraging the adoption of classroom observation more widely as part of the self-evaluation and improvement agenda in the effort to improve learning and teaching. These findings, endorsed by the broader study of Hulme et al. (2008), provide at least a partial indication of the reasons for the OECD judgment that Scotland's support for teacher induction is world class.

REFERENCES

Her Majesty's Inspectorate of Education (HMIE). (2007). *Teaching Scotland's children: A report on progress in implementing "A teaching profession for the 21st century."* Edinburgh, UK: Author.

Hulme, M., Elliot, D., McPhee, A., & Patrick, F. (2008). *Professional culture among new entrants to the teaching profession.* Edinburgh, UK: General Teaching Council for Scotland.

Matheson, I., & Hulme, M. (2009, September). *Models of support in the teacher induction scheme in Scotland: Experiences of head teachers and supporters: Analysis of focus group outcomes.* Paper presented at the British Educational Research Association Conference, Manchester, United Kingdom.

Pollock, S., Whyte, K., & Peake, H. (2006). *A mid-term report: A first stage review of the cost and implementation of the teachers' agreement "A teaching profession for the 21st century."* Edinburgh, UK: Audit Scotland.

Scottish Executive Education Department (SEED). (2000). *A teaching profession for the 21st century: The report of the committee of inquiry into professional conditions of service for teachers.* Edinburgh, UK: The Stationery Office.

Scottish Executive Education Department (SEED). (2001). *A teaching profession for the 21st century: Agreement reached following recommendations made in the McCrone report.* Edinburgh, UK: Author.

Scottish Executive Education Department (SEED). (2007). *OECD review of national policies for education: Quality and equity of schooling in Scotland.* Edinburgh, UK: Author.

24

Cooperating across Cultures: Professional Development in a Chinese Minority Region

Tasha Bleistein and Tao Rui

BACKGROUND

The Guyuan side street is choked with vendors hawking vegetables, dried wolfberries, grilled lamb, and steamed bread. Ms. Tasha Bleistein, an American teacher, slowly makes her way through the shoppers and onlookers who gather when she stops to haggle with a vendor. Her new home is a dusty apartment compound of mismatched, dilapidated buildings at the end of the street. Even at the beginning of the twenty-first century, cars are few in Guyuan, but three-wheeled vehicles and scooters make weaving through crowds a slow process.

Along the street, head coverings and *qing zhen*—the Chinese phrase for *halal*, which refers to strict adherence to dietary practices—signs above restaurant doors are a testament to the predominant local faith. Students walk beside farmers who struggle to eke out a living in an area that was deemed *unsuitable for living* by the United Nations in the 1970s (*China Daily*, 2009). As Ms. Bleistein approaches the apartment complex near the small teacher-training college where she works, she meets a new colleague for the first time. Ms. Tao Rui grew up, went to college, and found employment in this autonomous region in the desert of northwest China. Chinese autonomous regions, of which the most well known is Tibet, are special administrative regions with a large concentration of at least one minority group. Ningxia has a high concentration of Hui, a Chinese Islamic minority.

Ms. Bleistein and Ms. Tao worked together in the Foreign Languages Department at Guyuan Teachers College for two years. While preparing for her Intensive English classes, Ms. Tao often had questions about sentence structure or culture but could not find the answers in her books. Other Chinese colleagues were unable to help. She asked herself, "Why not consult my native-English-speaking colleagues?" It was this initial thought that led to the development of her collaborative relationship with Ms. Bleistein, who was eager to learn more about Chinese educational systems and methodologies. The two began observing each other's classes and exchanging feedback. Gradually, a professional partnership and personal friendship developed that led to further collaboration and growth.

DEEPENING COOPERATION

Ms. Tao and Ms. Bleistein began exploring the differences between traditional Chinese teaching methods and the Western teaching methodology. They sought a balance between the traditional Chinese approach and communicative methods. Ms. Tao discovered that her language skills had improved during this exploration, and her willingness to interact with native English speakers increased. Discovering the benefits of cooperation fostered increased collaboration. The two teachers assisted each other in their separate action research inquiries before moving on to pursue other opportunities. Three years later, both teachers had completed master's degrees and relocated to Yinchuan, the capital city of Ningxia. With more experience, Ms. Tao and Ms. Bleistein were both in supervisory roles at rival universities. They often discussed problems they encountered, seeking cultural insights to better understand how to communicate to departmental leadership or foreign teachers.

THE PROBLEM

In western China, opportunities are few for local teachers to enter the international world of professional development. Local teachers who do not leave minority regions might develop limited worldviews and fossilized English-language errors. In addition, the influence of the traditional Chinese teaching approach combined with time and energy constraints may cause them to distrust or ignore Western methods of professional development. Many Chinese teachers in the region believe professional development is achieved in isolation through self-reflection, reading, and individual research. With this belief, English-speaking Chinese educators rarely form groups and collaborate with each other, let alone cooperate with Westerners. Such collaboration usually only occurs when it is required.

In contrast, foreign teachers in China may have no specialized training and thus very little understanding of how to effectively teach. They may be little more than native speakers of English who entertain students. Even those with advanced degrees or experience in teaching English as a foreign language may not understand cultural differences or the education system in China.

In addition, foreign teachers often teach oral English classes, which are viewed by many students and faculty members as less important than grammar-heavy courses such as intensive reading or theoretical courses such as linguistics. Many foreign teachers have difficulty integrating into the Chinese university system and identifying other teachers who are willing to engage in professional cooperation. This chapter explores an attempt to navigate cultural differences and overcome other barriers in collaborating for professional development in a Chinese minority region.

THEORETICAL FRAMEWORK

Cooperation and collaboration have become educational buzz words because contemporary research has shown that learning often occurs best in community. Vygotsky (1978) called attention to the fact that learners achieve more when someone assists them in the learning process. This idea is a foundational tenet of the Dewey-influenced U.S. educational system. While most people agree that cooperation is beneficial for professional development, cross-cultural cooperation involves a unique set of challenges. Nonetheless, successful cross-cultural cooperation has great rewards. George (1995) observed these rewards in the data she analyzed from Fulbright scholars who taught in different parts of the world:

For most Americans teaching in a host country, colleagues and students become the best "guides" to the workplace and the most useful "informants"
on the culture. Indeed, these relationships become the small keyholes
through which American professors witness other ways of working, thinking, and being. (p. 95)

Strong professional friendships with local educators lead to true cultural engagement and deeper understanding. For their part, the benefits
local teachers receive via cross-cultural cooperation include (a) exploring
new teaching methods, (b) improving their language abilities, and (c)
broadening their understanding of the world.

While this cooperative development is potentially quite beneficial, it
can be difficult to establish, as evidenced by Liu's (2007) experiences
at Shantou University in China: "There are so many factors working
against it [cooperation] in the real world: Time and energy constraints,
'turf wars,' feelings of inadequacy or superiority with language and
pragmatics, and general inexperience with the idea of collaboration" (p.
120). Beyond logistical issues, Ms. Tao found that many Chinese teachers
avoided cooperation due to their belief that professional development was
an individual undertaking.

OVERCOMING CHALLENGES TO
COOPERATE CROSS-CULTURALLY

One means of cooperation that Ms. Tao and Ms. Bleistein explored is
teacher support groups (TSGs). Richards and Farrell (2005) defined TSGs
as "two or more teachers collaborating to achieve either their individual or
shared goals or both based on the assumption that working with a group is
usually more effective than working on one's own" (p. 51). These groups
have formed under a variety of names, including teacher development
groups, learning circles, action research groups, and teacher learning communities (Richards & Farrell, 2005; Wenger, 1998).

Richards and Farrell (2005) claimed that the most effective TSGs involve voluntary participation, which was also echoed by Lamie's (2006)
experiences with professional development in China: "Initiators of change
should be aware that change that is imposed on others, although not cer-

tain to fail, is likely to be poorly received. . . . Teachers that are involved in the process are more inclined to have a positive response, and attitude, to the change than those who are not" (p. 80).

While support groups and learning communities are increasingly common around the world, they rarely involve intercultural membership or voluntary participation in China.

Ms. Tao and Ms. Bleistein's teacher support group was birthed from the voluntary cooperation of lecturers from two neighboring universities in Yinchuan: Ningxia University and Beifang University of Nationalities. To establish the group, the facilitators invited seven teachers—both Chinese and foreigners—to dinner at a local restaurant to introduce the concept of a teacher support group. A visiting professor shared her process of professional growth as a successful published author. After meeting her and listening to the introduction about teacher support groups from Ms. Bleistein, all attendees expressed interest in participating in the cross-cultural teacher study group and agreed to meet biweekly.

The nine teachers focused on various professional development strategies during meetings. The group decided the overarching goal was to explore ways to increase teacher creativity and student autonomy in the classroom. Ms. Bleistein took responsibility for preparing activities for the group with input from Ms. Tao. The group explored professional development strategies, including journaling, observations, and case studies.

Journaling

Group members kept journals to record areas of their teaching that they hoped to improve. These areas were then analyzed and restructured into themes for the group to focus on during meetings. After analyzing members' needs, the group settled on the themes of student autonomy, teacher creativity, and innovative ways to teach reading.

Observations

Group members observed one or two other teachers in the group, focusing on teacher creativity and student autonomy. The observers suggested alternative teaching methods and approaches to help the teacher to think about his or her lesson in a new way. During group meetings, participants discussed the observations in pairs or smaller groups.

Case Studies

Group members wrote a case study about an especially challenging problem they encountered in the classroom. The case studies were discussed and suggestions were given in pairs and in the whole group. One case study was written about a News Reading course.

A SAMPLE CASE STUDY

I teach a News Reading course for junior English majors. Each week I try to introduce a reading strategy, grammar point, or information about a particular newspaper. I then have the students practice what they have just studied by reading news articles. The problem is that I don't know how to interest the students. I spend a lot of time choosing the news articles so that the articles are relevant and interesting. I even adapt them to fit the level of the students (for example, add Chinese, remove difficult phrases, or change the wording).

It seems like no matter what I do the students seem uninterested during the reading portion of the class. I generally have the students read alone, but sometimes we read as a class or they do small group/pair work. Students also seem to have the attitude that the course is *easy*, but they still are unable to understand the articles or use the skills that I am teaching. What are some of your ideas or suggestions?

Identification of Strengths and Weaknesses

Group members identified their strengths and weaknesses as educators through self-reflection, peer observation, and student surveys. They worked on a professional development plan that outlined specific steps for improvement based on the data collected. Teachers were then asked to work in pairs to achieve their goals.

Implementing New Strategies

Group members presented a successful lesson to the group. Other members were asked to implement one of the strategies presented by another group member and report back to the group on the success of the lesson using a new teaching strategy.

SUCCESSFUL OUTCOMES

Benefits

All participants benefited from the innovative experience and expressed interest in future group meetings. They enjoyed learning from each other and focusing on a collaborative approach to professional development. Through their experiences, the Chinese teachers and the foreign teachers recognized the benefits of cooperation between native- and non-native-English-speaking educators. From classroom observation and idea exchanges to co-writing and co-presenting, participants saw improvements in their professionalism and in their understanding. Native-English-speaking participants were especially grateful for the opportunity to learn about the Chinese educational system and to befriend Chinese teachers. For Chinese participants, some of the benefits of collaborating with native-English-speaking educators included feelings of increased communicative competence and the desire to continue to explore cross-cultural professional development.

Challenges and Solutions

Since China has a hierarchical culture, this trait fosters expectations for group leaders to be authoritarian, even in a voluntary support group. These expectations for authoritarian leadership made Ms. Bleistein uncomfortable. She wanted the group to be egalitarian and therefore hesitated to assert herself as the leader. As the meetings progressed, Ms. Bleistein realized that she was not just the organizer or even the facilitator; she was the leader of the group, and Ms. Tao was her co-leader and consultant. Ms. Bleistein's cultural and personal desire for an egalitarian environment and her fears of cultural imperialism were inhibiting her from taking a stronger leadership role in the group.

There were differing views on the need for authoritarian leadership. One member expressed frustration that work outside of group meetings was suggested and not required. The egalitarian environment caused some Chinese participants to experience a dissonance similar to that of Chinese students who are encouraged to be more autonomous in a collectivist society. Additionally, participants developed close personal relationships and fostered an atmosphere of collaboration among themselves. Meetings often lasted from two to three hours because teachers would linger to socialize. Close friendships were formed among participants and an awareness of the differences between their academic communities was enhanced. Every member of the group had the opportunity to develop positive relationships and to gain new insights, especially about intercultural communication. They all expressed a desire to participate in future teacher support groups.

IMPLICATIONS

For individuals like Ms. Tao and Ms. Bleistein, building collaborative relationships begins with a friendship that is open to exploring cultural differences. Collaborative professional relationships develop along the lines of deepening friendships so that both parties act as cultural informants who promote true cultural understanding in the other person. Participants in professional development groups must begin with a strong desire to connect with each other to ensure that their cooperative relationship will survive cultural friction, time limitations, and energy constraints. In addition, problem solving, creativity, and the willingness to learn all play essential roles in developing and maintaining successful cooperation across cultural boundaries.

For groups, successful cross-cultural collaboration between Chinese English-speaking and native-English-speaking educators mainly depends upon balancing different expectations and understandings of power. Should there be a powerful group leader who directs the group? Or should there be a more egalitarian relationship among group members? Discussing cultural differences and expectations can help to clarify and establish a successful cooperative relationship.

Chinese English-speaking educators in a collaborative group should not feel inferior to or less capable than native-English-speaking educators. Likewise, native English-speakers must not allow fears of cultural imperialism to stop them from acting more appropriately in the host culture. Open discussions of expectations and group organization are necessary for the group's success. Continued research and extensive collaboration are needed to explore the balance of power in high- and low-power-distance cultures to extrapolate its implications for voluntary, cross-cultural teacher support groups.

REFERENCES

China Daily. (2009, September 18). *They're laudable for decades of change.* Retrieved September 18, 2009, from http://www.china.org.cn/features/60years/2009–09/18/content_18552270.htm

George, P. G. (1995). *College teaching abroad: A handbook of strategies for successful cross-cultural exchanges.* Boston: Allyn & Bacon.

Lamie, J. M. (2006). Teacher education and training in China: Evaluating change with Chinese lecturers of English. *Journal of In-Service Education, 31*(1), 63–83.

Liu, J. (2007). Native and non-native collaboration in EFL. In J. Liu (Ed.), *English language teaching in China: New approaches, perspectives and standards* (pp. 107–123). New York: Continuum.

Richards, J. C., & Farrell, T. S. C. (2005). *Professional development for language teachers.* New York: Cambridge University Press.

Vygotsky, L. (1978). Problems of method. In M. Cole (Trans.), *Mind in society* (pp. 52–75). Cambridge, MA: Harvard University Press.

Wenger, E. (1998). *Communities of practice: Learning, meaning, and identity.* New York: Cambridge University Press.

25

Breaking the Mold to Mend the Wounds: An Innovative Model of Collaborative Practice to Further Aboriginal Student Learning

Lorenzo Cherubini

In Ontario, Canada, the story of Aboriginal students' lack of success in public schools is indeed heartbreaking. According to Cajete (2008), Aboriginal student achievement is affected by an array of historic realities that continue to contribute to their disconnection from formal schooling. In order to address the epistemic wounds of colonial education practices, the Ontario Ministry of Education's (OME) (2007) policy documents *Building Bridges to Success for First Nation, Métis, and Inuit Students* and *Ontario First Nation, Métis, and Inuit Education Policy Framework* are intended to close the achievement gap between Aboriginal and mainstream students in provincially funded public schools.

The policy documents recognize the injustices of the residential school experiences and self-declare the OME's commitment to provide a more equitable and respectable learning environment for Aboriginal students. Through these policies, the OME advocates for Aboriginal self-identification to better discern the needs of Aboriginal learners and gauge the success of the culturally sensitive programs being implemented in Ontario schools for the more than 50,000 Aboriginal students. Herein, however, lays the tension that has fueled a pivotal debate in Aboriginal communities across the province and is the impetus for this documentary account.

The ministry's request for Aboriginal students to self-identify has raised concerns across Aboriginal communities—concerns that are embedded in a sense of distrust in Eurocentric-based education systems that have historically betrayed Aboriginal peoples' cultural, linguistic, and epistemic identities (understood primarily as the study of knowledge and the process in which it is generated). This chapter documents a project led by an Aboriginal Education and Research Centre located in an Ontario university, a Catholic and a public school board located in the same jurisdiction, and Aboriginal community leaders. The objective of the project was to inform teachers and administrators, through consultation with Aboriginal communities, of Aboriginal peoples' perceptions related to policy and their storied experiences as they relate to their children's education.

LOCAL CONTEXT

The *Ontario First Nation, Métis, and Inuit Education Policy Framework* (OME, 2007) describes the importance for public school teachers to be aware of Aboriginal students' learning needs and proposes that teachers and principals become better informed of Aboriginal students' cultural and epistemic traditions to provide socially inclusive schoolwide practices. The second OME publication, *Building Bridges to Success for First Nation, Métis, and Inuit Students*, provides school boards with an outline to develop policies for voluntary and confidential Aboriginal student self-identification. In Canada, education is under the jurisdiction of provincial governments. By having Aboriginal students self-identify, the document suggests that the OME can collect reliable data specifically on Aboriginal student achievement as reported on the provincial large-scale standardized tests.

THEORETICAL CONTEXT

The issue of self-identification has an impact upon Aboriginal peoples' identities and is integral to their ancestral Native image and sense of self (Lomawaima & McCarty, 2006). In precontact Aboriginal communities, education perpetuated Aboriginal peoples' linguistic and cultural traditions and ensured the sustainability of their unique knowledge paradigms from one generation to the next (Elijah, 2002). Since colonial rule, Euro-centric educational practices have celebrated the superiority of Western knowledge and epistemologies at the peril of the same customs, traditions, and worldviews innately linked to Aboriginal identity (Battiste, 2002). It is critical, therefore, to account for the reality that mainstream educators may be unintentionally perpetuating practices that underscore frustrating experiences for Aboriginal students who better relate to "the living landscape [that is] encoded with their peoples' history and world view" (Lopez & McClellan, 2007, p. 29).

The fundamental ideological disconnect between Aboriginal and Eurocentric epistemic preferences has resulted in the profound underachievement of Aboriginal students in public education. The residential school experiences of generations past have severe implications for the intense devaluing of Aboriginal identity and, paradoxically, situate Aboriginal identity as static and resistant to change (Kirmayer, Simpson, & Cargo, 2003). Standardized tests are products of Eurocentric measures of student achievement and curriculum. There is a potential danger, according to Aboriginal communities, that the separate reporting of Aboriginal students' test scores from mainstream learners will further isolate this cohort of students from the larger mainstream population and deepen the epistemic and psychic wounds already inflicted.

AN INTERVENTION MODEL

The challenge was to invite discussion between Aboriginal communities and educators to further teachers' awareness and Aboriginal student learning. The method included seven Aboriginal community forums (scheduled eight weeks apart) dispersed across one large region in Ontario. Each forum included a drumming ceremony, dinner, and discussion. Attendees were invited to respond to four questions, including:

1. Before the forum tonight, how aware were you of the Ministry of Education's Aboriginal education initiatives?
2. What resources would you like to see made available to teachers, schools, and school boards to improve your child's learning experience?
3. What types of programs would you like to see implemented in the schools and by the school boards?

4. What concerns do you have about how these data will be interpreted
   or used by the school boards, the OME, and by publicly reporting
   the aggregation of the standardized test results?

Participants' responses yielded the data that were analyzed using a
grounded theory inductive approach by a bi-epistemic team of Aboriginal and mainstream researchers. Responses were analyzed for prevailing
codes (topics that reoccurred throughout the response) and later were collapsed into main themes. Both Aboriginal and non-Aboriginal scholars
participated in lengthy discussions to ensure that we accurately captured
participants' thoughts. In total, 170 people attended the community forums.

Furthermore, it would not be an overstatement to suggest that the success of the community forums was to a large extent an outcome of the
culturally appropriate interventions that allowed the Aboriginal communities to express their thoughts about the OME initiatives. The model broke
from traditional inservices that tend to be one-directional information
sessions and situated the voices of the Aboriginal community at the heart
of the consultations. Attendees were not passive recipients of the school
board's agenda but, instead, determined the direction of the discussion
and functionally linked their concerns to the implications related to policy.

OUTCOMES

Two specific threads woven throughout the stories of the Aboriginal communities were especially noteworthy: the affirmation of community social
agency and the centrality of Aboriginal values. The voices and reflections
of the attendees are shared anonymously throughout the chapter.

The Affirmation of Community Social Agency

The opportunity to gather Aboriginal community members in a public
forum provided a space conducive for individuals to listen to education
policy objectives, account for the voices of their community, and engage
in—what was for some—conversations about difficult experiences related
to schooling. Establishing a culturally appropriate space for discussion

allowed community members to affirm their assertiveness while empowering each other to negotiate critical thoughts related to their children's education. By understanding each other's challenges, community members engaged at a level of interaction that attested to their social agency.

The forums provided opportunities to affirm themselves amongst the social agency of their community in consultation with mainstream educators. Community members regularly voiced their appreciation of school practices that endorsed "more positive interactions with respect to the culture." Others were adamant that Aboriginal student identity could be addressed by curricular practices that "respect the territory the [school] building rests on."

Consistently throughout the response, community members suggested that more *accurate* histories of Aboriginal peoples be presented to all students (not just Aboriginal students) so that Aboriginal students could situate their identity in light of the ancestral heritage of place and land. By assembling as community, the attendees had what Giddens (1991) referred to as *social agency* whereby they developed their self and group consciousness to become more effectively involved in public policy directions.

The community had a genuine concern that Aboriginal student identity was not necessarily being fostered in all mainstream schools, given the lack of "cultural activities to build self-identity and self-confidence." Attendees felt at ease to admit their uncertainty with some of the policy initiative components but were affirmed by the community to express how their cultural, social, and epistemic distinctiveness was in some cases underrepresented in mainstream schooling practices.

Given this sense of community agency, attendees also expressed their concern regarding the anticipated consequences of the OME's intent to disaggregate data on Aboriginal student achievement on the provincial standardized tests. Community members stated their "concern how this information might stigmatize our people." They affirmed each other's hesitation to self-identify for fear that "the government may use this information to take even more away from our people," that the "data will be used in negative ways," and that "self-identification should not be associated with standardized testing."

The community was well aware of how the injustices of the past have negatively influenced their peoples' experiences in public school, and was determined to ensure that reporting of Aboriginal student achievement on standardized testing would not be a subtle means of colonial domination and suppression. They refused to be wounded again.

The Centrality of Aboriginal Values

Aboriginal values resonated in the voices of the community. The community was frustrated with a mainstream education system that has politicized their values in favor of Eurocentric interests. The community was critical of the fact that, as one individual wrote, "Learning through traditional [Aboriginal] methods" was not a component of the current curriculum. They wondered about the absence of "people who would share their knowledge of cultural values and beliefs to instill pride and dignity for those [students] who do not understand their own background."

The voices and reflections of the attendees conveyed strong messages to the educators in attendance that the community feels a great need to extend the influence of their values into the education of their children. Typical of others, one participant reflected, "I would like to see a program brought forward for Aboriginal students where they can get in touch with their cultural roots." The community was adamant that Aboriginal students' value statements, as they relate to their epistemic needs, are in many instances not being met. By representing Aboriginal values in their education, attendees believed that Aboriginal students will better appreciate the traditional and holistic teachings associated with Aboriginal worldviews.

Interestingly, several groups expressed their concern that mainstream teachers were not adequately prepared to represent Aboriginal values in their pedagogical practice. While they recognized that teachers' knowledge of Aboriginal values was in most cases quite scant, community members were fearful of the extent to which this reality unintentionally stifled Aboriginal students' learning and silenced their voices. Common in the community's observations were statements like this: "All teachers need to be more educated in Native history to build a better understanding of our background."

Another attendee reflected, "I would like every teacher in the district to learn about Aboriginal culture. This training should occur many times first until all teachers are culturally competent. Then it should be followed up yearly." There is ample research to suggest that preservice and inservice teacher education programs need to better prepare teachers to work with diverse students (Ladson-Billings, 2006; Sleeter, 2005). As King (2004) suggested, teachers have a limited understanding about pedagogical and epistemic issues related to diversity; "Dysconscious racism is a form of racism that tacitly accepts dominant White norms and privileges" (p. 73). The community questioned educators about how their children are being meaningfully engaged in their education if in fact teachers and administrators know very little about Aboriginal values and epistemic practices.

CONCLUSIONS

This model of collaborative practice endorses a community-based approach supported by culturally appropriate interventions. Further, the Aboriginal forums underscored the complexities and details of the communities' perceptions of schooling, policy, and practice. Aboriginal communities were not subjected to traditional inservice programs but instead were able to voice their stories and inform educators by discursively isolating their critical concerns. It resulted in two key outcomes that informed the sense of Aboriginal community agency and Aboriginal values in public education. In the process, various conclusions were drawn that reflected directly upon the community's objective to mend the wounds of dominant epistemology.

The community made clear that their stories of marginalization had to be heard by educators. The community believed that greater exposure to Aboriginal peoples' culture and traditions would benefit all students enrolled in public education. Peoples' written and verbal contributions emphasized the merits of exposing all children to Aboriginal customs. They suggested heightening teachers' awareness of Aboriginal students' epistemic preferences so that educators could incorporate them into their practice and translate these into authentic learning experiences for all students.

Also learned was that the creation of regional consultative teams lends itself to the successful implementation of Aboriginal Community Forums. Members of the consultative teams can offer their knowledge and resources during the planning of the forums and represent the interests of their stakeholders. Further, the forums themselves are a culturally appropriate means to honor the voices of Aboriginal peoples in a manner that is respectful of their past and present experiences in formal education. In essence, the voice of the community resonated long after the consultations, as parents told their stories so that teachers can better understand their students' struggles.

Last, there is significantly more work to be done. The colonial narrative runs deep into the hearts of Aboriginal peoples. Opportunities for parents to speak directly and candidly to mainstream educators foster critical thought and hopefully inspire revolutionary action. Only by changing the culture and pedagogy of public school classrooms will the proverbial achievement gap begin to close. Such a model decolonizes educational and institutional norms by paying closer attention to the thoughts and experiences of the communities that are affected most by public educational policy. By engaging the voices of the Aboriginal community, the forums aim to enact change in the well-intentioned teachers commissioned to teach *all* students.

Given the legacy of Aboriginal peoples' oppression that is generally misunderstood and seemingly never fully chronicled, this innovative model represents an ambitious intent to promote the cause that all teachers have in common—achievement for all students. In this context, therefore, mainstream educators can be made fully aware of Aboriginal peoples' punctuated epistemic pasts, and as a result, enable policy in each of their classrooms that is responsive to Aboriginal learners.

REFERENCES

Battiste, M. (2002). *Indigenous knowledge and pedagogy in First Nations education: A literature review with recommendations.* Ottawa, ON: Author.

Cajete, G. (2008). Sites of strength in Indigenous research. In M. Villegas, S. R. Rak Neugebauer, & K. R. Venegas (Eds.), *Indigenous knowledge and education* (pp. 204–210). Cambridge, MA: Harvard Educational Press.

Elijah, J. (2002). *Literature review: Language and culture.* Ottawa, ON: Author.

Giddens, A. (1991). Structuration theory: Past, present and future. In C. Bryant & D. Jary (Eds.), *Theory of structuration: A critical appreciation* (pp. 201–221). London: Routledge.

King, J. E. (2004). Dysconscious racism: Ideology, identity, and the miseducation of teachers. In G. Ladson-Billings & D. Gillborn (Eds.), *The Routledge-Falmer reader on multicultural education* (pp. 71–83). London: Routledge-Falmer.

Kirmayer, L., Simpson, C., & Cargo, M. (2003). Healing traditions: Culture, community and mental health promotion with Canadian Aboriginal peoples. *Australian Psychiatry, 11,* 15–23.

Ladson-Billings, G. (2006). From the achievement gap to the education debt: Understanding achievement in U.S. schools. *Educational Researcher, 35*(7), 3–12.

Lomawaima, K. T., & McCarty, T. L. (2006). *To remain an Indian: Lessons in democracy from a century of Native American education.* New York: Teachers College Press.

Lopez, A., & McClellan, H. (2007). Letting in the sun: Native youth transform their school with murals. *Reclaiming Children and Youth, 16*(3), 29–35.

Ontario Ministry of Education. (2007). *Building bridges to success for First Nation, Métis, and Inuit students.* Toronto, ON: Author.

Ontario Ministry of Education. (2007). *Ontario First Nation, Métis, and Inuit education policy framework.* Toronto, ON: Author.

Sleeter, C. (2005). *Un-standardizing curriculum: Multicultural teaching in the standards-based classroom.* New York: Teachers College Press.

26

Participatory Action Research for Teacher Development in Malawi

Liz Barber, Tom Smith, Alexander Erwin, Vanessa Duren-Winfield, Tenika S. Walker, Brian Mosleley, and James D. Worsley, with the following teachers from the Domasi Demonstration Primary School, Zomba, Malawi: Chifundo Ziyaya, Mirriam Sherriff, Ethel Chikapa, Beauty Kafuna, Liveness Mwanza, Ausman Ngwali, and Lucy Kapenuka

Since 2007, students and faculty from North Carolina Agricultural and Technical State University have traveled to Malawi to work with teachers in three primary schools to support the country's 1994 universal public education initiative. Many in Malawi teach without the equivalent of high school diplomas or have limited certificates and little formal preparation. Our innovative program came about when representatives from these schools requested the support of educators from the United States. This chapter is an example of participatory action research experiences as a form of teacher development for developing country settings.

RESEARCH BASE

Typically, the knowledge flow in developing nations has been outside-in, as in many nongovernmental organization efforts. Instead, we draw on feminist participatory action research, critical praxis, and social justice to honor local indigenous knowledges as a foundation for developmental efforts (McIntyre & Lykes, 2004). Documentation strategies include standard ethnographic methods of participant observation (Hammersley & Atkinson, 2007); life history methods, prompted recall and power sensitive conversations (Haraway, 1988); field notes, and photo- and video-ethnography.

Informant accounts are used as a data source, and case analysis is implemented as a research tool.

THEORETICAL CONTEXT

Our support for Malawian teacher development is situated within a sociopolitical context of turmoil: HIV/AIDS (*Malawi losing 10 people per hour to AIDS*, 2005; UNAIDS, 2008), recurring famines and failure of the country to attain *food sovereignty* (the ability to provide food for people where and when it is needed, as opposed to purchasing food, fertilizers, or pesticides from outside), as well as an ongoing struggle for democratic government. Our efforts take on life-and-death proportions understood within the context of the HIV/AIDS epidemic: One child in ten aged birth through fourteen years old tests positive, with staying in school forming the only correlate of remaining disease free. Yet, because pupils must take their eighth-grade exams in English, a language that few have mastered by that time, fewer than 17 percent score high enough to attend a free public secondary school.

IMPLEMENTATION OF THE COLLABORATIVE INITIATIVE

1. Collaborative projects have been negotiated across a year or more of planning, depending upon the initiative. Presentation of a laptop to the one school that has electricity has allowed for regular e-mail contact to supplement postal correspondence between Malawian and U.S.-based colleagues. Libraries have been established and maintained in three schools.
2. A child feeding program has been revived and maintained for one school, and a starvation months-only feeding established at another.
3. Permaculture maize farming was written into the curriculum and enacted to provide for sustainability of child feeding programs.
4. Bilingual teaching using commercially produced and teacher-authored Big Books (poster-sized books for classrooms of over 125 children), books on tape, books translated into local languages, and

correspondence with U.S.-based elementary school pen pals has been established.

5. A sister-school relationship established with a U.S.-based elementary school.

6. Scholarships provided for ten new pupils per year to attend secondary school.

7. Scholarships for three candidates to complete bachelor of education degrees in critical needs areas of literacy, science, and mathematics. Upon their graduation, these individuals will serve as teacher educators in their areas of expertise.

8. First aid kits maintained as appropriate for rural schools.

9. Medical supplies provided by a U.S.-based sister hospital for a village facility where medical staff attend to 500 mothers and babies as patients per day and provide them with anti-retrovirals.

10. Teacher development of culturally congruent HIV/AIDS instructional materials for Standards (grades) 1–8.

11. Maintenance of school facilities: blackboard painting, curriculum charts painted on walls, repairs to holes in concrete floors and broken glass windows, and padlocks for library doors.

12. Establishment of a career education curriculum for Standards 6–8.

All projects are ongoing and supported by students and faculty members at North Carolina Agricultural and Technical State University and two other U.S.-based institutions: Virginia Polytechnic and State University and Radford University. Occasionally organizations such as the National Council for the Social Studies (NCSS) provide items needed. Our conduit for the flow of ideas and initiatives is unique—an annual month-long summer service learning research study abroad involving students and faculty members from all three U.S.-based universities.

Working with Malawian colleagues, we aim to support projects that seed sustainable ideas. For example, until we established scholarships for three bachelor of education candidates, all college students were residential. As faculty and students at U.S.-based state universities, we lacked access to funds to sponsor this arrangement. At North Carolina Agricultural and Technical State University, a historic black university in Greensboro, North Carolina, most students work at outside jobs to help fund their education. However, when we negotiated with Domasi College of Education representatives in Malawi to pay tuition, books, and supplies for three day students who otherwise would be unable to pursue their education, donors began offering similar scholarships for other nonresidential students, significantly expanding the pool of candidates.

RECENT COLLABORATIONS

Our most recent collaboration involves preparations for a Literacy in the Mother Tongue (LTM) initiative for the summers of 2010–2011. The LTM Project—like our other collaborations prior to it—is defined by educators from two sides of the globe working side by side in a nonhierarchical setting. Early on, Malawian educators had been adamant that as English-language speakers our greatest contribution would be as supporters of their efforts to teach English literacy. Their pupils often failed to accurately demonstrate knowledge on end-of-grade exams because of a lack of skill with English literacy. While Malawi mandated LTM instruction, colleagues in our three partner schools in rural Domasi informed us that they lacked preparation in the method. During the summer of 2009, Domasi Demonstration Primary teachers in Standards 1 through 3 invited Liz Barber (coauthor) into their classrooms to observe and assist with devising the school's own teacher-led LTM initiative.

Despite the LTM mandate, currently Malawian schools teach in the ChiChewa language, with English taught as a second language in Standards 1 through 4. From Standard 5 on, all instruction and testing is conducted in English only. With seventeen indigenous languages spoken in Malawi (three in rural Domasi), many children lack the *bridge language* that would allow them to acquire literacy at all. In our experiences with pupils, we recognized that less than one third had sufficient English facility to understand even the simplest of instruction.

Working with Malawian educators and with faculty and student groups in the United States, we had been able to do something about the learners who came to school without pen or pencil, or an exercise book in which to write down their assignments. Working in concert we helped fill hungry bellies, obtained school uniforms made for pupils who needed them, and paid local artists to paint needed information on classroom walls. We provided libraries with books and collaborated to seed feasible and sustainable instructional strategies for classrooms of hundreds of children, such as teachers' writing their own Big Books for culturally comprehensible HIV/AIDS instruction (Duren-Winfield & Barber, 2006–2007). Now teachers wanted to work with us to develop a model for teacher education in LTM, to allow all pupils to acquire literacy and English through a bridge language of their own.

A DAY IN THE LIFE OF THE DOMASI LITERACY IN THE MOTHER TONGUE (LMT) PROGRAM

On July 1, 2009, Liz entered the Standard 2 classroom of Mirriam Sherriff and Chifundo Ziyaya with a steno pad and a camera. Mirriam and Chifundo had been the first to request Liz's visit as they chatted during tea break that morning. Early in our collaboration, tea break at the Demonstration School had established itself as a major sharing time; on our arrival each summer we caught up with news of each other's families, any changes in the school, and new teaching challenges. Over tea and drop scones (or sometimes roasted maize or steamed cassava root—some regional treats), we exalted over our children's successes and puzzled out possible solutions to challenges the teachers face in mass education in a country that can provide little supportive infrastructure.

In the Standard 2 classroom, Liz watched as Mirriam used vegetables and fruits to demonstrate ChiChewa words, which she pronounced and then wrote on the blackboard for over 100 children to copy in their exercise books. Negotiation of language was clear—not all children knew the ChiChewa words for these foodstuffs, but all of the children recognized the commonly grown objects and repeated their ChiChewa names with great enthusiasm. Once the pattern had been established, Mirriam invited the children to tell their various names for the same items, then reiterated the ChiChewa name as she wrote each one on the blackboard.

After she had introduced all the fruits and vegetables in this manner, Mirriam oriented the children to a textbook lesson that included these same ChiChewa vocabulary words. Using her fruits and vegetables, Mirriam reviewed each word on the blackboard twice in unison with the children, tapping word parts with a stick to point out and emphasize syllables. She then guided her pupils to locate the same words in the textbook—there were textbooks for every two to three children—and to *read* these aloud again in unison with her. Finally, Mirriam read the book sentences aloud and invited the children to repeat the sentences with her.

Next, Mirriam reoriented her pupils' attention to the blackboard, where she wrote each fruit or vegetable word in a new sentence, saying the words out loud as she wrote them. She then asked for volunteers to come use her stick to point out the word in each blackboard sentence that stood for the fruit or vegetable she held up for the children to see. Next, Mirriam guided the children to *read* the blackboard sentences aloud with her, and then copy them into their exercise books to practice at home (*exercise books* are made of 3x5 pages of blank lined newsprint stapled together inside a paper cover, available for the equivalent of 2 to 3 cents U.S. currency).

As the children copied the sentences, Mirriam and Liz both circulated to see how they were doing and to offer help. Some still needed pencil or paper, which Liz provided, and a number of children came to the floor at the front of the classroom to better see the blackboard as they copied their sentences. Mirriam asked the children who had finished early to draw a picture in their exercise books of what each sentence meant. Outside, as older child drummers began warming up for that afternoon's traditional intramural dance practice, several Standard 2 pupils broke into an irrepressible dance wiggle. Mirriam smiled at Liz, then the children, and dismissed her class at 11:20.

Later that afternoon, Mirriam and Chifundo met with Liz to debrief on the instruction observed and to plan together. Liz learned that both teachers speak Yao as well as ChiChewa—Yao and Ngoni are the other two major languages spoken in the Domasi region—and that children in the local Yao tribe usually speak both and need only a little help with ChiChewa. Liz also learned that from 8:30 until 9 a.m. each morning a *radio teacher* gives instruction in math, English, ChiChewa, and writing skills lessons that are broadcast all over the country. However, the radios given to the schools are all solar powered, so on cloudy days these are useless. Mirriam and Chifundo demonstrated the radio given to them, and the sound quality from it rendered it less than useful in a classroom of over 100 learners.

Despite the struggles, Chifundo and Mirriam were eager to brainstorm possibilities for an LTM Program with Liz, wanted to co-lead it with her, and offered the following as suggestions:

1. Materials needed included charts and markers, word cards, sentence strips, Big Books, writing and drawing materials for children and teachers, materials for making teaching games, and small books for children to take home for reading practice.
2. Training should take place after school on Mondays and Wednesdays (not on a market day, when teachers had opportunities to sell items to make money for their families, or to shop for needed items), in sessions based upon the staggered release times for the various standards.

Observations and follow-up conversations in other classrooms reiterated similar themes. Despite the large numbers of pupils, the language diversity, and a lack of formal preparation, all the early standard teachers evidenced a high level of pedagogical skill and keen responsiveness as they worked with their classes.

Powerful literacy strategies were already in place, and with these teachers as co-planners and co-teachers, the construction of an LTM Program would be feasible in two summers of workshops. Teachers at the Demonstration School had, in previous collaborative initiatives, developed skill in teaching from Big Books and established confidence in authoring their own instructional materials. Indeed, these practices had been written into the Malawian national curriculum by some of the same teachers as they worked on curriculum projects at the Malawi Institute of Education during the months immediately after our yearly visits.

Such efforts have consistently built empowerment for teachers in an instructional climate that has been, until recently, almost totally dominated by the influence of the old British lecture model that lacked respect for indigenous teacher knowledge and left learners to their own resorts in classrooms. Our hope is to arrange for each teacher who participates in the LTM Program to receive a certificate from the Malawi Institute of Education that will allow him or her to become a teacher trainer in LTM (in a

similar manner as participants in the U.S.-based National Writing Project
[www.nwp.org] become teacher trainers, themselves).

UNDERSTANDING AND SUPPORTING
TEACHER DEVELOPMENT ACROSS CULTURES

Within all of our collaborative projects, Malawian teachers define the focus and everyone has a voice in how we work together. Unlike the efforts
of most nongovernmental organizations (common providers of assistance
to developing countries), our collaborations exist as situated projects
that take into account distinct local cultures and indigenous knowledges
shared with us by those most affected in given social, political, and cultural contexts. As teachers and friends we come together, move apart, and
come together, our closeness facilitated by strategies that make spaces for
voicing one's realities.

Malawian teachers' desire to continue to collaborate with us constitutes
tacit approval of the ways our projects are conducted, although we cau-
tion ourselves in overreliance on positive feedback from colleagues in
developing country situations. Despite efforts to level the power relations,
educators in such settings rely largely on outside sources for support—
over 90 percent of the Malawian education budget comes from foreign
aid. It is difficult to imagine individuals living in a developing country
situation, regardless of how much they are encouraged to do so by outsiders, having the freedom to critique the ideas of those attempting to help.
In recent Malawian history, dissenters disappeared in the night, never to
return (Englund, 2002).

Working across power divides, we must remind ourselves of our posi-
tionings: As outsiders in the culture, we must strive for an *I don't know*
status to avoid approaching the social and cultural realities of our collaborators with a colonizing perspective (Mutua & Swadener, 2004). Etzioni
(2004) encouraged outsiders new to a culture to bring a service-learning
perspective to their experiences. Further, good cross-cultural collaboration requires sustained time within the cultural context.

Finally, as educators from the West working in developing countries
in the East, we must question the privilege we enjoy and the myth of
meritocracy, while strengthening our alliances to nudge at the centers of

power to which we have access. Our teacher colleagues in Malawi, and the children and families they serve, deserve no less.

REFERENCES

Duren-Winfield, V., & Barber, E. (2006–2007). Participatory action research as a form of mutual aid and self-help: The "Teachers, Children, AIDS, Photovoice Project" in Malawi, Sub-Saharan Africa. *International Journal of Self Help and Self Care, 5,* 203–225.

Englund, H. E. (2002). *Democracy of chameleons: Politics and culture in the new Malawi* (Kachere Books, No. 14). Blantyre, Malawi: Christian Literature Association in Malawi.

Etzioni, A. (2004). *From empire to community: A new approach to international relations.* New York: Palgrave Macmillan.

Hammersley, M., & Atkinson, P. (2007). *Ethnography: Principles in practice* (3rd ed.). London: Routledge.

Haraway, D. (1988). Situated knowledges: The science question in feminism and the privilege of partial perspectives. *Feminist Studies, 14,* 575–599.

Malawi losing 10 people per hour to AIDS (2005). Retrieved February 15, 2009, from http://www.aegis.com/news/ads/2005/AD050215.html

McIntyre, A., & Lykes, M. B. (2004). Weaving words and pictures in/through feminist participatory action research. In M. Brydon-Miller, P. Maguire, & A. McIntyre (Eds.). *Traveling companions: Feminism, teaching, and action research.* Westport, CT: Praeger.

Mutua, K., & Swadener, B. B. (Eds.). (2004). *Decolonizing research in cross-cultural contexts.* Albany: SUNY Press.

UNAIDS (2008). UNAIDS 2008 Report on the global AIDS epidemic. Retrieved February 15, 2009, from http://www.unaids.org/en/KnowledgeCentre/HIVData/GlobalReport/2008/

Afterword: Innovation as Hope

Tod Kenney

The purpose of an innovation is to create a novel strategy that results in improved performance outcomes. But what if the new approach is just a rejuvenated heirloom educational construct, albeit with a new nomenclature? For example, the popular phrase from many of today's inservice programs on curriculum development criticizes school curricula as being "a mile wide and an inch deep," which is an echo of Alfred North Whitehead's two commandments:

1. Do not teach too many subjects, and,
2. What you teach, teach thoroughly.

Whitehead's *Aims of Education* was published in 1929. But just because a strategy or program has a historical antecedent should not exclude its practice from being classified as an innovation. If a program is practiced in a new setting or in a new context, then it is, indeed, a novel strategy for that circumstance. Not wanting to get mired in the semantics of the term *innovation*, the basis for judgment should rest on a singular criterion: Will the innovation improve instructional practice and student performance?

Many of the current practices in preservice and inservice teacher education appear robust on paper, but the significant loss of teachers from the profession (as frequently cited in the literature and in this volume) should serve as a signal to examine the status of our profession. Wineburg's (2006) survey of 240 American Association of State Colleges and Universities found that the manner in which institutions assess the effectiveness of their programs varies widely in form, function, and fallibility: "In effect, everyone is trying to invent (or reinvent) wheels to produce evidence, albeit some of the wheels are without tires, some are broken, and some are not even round" (p. 3). This severe diagnosis serves as a clarion call for the need to carefully evaluate and change our educational practices.

Progress is being made. Hill's (2003) study of the organizational health of schools stated, "I witnessed pockets of innovation and random acts of implementation" (p. 60). But clearly we must move past sporadic improvements. Eisner (2005) declared that the vitality of our school systems depends on innovation and encourages the "cultivation of productive idiosyncrasy" (p. 168). The hope is that the productive idiosyncrasy/ innovation will transition to become the new normal.

Innovation implies a change in current practice, and inherent in that understanding is that it is a positive change. Geertz's (1973) commentary on innovation in cultures stated that "Everyone snaps them up as the *open sesame* of some new positive science, the conceptual center-point around which a comprehensive system of analysis can be built" (p. 3). The innovations outlined in *Breaking the Mold* provide hope that these practices can serve as the centerpiece for reform. In order to operationalize these reforms, many of the programs stress the importance of collaboration and best practices, as well as developing an enhanced sensitivity to diverse learner needs.

The range of demographics of the student population in and amongst schools has focused attention on the need to directly address the issue of diversity. This includes Darvin's use of *situated performances* to influence decision-making processes and Smagorinsky's course work designed to provoke reflection about cultural segregation. Whether you house your university's educational program on site in an urban elementary school, recruit from the local population to become certified teachers, or allow the Aboriginal people a voice in the school, the intent is to deliberately focus on diversity and its impact on the practice of teachers.

Developing a multicultural sensitivity or engaging the students' imagination are both strategies designed to stimulate student engagement. Dr. F. Louis Soldan, formerly the superintendent of schools in St. Louis, remarks on a teacher's use of student-centered instruction: "In conducting the lesson she has no thought of using it to display her own professional skill or brilliancy; but she puts the child in the foreground. . . . Her aim is to excite activity, and for this purpose she enlists his interests. . . . She not only serves the intellectual food, but also stimulates the appetite" (p. 54). Soldan's article was published in 1899! Stimulating student interest is an heirloom concept, but the contemporary lens of culturally responsive education serves to reinforce its relevancy.

Some innovations require a cognitive reordering. "The most sobering understanding is that there will be few innovative breakthroughs in practice as long as the current theory base remains unchallenged" (English, 2005, p. xx). Zavala's report on a network of teacher collaboration that coalesces around social justice is one example of how the social justice paradigm, as an emerging perspective in education, can serve as the vehicle to embolden innovative initiatives.

Collaboration is a quality that can help spread innovations and increase the robustness of their execution. Unfortunately, Miles and Miles's (1999) work on leadership found that collaboration has no philosophical heritage in Western civilization. A study in teacher discourse and collaboration also indicated that collaboration is not an automatic trigger for creativity or innovation (Scribner, Sawyer, Watson, & Myers, 2006). They state that the parties involved need to build capacity that fosters facilitation, interaction, and communication.

Fortunately, many of the programs outlined in *Breaking the Mold* embed both the principle of collaboration as well as the explicit teaching of its components in order to operationalize the concept. Collaboration is a vital component for innovations such as seminaring, creating Living Learning Communities for undergraduates, and Kennesaw State University's design of their doctoral program that explicitly enumerates collaboration as the expected mode of operation for their cohort of students. The value of collaboration is obliquely addressed in Sid Caesar's humorous metaphor; "The guy who invented the wheel was an idiot. The guy who invented the other three, he was a genius" (as cited in Pink, 2005, p. 138). Pink's book title, *A Whole New Mind*, aptly frames the perspective that innovations involve revolutionizing the way we think.

The genesis for creating an innovative practice requires being cognizant that change is necessary. Root-Bernstein's (2003) work in the *International Handbook on Innovation* informs us that *epistemology* is the study of how knowledge comes into being and *nepistemology* is the study of ignorance. He cited Witt's 1988 typology that identifies six forms of ignorance. Overcoming ignorance and recognizing that reform is required must then be coupled with action. McTamaney and Palmeri's chapter about the review of their university's program for NCATE accreditation is telling of the inertia of ignorance: "Admittedly, our prior framework had fallen into obscurity and, candidly, few of us noticed." Policies and protocols can become perpetual practices, which is the antithesis of innovation.

The absence of any initiative for change contrasts with the exclamation "innovate or die!" (Robbins & Decenzo, 2007, p. 432). The 2004 National Innovation Initiative, crafted by the Council on Competitiveness, stated, "For the past 25 years, we have optimized our organizations for efficiency and quality. Over the next quarter century, we must optimize our entire society for innovation" (as cited in National Center on Education and the Economy, 2007, p. 25). Producing an innovative practice is a creative act that may include revisiting an heirloom educational construct and revitalizing it into a productive strategy.

The book *Explaining Creativity: The Science of Human Innovation* defined creativity as the balance of imitation and innovation (Sawyer, 2006), which allows an innovation to emerge from a previous practice. As new generations of teachers enter our classrooms, our ultimate goal as educators is to maximize the preservice and inservice experiences for all teachers. The innovations contained within *Breaking the Mold* serve as templates for success and offer hope for improving our practice as educators in order to gain improvements in student performance outcomes.

REFERENCES

Eisner, E. W. (2005). Standards for American schools: Help or hindrance? In E.W. Eisner (Ed.), *Reimagining schools: The selected works of Elliot W. Eisner* (pp. 163–172). New York: Routledge.

English, F. W. (2005). Introduction: A metadiscursive perspective on the landscape of educational leadership in the 21st century. In F. English (Ed.), *The Sage handbook of educational leadership: Advances in theory, research, and practice* (pp. ix–xvi). Thousand Oaks, CA: Sage.

Geertz, C. (1973). *The interpretation of cultures: Selected essays by Clifford Geertz.* New York: Basic Books.

Hill, G. D. (2003). Organizational health. *School Administrator, 60*(6), 26–28.

Miles, R. E. & Miles, G. (1999). Leadership and collaboration. In J. A. Conger, G. M. Spreitzer, & E. E. Lawler, III (Eds.), *The leader's change handbook: An essential guide to setting direction and taking action* (pp. 321–343). San Francisco: Jossey-Bass.

National Center on Education and the Economy. (2007). *Tough choices or tough times*. San Francisco: Jossey-Bass.

Pink, D. H. (2005). *A whole new mind: Moving from the information age to the conceptual age*. New York: Riverhead Books.

Robbins, S. P., & Decenzo, D. A. (2007). *Supervision today!* (5th ed.). Upper Saddle River, NJ: Pearson Education.

Root-Berstein, R. (2003). Problem generation and innovation. In L.V. Shavinina (Ed.), *The international handbook on innovation* (pp. 170–179). Amsterdam, Netherlands: Elsevier.

Sawyer, R. K. (2006). *Explaining creativity: The science of human innovation*. Oxford: Oxford University Press.

Scribner, J. P., Sawyer, R. K., Watson, S. T., & Myers, Y. L. (2006). Teacher teams and distributed leadership: A study of group discourse and collaboration. *Educational Administration Quarterly, 42*(5), 1–34.

Soldan, F. L. (September, 1899). Efficient and inefficient teachers. *Teachers World, 11*(1), 54–55.

Whitehead, A. N. (1929). The aims of education. In A. N. Whitehead (Ed.), *The Aims of Education and Other Essays* (pp. 1–23). New York: Macmillan.

Wineburg, M. S. (2006). Evidence in teacher preparation: Establishing a framework for accountability. *Journal of Teacher Education, 57*(1), 51–64.

Contributors

Liz Barber, PhD, is an experienced teacher, literacy studies professor, and ethnographic researcher. She teaches in the Leadership Studies Doctoral Program at North Carolina Agricultural and Technical State University and conducts participatory action research projects in both Greensboro, North Carolina, and Domasi, Malawi. Her research focuses on writing, literacy, and leadership as these develop within cultures or communities of practice.

Harriet J. Bessette, PhD, is an associate professor of special education in the Inclusive Education Department at Kennesaw State University and also serves as the coordinator of the EdD and EdS programs in the Bagwell College of Education. She has participated in several Harvard Institutes on Critical Issues in Urban Special Education, where she collaborated with scholars across the nation to address accountability, assessment, and leadership practices in P–12 schools.

Tasha Bleistein, MA, currently teaches for Chemeketa Community College and Azusa Pacific University's MA TESOL program. She taught in China for nine years and is working on her PhD in intercultural education at Biola University, La Mirada, California.

Lace Marie Brogden, PhD, is an associate professor of education at the University of Regina, Canada. Her research interests include language teacher education and induction, autoethnographic and autobiographical texts within narrative inquiry, and the impact of architecture on identity performance/production.

Valerie B. Brown-Schild, PhD, is director of the Kenan Fellows Program for Curriculum and Leadership Development at the Kenan Institute for Engineering, Technology & Science at North Carolina State University.

Ruben G. Carbonell, PhD, director of the Kenan Institute for Engineering, Technology & Science, is the Frank Hawkins Kenan Distinguished Professor of Chemical Engineering at North Carolina State University.

Julie Causton-Theoharis, PhD, is an associate professor in the School of Education at Syracuse University in the Inclusive Elementary Education program. Her work centers on inclusion, differentiation, and collaboration for inclusive schooling. She has a new book entitled *The Paraprofessional's Handbook for Effective Support in Inclusive Classrooms* (Brookes Publishing, 2009).

Lorenzo Cherubini, EdD, is an associate professor in the Faculty of Education, Brock University (Canada). The focus of his research is policy analysis, Aboriginal education, and teacher development. His research is supported by the Social Sciences and Humanities Research Council of Canada (SSHRC).

Anne Chodakowski, PhD, is a postdoctoral fellow with the Imaginative Education Research Group at Simon Fraser University in Vancouver, Canada. Her current research interests include imaginative teacher education, practitioner research, drama, literacy, and oral language development.

Charles R. Coble, EdD, is a former vice president of the University of North Carolina system, dean of the School of Education at East Carolina University, and chair of the Kenan Fellows Program Board of Advisors. He is cofounder and partner with the Third Mile Group.

Soria E. Colomer, MA, is a doctoral candidate of language and literacy education at the University of Georgia in Athens, Georgia. She is a National Board Certified teacher and her research interests include foreign language and ESOL teacher education.

James Cope, PhD, is the chair of the Department of Elementary and Early Childhood Education at Kennesaw State University, Georgia. His research interests are the development of lifelong readers, integration of technology into literacy classrooms, and using technology to engage students' interests. Prior to his work in higher education, Dr. Cope taught at the elementary, middle, and high school levels.

Joseph Corriero, EdD, is an assistant professor at Monmouth University and co-coordinator of the Educational Leadership program. He is a former public school principal and central office administrator. His research interests include new teacher induction, university/school partnerships including Professional Development Schools, and school leadership.

Jacqueline Darvin, PhD, is an assistant professor of literacy education at Queens College of the City University of New York. She is a former middle and high school English teacher. Her research interests include the sociopolitical and cultural aspects of literacy teaching and learning, pedagogy in teacher education, and literacy in the content areas and vocational contexts.

Vanessa Duren-Winfield, PhD, is an assistant professor and director of research at Winston-Salem State University. She has seventeen years of experience as a health disparities researcher with special emphasis on disparities in quality of care for minority populations to include health literacy, HIV/AIDS and cardiovascular disease. Her research in Malawi, utilized participatory action research as a framework to explore and expand upon health literacy on the prevention and treatment of HIV/AIDS among Malawian schoolchildren.

Kieran Egan, PhD, is a professor of education at Simon Fraser University in British Columbia, Canada. He is the author of approximately twenty-five books, including *The Educated Mind: How Cognitive Tools Shape our Understanding* (University of Chicago Press, 1997). His new book is *Learning in Depth: A Simple Innovation That Can Transform Schooling* (University of Chicago Press, 2010).

Alexander Erwin, PhD, directs the innovative Interdisciplinary Leadership Studies doctoral program at North Carolina A&T State University. A revered leader, Dr. Erwin is an experienced educator in his own right, and has earned Principal of the Year honors in his career in public school education, prior to entering academe. He has worked incessantly to further the development of teacher leaders in the southern United States and in Malawi.

Andrew Ferdinandi, EdD, a former middle school teacher and counselor in New York City, is associate professor in St. John's University's School of Education. He teaches future school counselors and mental health counselors at the master's level.

Douglas Fisher, PhD, is a professor of language and literacy education in the School of Teacher Education at San Diego State University and a classroom teacher at Health Sciences High and Middle College. He is a recipient of the Celebrate Literacy Award from the International Reading Association.

Mary Ellen Freeley, EdD, is an associate professor at St. John's University in Queens, New York, and past president of ASCD. In her forty years as an educator, Dr. Freeley has been a superintendent of schools for twelve years as well as a teacher, principal, and professor, and her work with ASCD has included numerous international visits to schools in St. Maarten, New Zealand, China, India, Australia, and Singapore.

Thomas R. Guskey, PhD, is a professor of psychology at the University of Kentucky and an expert in research and evaluation. He has authored or edited seventeen books, including *Evaluating Professional Development* (Corwin, 2000).

Thomas Hamilton, MEd, is the director of educational policy at the General Teaching Council for Scotland. His research interests are in the field of teacher quality and regulation.

Victoria Hasko, PhD, is an assistant professor of foreign language education at the University of Georgia. Her research interests include second/

foreign language acquisition and pedagogy, computer-assisted language teaching, and bilingual education.

Lisa B. Hibler, BS, teaches chemistry at Athens Drive High School in the Wake County Public School System in Wake County, North Carolina. She is a Kenan fellow in the class of 2010.

Yi-Ping Huang, PhD, currently serves as the accreditation coordinator, assessment director, and associate professor for the Education Department at University of Maryland, Baltimore County (UMBC).

Patricia A. Jennings, PhD, is a faculty researcher with the Prevention Research Center at Pennsylvania State University and director of the Initiative on Contemplation and Education at the Garrison Institute in Garrison, New York. Dr. Jennings develops and tests interventions to promote teacher social and emotional competence and the effect of these interventions on classroom climate and student social, emotional, and academic outcomes.

Laura R. Kates, EdD, joined the faculty of Kingsborough Community College of the City University of New York as an assistant professor in the fall of 2006. Prior to doing so, she was a teacher and curriculum consultant in the New York City public schools for fifteen years. Her research interests include teacher education pedagogy, policy and program design, and students' perspectives on their learning experiences.

Tod Kenney, EdD, has taught in the secondary schools in Connecticut for twenty-eight years and is currently a curriculum specialist in the East Hartford Public Schools, Connecticut. His work explores the construct of educational leadership and its relationship to student performance outcomes. He received his doctorate from Central Connecticut State University.

Dawn Latta Kirby, EdD, is associate dean, College of Humanities and Social Sciences, and professor of English and English education at Kennesaw State University. She is the coauthor of *Inside Out: Strategies for Teaching Writing* (Heinemann, 2004) and of *New Directions in Memoir:*

A Studio Workshop Approach (Heinemann, 2007). She is currently working on a book on writing and teaching inquiry and the contemporary essay.

Diane Lapp, EdD, is distinguished professor of education in the School of Teacher Education at San Diego State University. She is currently a teacher at Health Science High and Middle College and has taught in elementary and middle schools as well.

Corey S. Mackenzie, PhD, is a clinical psychologist and assistant professor in the Department of Psychology at the University of Manitoba. Dr. Mackenzie's research interests focus on ways of improving older adults' mental health.

Ian Matheson, PhD, is educational planning and research officer at the General Teaching Council for Scotland, Edinburgh. His research interests include initial teacher education and professional development for teachers.

Mairi McAra, BEd, is a professional officer (Early Professional Learning) at the General Teaching Council for Scotland. Her research interests are in building teacher capacity through continuing professional development.

Morva McDonald, PhD, is an associate professor of curriculum and instruction and teacher education in the College of Education at the University of Washington, Seattle. Her research focuses on organizational aspects of teacher education and social justice teacher education. She uses sociocultural theories of learning to frame and understand teacher preparation and prospective teachers' opportunities to learn

Sheryl L. McGlamery, PhD, is a full professor in the College of Education (Teacher Education Department) at the University of Nebraska at Omaha. Her current research interests include imaginative teacher education, practitioner research, drama, literacy, and oral language development.

Catherine McTamaney, EdD, is a lecturer in the Department of Teaching and Learning at Vanderbilt University's Peabody College. She is a former school head, community and parent educator, and classroom teacher. Her research interests include Montessori education, school leadership, and teaching as a vocational practice.

Brian Mosleley, MS, is a doctoral student in instructional design and technology at Virginia Polytechnic Institute and State University. He has worked in business for five years in management and career development. He is interested in designing educational tools for instructional development in third world settings.

Jana Noel, PhD, is a professor in the Department of Teacher Education at California State University, Sacramento, and is the university's Community Engagement Faculty Scholar. She has received Sacramento State's Outstanding Community Service Award as well as the university's Research and Creative Activities Capstone Award for research that makes national and international contributions to the field. Dr. Noel has published two books and numerous articles on urban teacher education and multicultural education.

Amy Palmeri, PhD, is an assistant professor of the practice at Vanderbilt University's Peabody College. She is a former preschool teacher and currently directs Peabody's Early Childhood Education Program. Her research interests include prospective teachers' content and pedagogical learning, beginning teacher development, and science teaching and learning.

Nita A. Paris, PhD, is the associate dean for graduate study and associate professor of educational psychology in the Bagwell College of Education at Kennesaw State University. She has authored and coauthored numerous manuscripts on metaphorical and analogical thinking and developing teaching expertise.

Susan K. Parry, MEd, is assistant director for partnerships at the Kenan Fellows Program for Curriculum and Leadership Development at the Kenan Institute for Engineering, Technology & Science at North Carolina State University.

Paul Pedota, PhD, is the director of Alternative Teacher Certification Programs and Field Experiences at St. John's University, Queens, New York, and is a former principal of a New York City secondary school.

Beth A. Peery, EdS, has thirty-four years of experience in the education field. She is a retired elementary principal whose focus has been on rigor and relevance in the classroom. Her experiences help her to make learning relevant and authentic for teacher candidates.

Patricia A. Poulin, PhD, is a postdoctoral fellow in psychology at the Ottawa Hospital and a shiatsu therapist. Her research focuses on the integration of mindfulness and traditional healing in health-care and educational settings.

Traci Redish, PhD, is an associate professor in the Instructional Technology Department at Kennesaw State University (KSU). Her current research interests include the study of technology leadership and policy, technology integration, professional development, and online learning.

Lynn Romeo, EdD, is dean of the School of Education at Monmouth University and also directs the Office of Certification, Field Placements, and School Partnerships. She is a former public school teacher, reading specialist, and administrator. Her research interests include mentoring, school partnerships, technology integration, Literacy Exploration Labs, and literacy instruction.

Tao Rui, MA, is currently a lecturer at Beifang University of Nationalities. Her master's degree is in applied linguistics from Nanyang Technological University in Singapore. Her research interests include teacher education and applied linguistics.

Twyla Salm, PhD, is an associate professor of education and director of the Professional Development Office at the University of Regina, Canada. Her research interests include interprofessional education in teacher education and studying how interprofessional collaboration can improve health and learning for students.

Saundra L. Shillingstad, EdD, is an associate professor in the College of Education at the University of Nebraska at Omaha, where she has taught for the past eleven years in the Teacher Education Department. Her current research interests include practitioner research, assessment literacy, and teacher induction.

Elizabeth A. Skinner, PhD, is an assistant professor of bilingual education in the Department of Curriculum and Instruction at Illinois State University. She is based in Chicago and works with students enrolled in ISU's Professional Development Schools in Elgin, Illinois, and Chicago.

Peter Smagorinsky, PhD, is a professor of English education at the University of Georgia. In 2010, he was named a fellow of the American Educational Research Association. His research includes a line of inquiry that centers on English teachers' development of pedagogical concepts; this chapter represents one effort to promote a conception of diversity education early in teacher candidates' university education.

Tom Smith, PhD, teaches courses in educational foundations and service learning. He is coauthor of a recent book on chaos theory, classroom dynamics, and cognition. He has an abiding interest in social justice, critical literacy, and other empowering pedagogies of hope. He is cofacilitator of the Malawi Literacy in the Mother Tongue initiative.

Geoffrey B. Soloway, MEd, is a doctoral candidate and instructor at OISE of the University of Toronto. His teaching and research focus on mindfulness training for preservice teachers and wellness in education.

Cherry O. Steffen, PhD, is an associate professor in the Department of Elementary and Early Childhood Education at Kennesaw State University, Georgia. She has used problem-based learning and various forms of technology to facilitate the development of teachers who are equipped to teach in the twenty-first-century classroom.

George Theoharis, PhD, is an associate professor in the School of Education at Syracuse University in educational leadership and inclusive elementary education. His work and research focuses on issues of school leadership, equity and social justice, school reform, and inclusion. He has a new book, *The School Leaders Our Children Deserve* (Teachers College Press, 2009).

Tenika S. Walker, MS, is a graduate of North Carolina A&T State University, where she studied psychology and earned a master's degree in rehabilitation counseling. She worked with teachers and children in the Malawian schools during the summer of 2008. Nikki has dedicated herself and her education to working with disabled and underserved populations cross-culturally in hopes of bridging the gap to increase social awareness.

Sharon Walpole, PhD, is an associate professor in the School of Education at the University of Delaware. She teaches undergraduate courses on language and literacy development in kindergarten and first grade, master's courses on content area reading instruction and on organization and supervision of the reading program, and doctoral seminars on literacy and educational policy.

Mark Warner, EdD, is an associate professor at Kennesaw State University, Georgia. His primary research interest is integrating problem-based learning and technology into the twenty-first-century classroom. Prior to his work in higher education, Dr. Warner was a school principal and taught grades 5–8 math, social studies, and language arts for fifteen years.

Thomas DeVere Wolsey, EdD, is the course lead for literacy and learning as well as the adolescent literacy and technology master of science in education specializations at Walden University. He previously taught English, social studies, and elective courses for more than twenty years in public schools.

James D. Worsley, PhD, is a recent graduate in leadership studies at North Carolina A&T State University; his dissertation research examined upward mobility for African American leaders in the parks and recreation field. Worsley is a regional manager in the Parks and Recreation Department with the Mecklenburg County government. He has a passion for education leadership among teachers and youth in Malawi.

Miguel Zavala, PhD, received his degree from the Graduate School of Education and Information Studies at the University of California, Los Angeles. He is an assistant professor in the Department of Secondary Education at California State University, Fullerton.

Ken Zeichner, PhD, is the Boeing professor of teacher education and director of teacher education, University of Washington, Seattle. His current research focuses on the different ways in which various forms of knowledge (academic, school based, community based) interact in social justice–oriented preservice teacher education programs.

Breinigsville, PA USA
17 January 2011
253391BV00006B/1/P